POSTMODERNISM AND POPULAR CULTURE

Angela McRobbie

London and New York

First published 1994
by Routledge
11 New Fetter Lane, London EC4P 4EE

Simultaneously published in the USA and Canada
by Routledge
29 West 35th Street, New York, NY 10001

Reprinted 1995, 1996, 1997, 1998

© 1994 Angela McRobbie

Typeset in Times by Intype, London
Printed and bound in Great Britain by
T.J. International Ltd, Padstow, Cornwall

British Library Cataloguing in Publication Data
A catalogue record for this book is available from the British Library

Library of Congress Cataloging in Publication Data
A catalog record for this book is available from the Library of Congress

ISBN 0–415–07712–5 (hbk)
ISBN 0–415–07713–3 (pbk)

POSTMODERNISM AND POPULAR CULTURE

Cultural studies started life as a radical political project, establishing the cultural centrality of everyday life and of popular culture. In a postmodern world where old certainties are undermined and identities fragmented, the way forward for those working with popular culture has become less clear. In contrast to more pessimistic readings of the possibilities of postmodernity, *Postmodernism and Popular Culture* engages with post-modernity as a space for social change and political transformation.

Ranging widely over cultural theory and popular culture, Angela McRobbie engages with everyday life as an eclectic and invigorating interplay of different cultures and identities. She discusses new ways of thinking developed with the advent of postmodernism, from the 'New Times' debate to political strategies after the disintegration of western Marxism. She assesses the contribution of key figures in cultural and post-imperial theory – Susan Sontag, Walter Benjamin and Gayatri Chakravorty Spivak – and surveys the invigorating landscape of today's youth and popular culture, from second-hand fashion to the rave scene, and from moral panics to teenage magazines.

McRobbie argues throughout for a commitment to cultural studies as an 'undisciplined' discipline, reforming and reinventing itself as circumstances demand; for the importance of ethnographic and empirical work; and for the need for feminists to continually ask questions about the meaning of feminist theory in a postmodern society.

Angela McRobbie is Principal Lecturer in Sociology at Thames Valley University, London. She has written extensively on popular culture, gender and youth culture, and is also a regular contributor to newspapers and magazines. Her current research is on the fashion industry.

CONTENTS

ACKNOWLEDGEMENTS

I would like to thank the following people for lending me books, talking to me on the phone, or, even better, making me tapes to listen to during the slow process of writing these pieces and then eventually of putting them together for this collection: Charlotte Brunsdon, Martin Culverwell, Marcella Evaristi, Mike Fitzgerald, Simon Frith, Paul Gilroy, Mica Nava, Sarah Thornton, Vron Ware.

Thanks to the following people and institutions for inviting me to present some of these chapters as papers at conferences: Lisa Appignanesi at the Institute of the Contemporary Arts, London, Kathy Woodward at the University of Milwaukee at Wisconsin, USA, Larry Grossberg at the University of Illinois at Urbana-Champaign, USA, Brian Winston at Penn State University, USA, Jane Feuer at Pittsburgh University, USA, Graham Murdock at Loughborough University of Technology, UK, Lidia Curti and Iain Chambers at Naples University, Italy, and Alison Kirton at the Institute of Education, London. For their writing and ideas, thanks also to Stuart Hall and Dick Hebdige.

Final thanks to the MA in Cultural Studies students at Thames Valley University, London, for their enthusiasm and dedication, to Martin Chalmers for encouraging me to go to clubs and listen to live music, especially ON-U-Sound and Tackhead, and also to Hanna Chalmers and her friends for criticizing me and keeping me in touch.

The author and publishers would like to thank the following journals and institutions for granting kind permission to reprint some of the material in this collection: *Cultural Studies, Feminist Review, New Formations*, Macmillan Publishers, *Theory, Culture and Society*.

INTRODUCTION

HB is back from Newcastle
But gone out – the washing
Machine is roaring away
And the fridge is defrosting
These are his favourite sounds.
(Derek Jarman, *Blue*, *Guardian*, 15 September 1993)

The plastic dress is deliberately fake. Ragga is fiercely postmodern
and the clothes are glaringly man-made. There is no interest in the
authentic, the matured, the antique (in contrast to white street style
with its second-hand poor-look grunge aesthetic). Instead, fabric and
detailing is trashy and vulgarly feminine. Ric-rac braid to trim a
blouse turns up as tramlines stitched on to the functional Lycra
leggings, radically altering their high active message.
(Kowdo Eshun, *The Independent*, 2 September 1993)

This book comprises a number of essays, the first of which was written
in the mid-1980s for the Postmodernism conference at the Institute of
the Contemporary Arts (ICA) in London. The collection takes its title
from this piece and the articles which follow chart the growth of a new
set of interests in cultural studies and in sociology since then. Instead of
providing, by way of an introduction, a short summary of the contents
of this book, I think it is more useful for the students and teachers whom
I envisage reading *Postmodernism and Popular Culture* to indicate, in a
less academic tone, why the various chapters in this book point in favour
of a feminist postmodernism.

It seems that to talk seriously about postmodernism today, one is still
by definition being defensive. This is because postmodernism has become
everybody's favourite *bête noire*, while at the same time not only generously providing something solid to argue against, when so many other
things have been 'melting into air', but also, in some mysterious way,
being a concept in the right place at the right moment. Postmodernism
has therefore served this function of shifting the paradigms in cultural

1

studies and sociology, doing that kind of intellectual work which inevitably provokes controversy and protest, all the more so when what seem to be at stake are precisely those terms like history, society and politics that have given substance and direction to the kind of work we do as teachers and researchers and the reasons why we do it.

 My suggestion in this book is that a feminist postmodernism forces us to confront questions which otherwise remain unasked and that in engaging with them we also find our academic practice and our politics undergoing some degree of transformation and change. There is much to be said for opening discussion out, for taking risks with our ideas, for exercising our disciplines, taking them for a walk and exploring the points at which they seem to reach a limit. This is a necessary strategy not a self-indulgent activity.

In the mid-1980s when postmodernism first appeared on the horizon, imported from France and taken up immediately by American academics like Fred Jameson (Jameson, 1984), it was responded to truculently, to say the least, at the ICA conference in London in 1984. Truculently perhaps because midway through the Thatcher years many on the left wanted unity and argued that any sort of questioning of the foundations of radical political thought, and any visible loss of faith, was simply another sign of the gradual success and the insidious power of the new right. I was accused of moving in this direction precisely because to me it seemed like the right moment to 'take a breather', to ask where we had gone wrong, or more precisely why, if our analysis was right, we had such difficulty in convincing more than just a tiny number of people. At the conference I argued that there was much that was exciting and useful in the postmodern writing which was becoming available. I also wanted at that time to think on the upbeat, and to interpret postmodernism not in terms of Baudrillard's catastrophe scenarios (Baudrillard, 1983) or of Jameson's desire for a return to the strong values of modernity. I argued that living along the fault-lines of the postmodern condition meant engaging with questions and dilemmas and differences which were there on the surface and no longer 'hidden from history' (Rowbotham, 1973).

At that time there were two approaches to postmodernism, each of which raised important questions for sociologists. First there was postmodernism in the field of the arts and in visual culture. From architecture to fine art, from remakes of B movies to the cinema of David Lynch, from Talking Heads to Laurie Anderson, what was becoming increasingly apparent was indeed a concern with surface, with meaning being paraded as an intentionally superficial phenomenon (what Jameson labelled 'waning in effect' or depthlessness). Not only was meaning in art or in culture all there, for all to see, stripped of its old hidden elitist difficulty, but it also, again as Jameson pointed out, seemed already familiar, like the faint memory of an old pop song, a refrain, a chorus, a tune, a 'cover

2

version' of an original which never was. (I still think the best example of this is the music of Blondie in the early 1980s with its tinny, self-consciously 'poppy' format, its tinsel tin-pan alley sound delivered by a breathless, tousled peroxide blonde, with a clear preference for perfect pop lyrics about being left 'hanging on the telephone'.)

Postmodern culture, like *The Big Breakfast* show of today, also seemed to be full of jokes; it refused to take itself seriously and for this reason found itself subject to criticism. Where this playfulness seemed also to penetrate the walls of academia, the response was heavily condemning. As McLennan has recently put it, 'the world remains too ravaged by oppression, ignorance and malnutrition ... for privileged intellectuals to trade in seriousness for the sparkling interplay of language games' (McLennan, 1992a: 18). In the collection that follows I take issue with McLennan and argue in favour of having, on occasion, a playful disposition. This need not in my opinion imply a forgetfulness or abandonment of politics. What it can do is force us to reconsider the foundations of our modern thought. It can also force us to think seriously about the trivial. Looking back it seems strange that exactly at that point in the 1980s when the left was trying to be popular and to plug into popular pleasures, it should react so disapprovingly. But there was a clearly hostile response to commentaries on postmodernism other than those of critique and condemnation.

In this context Jameson's seminal analysis of postmodern culture as the 'logic of late capitalism' occupies the moral high ground. Jameson offers a wonderfully rich account of the new world of the visual image where culture is dominant, while also showing this to be the logical product of a post-industrial capitalism. The force of his critique lies in the deathly quality of the products. There is nothing new, only the old, the recycled, the second-hand, and with this the increasingly intensive plundering of the past in the hope of discovering some mothballed velvet flares or a forgotten Biba dress (my examples) which can be reinserted into the world of the image and given meaning as simultaneously old and new. This represents the death of the imagination, the death of politics and virtually the death of the social, and according to Jameson it is connected with different and more fragmented identities or subjectivities. Lack of unity or thrust in culture is reflected in the lack of unity in the self. And this is and was at the heart of my critique on Jameson and his account of postmodernity. In Part III of this book, 'Youth, media, postmodernity', I attempt to show how second-hand, do-it-yourself plundering of culture, particularly on the part of both black and white young people who are as yet unformed as adults, and relatively powerless as a result, can give them space to impregnate a scornful, often condemning adult social order with the politics of their adolescent identities.

In *Postmodernism and Popular Culture* I also make two quite simple

3

suggestions. I suggest that the superficial does not necessarily represent a decline into meaninglessness or valuelessness in culture. Analysis of the so-called trivial should not remain at the level of the semiotic reading. In this sense postmodernism emerged like a breath of fresh air allowing cultural critics to shift their gaze away from the search for meaning in the text towards the sociological play between images and between different cultural forms and institutions. The glossy surface of pop, the intertextual referencing between film and advert and television programme, where Spender, in the TV crime series of that name, looks like an advert for designer beer, where adverts for Levi 501s re-enact Hollywood classics kaleidoscoped into trailers of 45 seconds, and where new Hollywood films like *9½ Weeks* take their lead from successful adverts, all this criss-crossing and fast cutting need not be seen as heralding the death of politics in culture but it does mean that we have to develop a critical vocabulary which can take this rapid movement into account. To my mind, postmodern criticism was better able to do this than semiology or structuralism.

But more important was Jameson's critique of surface. Drawing on the case of camp, and on Susan Sontag's well-known essay, 'Notes on "camp" ' (Sontag, 1967) I argue that to opt for the superficial can be a deliberate political strategy. Only by theorizing the producers of culture (in this case gay men) and by paying closer attention to the social practices of consuming culture, can we get a better understanding of how the tinsel and the glitter can produce meaning, in a different but no less significant kind of way than the great deep works of modernism.

I also want to query Jameson's notion of schizophrenic subjectivity and its integral connection with the depthlessness of postmodern culture. The obvious question to ask is which social subjects have had the privilege of being whole, or 'healthy', and thus fully inscribed in history and in culture? Who have been best able to represent the voice of their generation in culture? Who have been the spokesmen and spokeswomen of society? To lament the decline of full wholesome subjectivity is literally to cast aspersions on unwholesome, un(in)formed, partial and hybridic identities. It is to refuse the challenge of the invented, fabulous identities of the DJs and MCs of black culture, to close the ears to the musical sounds and samples which by playing with the names and the uncertain origins of the cultural producers mock and resist the whole heavily authorial game of western art and artistic production, and disguise themselves and their artistry in the costume ball of fun and funk. (I am thinking here perhaps of the mad musical inventiveness of George Clinton, the anarchic, falling-over-the-edge tracks of Parliament, Brides of Funkenstein and many others which provided an 'origin unknown' sample mix for a thousand other samplers and mixers ten years later.)

The second way of looking at postmodernism back in the 1980s was to consider it as an anti-foundationalist form of anti-social theory – that is, a form of criticism which interrogated and exposed the (cruel) foundations upon which modern social thought had been based. This approach, which became more familiar in the late 1980s, suggested that there could no longer be one theory of society, no one 'big picture'. At best there were a number of snapshots of the same view, each aware of the limits of its own field of vision. Here, too, we can detect a playfulness, a disrespect for the meta-narratives of history, a refusal to play the game of philosophy and a desire instead to enjoy a wilful breaking of the rules in favour of epithet, contingency, discontinuity. No wonder the work of postmodern theorists like Lyotard and Baudrillard infuriated the British left and the sociologists who were rightly wearied and frustrated after ten years of Thatcherism.

None the less it still seems to me that there is much to make use of here. Baudrillard's work on the real finding a reference point and a reality within the world of the mass-produced image remains of critical importance to the new sociology of the mass media. Real life means talking about what was on TV last night. Reality is the *News at Ten* and the images on the news become a reference point for the further experiencing of and construction of reality. The image of Joan Collins is as real as, if not more real than, Joan Collins in real life where she is 'realized' by her image-makers (hairdressers, makeup artists and stylists) for the pictures that will be taken of her on and off screen, at home (in *Hello!*) and in the street. She exists therefore to be 'snapped at'.

If Baudrillard remains the scourge of media sociologists for his scrambled channel-flicking style of writing, Lyotard infuriates others by appearing to play philosophical games with 'the foundations of modern thought'. He argues that the disavowal of fictions, narratives and stories with the growth of the age of science, reason and the enlightenment, disguised the fact that these were constructed within great overarching narratives and stories (of the freedom of the market, of progress and even of science itself). Capitalism and Marxism both depended on stories of progress, emancipation, revolution and success. The science which promised knowledge of and mastery over nature was part of a much bigger story of conquest, decimation and militarization. Lyotard is wary of big pictures too. Does this mean the end of history, politics, or society? Not at all. It means being attentive to the assumptions which shape social theory, the criteria which it uses and the pillars which support it. It means that we should also be alert to boundary-marking and to what exactly is being excluded from or included in the fields of knowledge which are now part of the information landscape of contemporary culture.

The other 'big issue' at the end of the 1980s was the future of Marxism in a postmodern sociology or cultural studies. Lyotard's critique of the meta-narratives of history coincided with the emergence of the post-colonialist critic, the subaltern subject who could not find a comfortable space of identity for him or herself within the Marxist class analysis of history. This coincided with the demise of the so-called Marxist regimes and the apparent fragmentation of the working classes of the western world as the old world of industrial labour gave way to the service sector, to core and periphery models of employment, and to forms of identity which were not constructed around work, class and community but instead around other constellations of strong cultural meaning: the body, sexuality, or ethnicity, for example; nationality, style, image, even subculture. A critique of Marxism inside cultural studies became inevitable. Laclau's *Reflections on the New Revolutions of Our Times* (Laclau, 1991) proposes the possibility of being post-Marxist. This is an important work for two reasons which are explored in more depth in one of the articles in this collection, 'Post-Marxism and cultural studies' (chapter 3).

First, Laclau insists on the 'radical incommensurability' of different social groupings and divisions (age, sex, ethnicity, class, nationality) and takes as his starting-point the unlikeliness of their unity, outside the incidental, the unplanned, the contingent. Post-Marxists have to begin to think through consequences of difference and divergences, boundaries and borders. Second, Laclau reminds us that in Gramsci's thought, hegemony was not just how the dominant social order practised government, it was also what the fundamental class (i.e. the working class) had to achieve. Alliances were not enough, achieving hegemony required leadership and a unity which would inevitably entail at specific points in time a smothering of difference. Gramsci is not being rejected outright, but in moving decisively away from unity and alliances, Laclau is also shifting into a post-Marxist mode.

This poses an equally important question for feminism. What happens to feminism when it confronts questions of difference and fragmentation, when as a universalist movement, feminism finds itself under attack from women who want to state their difference? Can the term post-feminism occupy any useful place in cultural theory and in sociology?

IN THE YEARS OF LIVING DANGEROUSLY

In the field of social theory the place of women in modernity has recently been posed against the politics of feminism in a postmodern society. It has become standard either to remain uncommitted in relation to postmodernism or else, rather reluctantly, to defend modernity. Why has this been the case? Modernity, it has been argued, provided the spaces for a discourse of freedom, emancipation and equality to emerge. The Enlightenment also freed people from the grip of superstition, mysticism and religious dogma. However, the difficulty of trying to fit women into the philosophical framework of the Enlightenment and of modern social thought has required a good deal of mental gymnastics. And what has happened is that either feminists have argued for the retention of 'large narratives' or for a postmodern feminist theory which would be 'pragmatic and fallibilistic' (Wolff, 1990), or else a few have abandoned the search to fit women in and have explored what happens when they wave good-bye to modernity and fully confront the consequences of postmodern social criticism. This debate is one which I explore in chapter 4, closing Part I of this book. What is at stake in abandoning modernity as an enabling structure is the fear of losing the notion of the women's move-ment, losing the idea of what it is to be a woman, and losing with this a politics of representation, that is able to speak on behalf of 'women'. This is because postmodern theory explores the foundations which secure and support this idea of a single womanhood and in so doing point to who is excluded. Feminist postmodern theory insists that we listen to the voices of those who dispute the terms of representation and who say 'This is not us'. That these voices are often those of black women is not insignificant.

An alternative way of thinking through feminism, modernism and post-modernism has been to set feminism alongside questions of culture. Nava (1992) and Bowlby (1992) argue that far from being invisible in modernist culture women played a key role in the new public spaces of the modern city and in so doing came to represent the growth of capitalist consumer culture. Modernity was symbolized in the strikingly fashionable figure of the modern woman. According to these writers there is a case to be made for positioning women strongly inside modernity. The temperature is also less heated when feminists engage with postmodernism as an artistic practice. Here we can see a lively debate around postmodern strategies in painting, in film and photography, and also in writing. My own feeling is that some of this work is flawed by what is done to postmodern theory to make it compatible with feminist cultural criticism. It is first given a historical place which is in line with and connected to its modernist predecessor, and then slotted into a recognizable radical tradition. Janet Wolff appears to endorse Craig Owens's definition of postmodern art as work which 'undermines representation and which operates a deconstruc-tive action within art. . . . This is to return to a view of postmodern cultural practice which connects with poststructuralist and postmodern theory, and whose radical project is the destabilizing of the image' (Wolff, 1990: 195). By locating postmodernism within the radical tradition in art in this way and by disavowing the radical break marked by this way of thinking, to my mind Janet Wolff ends up rather lamely suggesting that 'the best kind of postmodern theory and practice is in fact a kind of modified modern-ism' (ibid.: 205). If she is right then there is no real case to be made for a distinctively feminist postmodernism. Instead there is an agreed line leading from modernity into postmodernity and the question for feminists revolves around the point of connection.

McLennan would agree with the need for this sense of connection and continuity and he would also opt for modifying modernity. He reminds us that the Enlightenment meant the idea of making better the society in which we live. The development of the social sciences was part of that project. He warns against the dangers of disavowing the ideals of modernity in favour of relativism which he argues encourages 'indifference'. There must be universals, he says. Without them discussions about what is good and what is true cannot take place.

Stuart Hall (1992) explores a different set of possibilities. He argues that the new world is a very different one. There are moving boundaries and borders, new maps, new nationalisms and transnationalisms. He seems to be suggesting that what we have to do as sociologists is to explain these changes. Instead of defending modernity Hall reminds us of its 'other side'. Where some have seen order, reason and achievement, humanity and vision, he sees savagery and turbulence. His is a postcolonialist voice. The question this poses for feminists is whether we also should explore the other side of modernity. Can we afford to leave it behind and think through, with all the effort it entails, what a politics of feminism might look like from a postmodern perspective and what kind of sociological practice might emerge from such a position?

Braidotti (1992), Butler (1992), Flax (1992a, 1992b) and, from a feminist postcolonialist position, Gayatri Chakravorty Spivak (1992) help us to do this by pursuing a radical critique of modernity. Reason, humanity and even equality are 'domination' Enlightenment concepts. To enlighten some was to regulate many others. The great achievements of rationality and knowledge were founded on disciplinary practices of a new order and dimension. This kind of questioning, however, need not mean the abandonment of all reason; instead it asks after the construction of reason or rationality. We also have to think about thinking. On whose behalf do we do it? Why? What is it to be a feminist intellectual or a feminist sociologist? If feminism is one of the products of modernity and if it cannot and should not represent all women, how do we create a politics of feminism, to whom do we speak? Both Butler and Spivak talk about the important moment being the one when 'other' women say that they are not being spoken to. So when black women make this comment they too are creating and asserting a different identity as women. Likewise with younger women; influenced by feminism as good sense but enraged by the attempts of teachers, mothers and others to make them into good feminists, they show decisively how the old polarity between feminism (good) and femininity (bad) has, as Charlotte Brunsdon (1992) has shown, gone for good. Things are much more complex now. We have to look for what emerges from between feminism and femininity, and we have to attend to the inventiveness of women as they create new social categories, some of which cause grave concern on the part of the social order.

Studying single mothers and the new fluid relations of family life would therefore be an excellent starting-point for a feminist postmodern sociology.

Flax takes some of Butler's points even further. It is frightening to believe no longer that reason will triumph and save us from the threat of unreason. The failure to face up to the limits of reason, truth and knowledge, is predicated on a fearfulness of letting go. Go on, she says. And I would agree. Not to live with fear and danger is to block out so much of daily lived experience. If postmodernism forces uncertainty on to the agenda, if we have to look beyond reason, then at least we are forewarned. Our politics can begin to reflect the multiple realities of social insecurity. We have to deal with our own personal as well as political 'moral panics'.

This also gives us a way of constructing a kind of feminist postmodernism in sociology and cultural studies which refuses the lure of believing that if we try hard enough we can reproduce our feminist selves and our feminist theory in our daughters and with our students. Post-feminism and postmodernism in the social sciences must mean being able to see the deep problem with this kind of thinking. We have to respect difference and that includes the experience of young women for whom feminism, as we know, is not necessarily the political space they choose, even if they feel and express a desire to achieve equality. We have to let go and recognize the limits of our skills of analysis and our critical insight. They have to be credited with the ability to make their own judgements about what it is to be a young woman in Britain. Allowing this kind of gender space-for-difference makes teaching and research a more exciting project. It forces us to ask all the time why are we teaching this, does it still apply, is it relevant to our students? Each of the essays in this collection addresses some aspect of social change. How social relations are conducted within the field of culture, and how culture in turn symbolizes the experience of change, provide the points of reference for this body of work. And as each of the authors quoted at the beginning of this introduction indicates, much of the attention in cultural studies, and in this collection, is paid to the important but often unnoticed dynamics of everyday life: the sounds in the kitchen, the noises in the home, and the signs and styles on the street.

REFERENCES

Baudrillard, Jean (1983) *In the Shadow of the Silent Majorities*, New York: Semiotexte.

Berman, Marshall (1984) *All That Is Solid Melts into Air: The Experience of Modernity*, London: Verso.

Bowlby, Rachel (1992) *Still Crazy After All These Years*, London: Routledge.

Braidotti, Rosi (1992) 'On the feminist female subject or from she-self to she-other', in G. Bock and S. James (eds) *Beyond Equality and Difference: Citizenship, Feminist Politics and Female Subjectivity*, London: Routledge, pp. 176–92.

Brunsdon, Charlotte (1992) 'Pedagogies of the feminine: feminist teaching and women's genres', *Screen* 32, 4: 364–82.

Butler, Judith (1992) 'Contingent foundations: feminism and the question of "postmodernism"', in J. Butler and J. W. Scott (eds) *Feminists Theorise the Political*, London: Routledge, pp. 3–22.

Flax, Jane (1992a) 'Beyond equality: gender, justice and difference', in G. Bock and S. James (eds) *Beyond Equality and Difference: Citizenship, Feminist Politics and Female Subjectivity*, London: Routledge, pp. 192–209.

Flax, Jane (1992b) 'The end of innocence', in J. Butler and J. W. Scott (eds) *Feminists Theorise the Political*, London: Routledge, pp. 445–64.

Hall, Stuart (1992), 'The question of cultural identity', in S. Hall, D. Held and D. McGrew (eds) *Modernity and Its Futures*, Oxford: Polity Press, pp. 273–327.

Jameson, Fredric (1984) 'Postmodernism, or the cultural logic of capital', *New Left Review* 146: 53–92.

Laclau, Ernesto (1991) *Reflections on the New Revolutions of Our Times*, London: Verso.

Lyotard, Jean-François (1984) *The Postmodern Condition*, Manchester: Manchester University Press.

McLennan, Gregor (1992a) 'Sociology after postmodernism', inaugural address, Faculty of Social Sciences Occasional Papers, Massey University, Palmers Bag, New Zealand, pp. 1–22.

McLennan, Gregor (1992b) 'The enlightenment project revisited', in S. Hall, D. Held and D. McGrew (eds) *Modernity and Its Futures*, Oxford: Polity Press, pp. 327–79.

Nava, Mica (1992) *Changing Cultures: Feminism, Youth, Consumerism*, London: Sage.

Rowbotham, Sheila (1973) *Hidden from History*, London: Pluto Press.

Sontag, Susan (1967) 'Notes on "camp"', in S. Sontag, *Against Interpretation*, London: Eyre & Spottiswode, pp. 35–64.

Spivak, Gayatri Chakravorty (1992) 'French feminism revisited', in J. Butler and J. W. Scott (eds) *Feminists Theorise the Political*, London: Routledge, p. 54–86.

Wolff, Janet (1990) 'Postmodern theory and feminist art practice', in R. Boyne and A. Rattansi (eds) *Postmodernism and Society*, London: Macmillan, pp. 187–208.

Part I

POSTMODERNITY AND CULTURAL STUDIES

1

POSTMODERNISM AND POPULAR CULTURE

THE 'SOWETO DASH'

Rather than starting with a definition of postmodernism as referring either to a condition of contemporary life, or to a textual, aesthetic practice, I want to begin by suggesting that the recent debates on postmodernism possess both a positive attraction and a usefulness to the analyst of popular culture. This is because they offer a wider, and more dynamic, understanding of contemporary representation than other accounts to date. Unlike the various strands of structuralist criticism, postmodernism considers images as they relate to and across each other. Postmodernism deflects attention away from the singular scrutinizing gaze of the semiologist, and asks that this be replaced by a multiplicity of fragmented, and frequently interrupted, 'looks'.

The exemplary text or the single, richly coded image gives way to the textual thickness and the visual density of everyday life, as though the slow, even languid 'look' of the semiologist is, by the 1980s, out of tempo with the times. The field of postmodernism certainly expresses a frustration, not merely with this seemingly languid pace, but with its increasing inability to make tangible connections between the general conditions of life today and the practice of cultural analysis.

Structuralism has also replaced old orthodoxies with new ones. This is apparent in its rereading of texts highly placed within an already existing literary or aesthetic hierarchy. Elsewhere it constructs a new hierarchy, with Hollywood classics at the top, followed by selected advertising images, and girls' and women's magazines rounding it off. Other forms of representation, particularly music and dance, are missing altogether. Andreas Huyssen in his 1984 introduction to postmodernism draws attention to this 'high' structuralist preference for the works of high modernism, especially the writing of James Joyce or Mallarmé. 'There is no doubt that centre stage in critical theory is held by the classical modernists: Flaubert . . . in Barthes . . . Mallarmé and Artaud in Derrida, Magritte . . . in Foucault . . . Joyce and Artaud in Kristeva . . . and so on *ad infinitum*'

(Huyssen, 1984: 39). He argues that this reproduces unhelpfully the old distinction between the high arts and the 'low', less serious, popular arts. He goes on to comment: 'Pop in the broadest sense was the context in which a notion of the postmodern first took shape ... and the most significant trends within postmodernism have challenged modernism's relentless hostility to mass culture' (Huyssen, 1984: 16). High theory was simply not equipped to deal with multilayered pop. Nor did it ever show much enthusiasm about this set of forms, perhaps because pop has never signified within one discrete discourse, but instead combines images with performance, music with film or video, and pin-ups with the magazine form itself. As a *Guardian* journalist recently (3 January 1986) put it, 'Rock and pop performers today have to speak in multi-media tongues'.

With the exception of Barthes, 'heavy-weight' criticism has been focused towards memorable texts, while light-weight cultural analysis is given over to the more forgettable images of everyday life. And the 'purity' of the about-to-be-decoded image is reflected in the pivotal position occupied by semiology and structuralist criticism in media courses up and down the country. Despite gestures towards intertextuality and interdisciplinarity, this centrality given to the *structuralisms* in effect squeezes out of the picture all the other complex relations which locate the text, or the image, and allow it to produce meaning. These relations include those which mark out its physical place within the world of commodities, its sequencing, and its audience as well as consumers. Such issues are frequently relegated, with some disregard, to the realm of sociology or 'empiricism' as though these were the same thing. And while critics argue that this outside reality is really nothing more than a series of other texts, they are in the meantime happy to treat questions about consumers, readers, audience and viewers, as intrinsically uninteresting, as though this entails hanging about street corners with a questionnaire and clipboard.

Postmodernism allows what were respectable sociological issues to reappear on the intellectual agenda. It implicitly challenges the narrowness of structuralist vision, by taking the deep interrogation of every breathing aspect of lived experience by media imagery as a starting-point. So extensive and inescapable is this process that it becomes conceptually impossible to privilege one simple moment. So far only Dick Hebdige's (1979) *Subculture: The Meaning of Style* has broken out of this inadvertent reproduction of the old divide between high culture and the pop arts, as well as between representation and reality. In *Subculture*, Hebdige recognizes that familiar objects warrant analysis as signs and repositories of organized meaning, as much as linguistic or 'pure' visual signs. Under the conceptual umbrella of subculture, he brings together art, literature, music, style, dress and even attitude, and places these on the same analyti-

14

cal plane. Hebdige also brings a speed and an urgency to the business of interpreting the familiar marks of contemporary life.

It is surprising, then, that in a more recent article, where he engages directly with the question of postmodernism, Hebdige (1988) disavows the playful elements in *Subculture . . .* and, more manifestly, in the new fashion and style magazines. In contrast with what he sees now as an *excess* of style, a celebration of artifice and a strong cultural preference for pastiche, Hebdige seeks out the reassuringly real. He suggests that the slick joky tone of postmodernism, especially that found on the pages of *The Face*, represents a disengagement with the real, and an evasion of social responsibility. He therefore insists on a return to the world of hunger, exploitation and oppression and with it a resurrection of unfragmented, recognizable subjectivity. He only fleetingly engages with what Jameson (1984) has described as an important characteristic of the postmodern condition, that is, the death of subjectivity and the emergence, in its place, of widespread social schizophrenia. Hebdige seems to be saying that if this rupturing of identity is what postmodernism is about, then he would rather turn his back on it. What I will be arguing here is that the terrain of all these surfaces Hebdige mentions – pop, music, style and fashion – is neither as homogeneous nor as limited as he (or *The Face*) would have it. This landscape of the present, with its embracing of pastiche, its small defiant pleasure in being dressed up or 'casual', its exploration of fragmented subjectivity – all of this articulates more precisely with the wider conditions of present 'reality': with unemployment, with education, with the 'aestheticization of culture', and with the coming into being of those whose voices were historically drowned out by the (modernist) meta-narratives of mastery, which were in turn both patriarchal and imperialist.

Postmodernism has entered into a more diverse number of vocabularies more quickly than most other intellectual categories. It has spread outwards from the realms of art history into political theory and on to the pages of youth culture magazines, record sleeves and the fashion spreads of *Vogue*. This seems to me to indicate something more than the mere vagaries of taste. More, also, than the old Marcusian notion of recuperation, where a radical concept which once had purchase, rapidly becomes a commodity, and in the process is washed, laundered and left out to dry. Later on in this chapter I will locate this coming together of the worlds of intellectual analysis and pop journalism (as well as pop production) around postmodernism, by considering the role of education, and in particular 'cultural studies'. Here it is sufficient to point to the extensiveness and flexibility of the term.

Postmodernism certainly appeared in the UK like a breath of fresh air. It captured, in a word, a multitude of experiences, particularly what Baudrillard (1985) has called the 'instantaneity of communication'. This refers to the incursion of imagery and communication into those spaces that once were private – where the psyche previously had the chance at least to explore the 'other'; to explore, for example, alienation. Baudrillard claims that this space has now been penetrated by the predatory and globally colonialist media. But as the frontiers of the self are effaced and transformed, so too are the boundaries which mark out separate discourses and separate politics. Baudrillard interprets the new associative possibilities thrown up by 'instantaneity' gloomily. 'Everything is exposed to the harsh and inexorable light of information and communication' (1985: 130), which in turn generates only an 'ecstasy of communication'. But need Baudrillard be quite so pessimistic? Why must this speeding-up process, this intensification of exchange, be greeted with such foreboding?

The remainder of this chapter will be given over to arguing the case for postmodernism. It will suggest that the frenzied expansion of the mass media has political consequences which are not so wholly negative. This becomes most apparent when we look at representations of the Third World. No longer can this be confined to the realist documentary, or the exotic televisual voyage. The Third World refuses now to be reassuringly out of sight of 'us', in the West. It is as adept at using the global media as the old colonialist powers. Equally the 'we' of the British nation no longer possesses any reliable reality. That spurious unity has been decisively shattered. New alliances and solidarities emerge from within and alongside media imagery. A disenchanted black, inner city population in Britain, can watch in an 'ecstasy of communication' as black South Africans use every available resource at hand to put apartheid into crisis. Jokily, and within a kind of postmodern language, Dick Hebdige wrote, in *Subculture*, that TV images of Soweto in 1976 taught British youth 'the Soweto dash'. Ten years later this connection has amplified. The image is the trigger and the mechanism for this new identification.

IMPLOSION

Of course it's not quite so simple. The South African government has recently [1985] banned journalists from the black townships. And in less politically sensitive arenas, the media continue, relentlessly, to hijack events and offer in their place a series of theatrical spectacles whose relevance to what is going on is only tangential and whose formal cues come from other, frequently televisual, forms of representation. The year 1985 was rich in examples. Reagan's illness was relayed to the public, overwhelmingly in the language of soap opera. A *Guardian* correspondent pointed out that nobody would have been convinced if his doctors had not appeared at the press conferences dressed in white coats. A few weeks earlier Shi'ite militiamen took over a TWA airline office in Athens. In what was largely a bid for space on western prime-time television, the captors could afford to appear smiling and jubilant as they offered their victims a Lebanese banquet, against a backdrop of random gunfire at the ceiling, before packing them off to the United States.

This easing out of the real in favour of its most appropriate representation makes it more difficult to talk about the media and society today. It creates even greater difficulties in assessing the relationship between images, or between popular cultural forms, and their consumers. The consciousness industries have changed remarkably over the last ten years, but so have the outlook and the expectations of their audiences.

Against a backdrop of severe economic decline, the mass media continue to capture new outlets, creating fresh markets to absorb their hi-tech commodities. Symbolically the image has assumed a contemporary dominance. It is no longer possible to talk about the image and reality, media and society. Each pair has become so deeply intertwined that it is difficult to draw the line between the two of them. Instead of referring to the real world, much media output devotes itself to referring to other images, other narratives. Self-referentiality is all-embracing, although it is rarely taken account of. The Italian critic and writer Umberto Eco recently (1984) contrasted what TV was (paleo-TV) with what it now is (neo-TV). 'Its prime characteristic is that it talks less and less about the external world. Whereas paleo-television talked about the external world, or pretended to, neo-television talks about itself and about the contacts it established with its own public' (1984: 19).

Self-referentiality occurs within and across different media forms. One TV programme might be devoted to the production of another (Paul Gambaccini 'on' *The Tube*), just as television films based on the making of other large-scale cinema productions are becoming increasingly common. There is a similar dependency for material and content, as well as a relatively recent redefinition of what is interesting, and what readers and viewers want, in the print media's use of televisual stories. *The Face* magazine ran a piece on *The Tube* and, more recently, one on Michelle, the pregnant schoolgirl in *EastEnders*; The *New Musical Express* carried a major feature on *Brookside*, and *City Limits* sent two journalists to the *Coronation Street* set for a week. It's not so much that fiction is being mistaken for fact; more that one set of textual practices (in this case British soap) has become the reference point for another (reading the newspaper or glancing at a headline).

Media interdependency is both an economic and a cultural imperative. Children's TV on a Saturday morning evolves entirely around the pop music industry, offering an exclusive showcase for new 'promo' videos. The contents of these programmes are orchestrated around all the familiar pop business, phone-in to the stars, interviews, the new single, the talent competition for young hopefuls. This shows the feeding-off effect between mass media today. Where once the middle-class world of *Blue Peter* documented children's initiatives for charity, now Capital, in the form of culture and visual communications, penetrates further into the youth market. In the classless world of these programmes this means pushing back the frontiers of young people as consumers by transforming children and even toddlers into fans and thus part of the record-buying public.

The implications of this endless cross-referencing are extensive. It creates an ever-increasing, but less diverse, verbal and visual landscape. It is these recurring fictions and the characters who inhabit them which feed into the field of popular knowledge, and which in turn constitute a large part of popular culture. It would be difficult not to know about Victoria Principal, it would be impossible not to know about *Dallas*.

Texts have always alluded to or connected with others. Simone de Beauvoir's (1984) *Memoirs of a Dutiful Daughter* gives up many pages to all the books she read during her childhood, adolescence and early adult years. Indeed this critical bibliography forms a major strand of the work. The difference now is that the process is less restricted to literature, more widespread, and most apparent in the commercial mass media where there are more spaces to be filled. And such an opening up doesn't necessarily mean an extension of rights of access, only rights of consumption. More often it means a form of cosy, mutual congratulatory, cross-referencing and repetition (Wogan in *Denver*, Clive James in *Dallas*). Baudrillard greets these recent changes with some cynicism. He claims that more media offers less meaning in the guise of more information: 'All secrets, spaces and scenes abolished in a single dimension of information' (Baudrillard, 1985: 130). Eco follows this when he describes the scrambling effect of multi-channel choice on TV: 'Switching channels reflects the brevity and speed of other visual forms. Like flicking through a magazine, or driving past a billboard. This means that "our" TV evenings no longer tell us stories, it is all a trailer!' (Eco, 1984: 25).

Images push their way into the fabric of our social lives. They enter into how we look and what we earn, and they are still with us when we worry about bills, housing and bringing up children. They compete for attention through shock tactics, reassurance, sex and mystery, and by inviting viewers to participate in series of visual puzzles. Billboard advertisements showing an image without a code impose themselves, infuriatingly, on the most recalcitrant passer-by.

However, what is often forgotten is that the media also enter the classroom. This remains an undocumented site in the history of the image. But in seminar rooms across the country, slides are projected and students prise open new readings. The educational incorporation of contemporary mass media represents something other than the simple consumption of images, but it is also part of the widening-out process I mentioned earlier. People's usage of and experience of the media increases not just because there is more of it, but because it crops up in different places. Almost all the new disciplines in the arts and social sciences make use of pop imagery, whether in adult education, in degree courses, or on project work with unemployed young people. This gives rise to a rather more optimistic reading of the mass media than that offered by Baudrillard. The invasive impact of these new technologies, because they now occupy a place within these institutions, provides a basis for the production of new meanings, new cultural expressions. There is a myth that radical or challenging media forms come 'from the street'. In fact it is in the media workshops, in the creative writing classes and the college studios that such work emerges. Art students specializing in graphics and a dissertation on 'left imagery' go on to work freelance for *The Face*; others opt for mainstream advertising agencies while working unpaid for the Labour Party, or the women's movement, or new black cultural groups. (This was certainly my experience in teaching art students at St Martin's School of Art in London.) And of course the history of British pop music is one which grew out of the expansion of the art schools in the 1960s and the flooding into them of bright young working-class boys.

It is not absolutely necessary for my argument that these new forms of pop culture are and have been of a homogeneously high standard. It is much more important that the work itself is considered both in terms of where it comes from and who made it, and of what groups have, in turn, taken it up.

Twenty years ago Susan Sontag (1967) offered an interesting perspective on those forms of popular culture which are good because they are so awful. This was reflective of a *camp* sensibility, the essence of which is 'its love of the unnatural: of artifice and exaggeration'. Until then this was a widely felt but as yet untheorized popular aesthetic. In her essay Sontag stressed the importance of the knowing audience, one which could allow itself absorption because it was equally capable of detachment. This is useful to us here because it offers a fruitful way forward in understanding the more combative side, particularly in young people's engagement with culture. We can use both the notion of camp and that of the knowing audience to extend Jameson's (1984) recent attempt to make sense of the ever-accumulating and stultifyingly banal images which form such a staple part of the media output. He describes this as a new kind of depthlessness, a 'waning in effect'. Jameson applies the term pastiche to describe these circulating forms. This certainly has an immediate resonance. In both pop music and in the popular soap operas, pastiche is a dominant motif. According to Jameson pastiche 'without that still latent feeling that there exists something normal compared to which what is being imitated, is rather comic. Pastiche is blank parody' (1984: 114).

In *Dallas* and *Dynasty* this is the most appropriate way of describing the heightening of reality which becomes in turn a deadening unreality. These soaps signal a realism in which they have absolutely no investment.

The practised sincerity of the pop performer, his or her anxiety to convey real, recognizable and searing emotions, carries the same quality. In each case the reference back to real life or real emotions is purely formal or stylistic; a mannerism pointing nowhere. But Jameson's accurate account of this 'speech in a dead language' fails to engage with its reception. Perhaps this is because the bulk of his analysis of the 'postmodern condition' is focused towards art rather than popular culture, and in this arena little academic concern has been shown for audiences or consumers. However, in the field where Jameson's thesis is most markedly appropriate, that of pop music and its subsidiaries, there is no question of denying the consumers or fans their place. But how this integration is understood conceptually remains more problematic. Sontag's linking of pastiche with its favoured audience, gay men, is instructive because she shows how a relationship evolved around a social minority making a bid for a cultural form in which they felt they could stake some of their fragmented and sexually deviant identity. The insistence, on the way, on both style and pleasure made the product attractive to those outside as well as inside. The result was the absorption of camp style into the mainstream of popular taste. Sontag's approach is useful because she is not so much talking about pure or original 'artistic' invention, but rather describing how forms can be taken over and reassembled to suit the requirements of the group in question. This often means outstripping their ostensible meaning and ostensible function. In this capacity male gay culture has in the last few years had a remarkable impact. It has been explicit and outspoken, while holding on to both an aesthetic and a political discourse. In pop music, groups like Frankie Goes to Hollywood and Bronski Beat as well as performers like Marc Almond and Boy George have utilized many of the pastiche elements which Sontag describes, achieving mainstream success without blunting the edges of a celebratory homosexuality.

The advantages of Sontag's comments are that they emphasize *agency*. She brings the audience, the consumers, the 'camp followers' into the picture without sidetracking into 'empiricism'. The same would have to be done with pop music and contemporary youth culture. It is impossible to understand Boy George and Culture Club's rise to prominence without considering the punk, art-school, London, 'educated' subculture from which they emerged.

And, if media forms are so inescapable, 'if unreality is now within everyone's grasp' (Eco, 1984), then there is no reason to assume that the consumption of pastiche, parody, or high camp is, by definition, without subversive or critical potential. Glamour, glitter and gloss should not so easily be relegated to the insistently apolitical. For the left, necessarily committed to endorsing the real and the material conditions of people's lives, there remains still an (understandable) stiffness about Neil Kinnock's appearance in a Tracy Ullman video. This need not be the case.

If, as Jameson suggests, life has been dramatized to the level of soap, if love is always like a *Jackie* story, then yes, the sharp distinction between real life and fictional forms must give way to a deep intermingling, unmeasurable and so far captured most precisely in fictive or cinematic forms. Scorsese's *King of Comedy* traced this 'overdetermination by the image'; so did Woody Allen's *Stardust Memories*, as well as his more recent *Zelig* and *The Purple Rose of Cairo*. But Gore Vidal's (1983) novel *Duluth* outstrips all of these. It is a model of postmodern writing. Gore Vidal has his tongue firmly in his cheek. *Duluth* is a witty multilayered fiction which moves from the town of the title, to the soap series based on the place, outwards to the novel of the soap, backwards into the historical romances favoured by the town's top woman cop, and forwards into a science fiction setting where Roland Barthes makes a guest appearance. Obligingly Vidal ends the novel by handing it over to a word processor.

All of this comes close to what Baudrillard (1981) infuriatingly calls implosion. It's a vague but appropriate term. It implies an outburst of energy which is none the less controlled and inclining inwards. Baudrillard, Eco and Jameson all see this as a totalizing and all-immersing process. But none of them considers the new associations and resistances which have come into prominence by way of these processes in the last fifteen years. Many of these share more in common with the shattered energy of implosion, with Jameson's fragmented schizophrenic consciousness, than with the great narratives of the old left.

> It was especially the art, writing, film-making and criticism of women and minority artists, with their recuperation of buried and mutilated traditions, their emphasis on exploring forms of gender- and race-based subjectivity in aesthetic productions and experiences, and their refusal to be limited to standard canonizations, which added a whole new dimension to the critique of high modernism and to the emergence of alternative forms of culture.
>
> (Huyssen, 1984: 27)

In the British context one would want to append to this formidable production not just the proliferation of pop culture and the challenge it has mounted to the mainstream arts, but also the involvement of youth in the creation of an egalitarian avant-garde. Of course this is no longer an avant-garde proper, since the privileging of the forms has been abandoned in favour of a cross-referencing between forms, and notably between pop music and 'art', between aesthetics and commerce, between commitment and the need to make a living. This leads directly to a further failing in Jameson's account. There is no recognition that those elements contained within his diagnosis of postmodernism – including pastiche, the ransacking and recycling of culture, the direct invocation to other texts and other images – can create a vibrant critique rather than an inward-looking, second-hand aesthetics. What else has black urban culture in the last few years been, but an assertive reassembling of bits and pieces, 'whatever comes to hand', noises, debris, technology, tape, image, rapping, scratching and other hand-me-downs? Black urban music has always thrived on fake, forged identities, creating a façade of grand-sounding titles which reflect both the 'otherness' of black culture, the extent to which it is outside that which is legitimate, and the way in which white society has condemned it to be nameless. Who, after all, is Grandmaster Flash or Melle Mel? Or who was Sly and the Family Stone? Who mixed the speech by Malcolm X on to a haunting disco funk backing track? Reggae also parodies this enforced namelessness. Many of its best-known musicians suggest a deep irony in their stage-names: Clint Eastwood, Charlie Chaplin, and so on.

In America graffiti remain the best example of fleeting, obsolescent urban aesthetics, giving their creators fame once they get into the galleries but otherwise only faint notoriety.

> It is a cultural identity which half mocks, half celebrates, the excesses of mainstream white culture. The graffiti painter is the Spiderman of the ghettos, projecting pure fantasy. A terminal vantage point on white consumer culture. Hip hop is a subculture which feeds for its material upon the alien culture which need make no concession to blacks. The spray paints and comic book images of graffiti painting, to the disco beats and found sounds of rapping, are diverted from their mainstream domestic use and put out on the streets as celebration. For the white middle-class kid, the comic heroes occupy a space of boredom. For the black ghetto kid they are transformed by graffiti art into fantastic visions invested with secret meanings.
>
> (Atlanta and Alexander, 1981)

Alongside these largely male forms must be placed the writing of black women, the great explosion of the written word which writes a history otherwise condemned to remain only within popular memory. Toni Cade Bambara's (1983) prose is closest in rhythm to the jazz sounds of the city. It is breath-taking, agile writing, insisting on the pleasure, the wit and the idiosyncrasies of a community more often characterized as monolithic and deprived. All of this is taking place within the cracks of a crumbling culture where progress is in question and society seems to be standing still.

There *is* no going back. For populations transfixed on images which are themselves a reality, there is no return to a mode of representation which politicizes in a kind of straightforward 'worthwhile' way. *Dallas* is destined to sit alongside images of black revolt. And it is no longer possible, living within postmodernism, to talk about unambiguously negative or positive images. But this need not be seen as the end of the social, or the end of meaning, or for that matter the beginning of the new nihilism. Social agency is employed in the activation of *all* meanings. Audiences or viewers, lookers or users are not simple-minded multitudes. As the media extends its sphere of influence, so also does it come under the critical surveillance *and* usage of its subjects.

The reason why postmodernism appeals to a wider number of young people, and to what might be called the new generation of intellectuals (often black, female, or working-class) is that they themselves are experiencing the enforced fragmentation of impermanent work and low career opportunities. Far from being overwhelmed by media saturation, there is evidence to suggest that these social groups and minorities are putting it to work for them. This alone should prompt the respect and the attention of an older generation which seems at present too eager to embrace a sense of political hopelessness.

This article first appeared in *Postmodernism* (1986), ICA Documents 4 and 5, ed. Lisa Appignanesi, London: Institute of Contemporary Arts, pp. 54–8.

REFERENCES

Atlanta and Alexander (1981) 'Wild style . . . graffiti painting', *ZG* 6.
Bambara, T. C. (1983) *Gorilla, My Love*, London: Women's Press.
Baudrillard, J. (1981) *For a Critique of the Political Economy of the Sign*, trans. C. Levin, St. Louis, MO: Telos Press.
Baudrillard, J. (1985) 'The ecstasy of communication', trans. J. Johnson, in H. Foster (ed.) *The Anti-Aesthetic*, Port Townsend, WA: Bay Press, pp. 126–34.
de Beauvoir, S. (1984) *Memoirs of a Dutiful Daughter*, Harmondsworth, Mx: Penguin.
Eco, U. (1984) 'A guide to the neo-television of the 1980s', *Framework* 25: 18–27.
Hebdige, D. (1979) *Subculture: The Meaning of Style*, London: Methuen.
Hebdige, D. (1988) 'The bottom line on Planet One: squaring up to *The Face*', in D. Hebdige, *Hiding in the Light*, London: Routledge/Comedia, pp. 155–81.
Huyssen, A. (1984) 'Mapping the postmodern', *New German Critique* 33: 5–52.
Jameson, F. (1984) 'Postmodernism and consumer society', in H. Foster (ed.) *The Anti-Aesthetic*, Port Townsend, WA: Bay Press, pp. 111–25.
Sontag, S. (1967), 'Notes on "camp" ', in S. Sontag, *Against Interpretation*, London: Eyre & Spottiswode, pp. 35–64.
Vidal, G. (1983) *Duluth*, New York: Random House.

2

NEW TIMES IN CULTURAL STUDIES

The study of culture has, over the last few years, been quite dramatically transformed as questions of modernity and postmodernity have replaced the more familiar concepts of ideology and hegemony which, from the mid-1970s until the mid-1980s, anchored cultural analysis firmly within the neo-Marxist field mapped out by Althusser and Gramsci. Modernity and postmodernity have also moved far beyond the academic fields of media or cultural studies. Hardly one branch of the arts, humanities or social sciences has remained untouched by the debates which have accompanied their presence. They have also found their way into the 'quality' press and on to TV, and of course they have entered the art school studios informing and giving shape to the way in which art practitioners including architects, painters and film-makers define and execute their work. Good or bad, to be welcomed or reviled, these terms have corresponded to some sea-change in the way in which cultural intellectuals and practitioners experience and seek to understand the world in the late 1980s and into the 1990s. So deeply interrogative has been the notion of postmodernity that it has proved not just permissible, but necessary, to bring together *postmodernism* as an aesthetic/cultural movement whose impetus derives from the break it marks out with modernism and the avant-garde, and whose impact lies in its turning away from linearity and teleological progress towards pastiche, quotation, parody and pluralism of style, with *postmodernity* as a more general condition. As Boyne and Rattansi argue:

> What allows us an extension of the term postmodernism to both the fine arts and trends within the disciplines of literary theory, philosophy and the social sciences is that they share a common condition which we would characterise as a crisis in 'representation' ... in which older modes of defining ... the objects of artistic ... and social scientific languages are no longer credible.... It is arguable that the idea of 'crises of representation' can be extended to cover the crises of social class-dominated politi-

24

cal movements and discourses and some of the problems of political representation now apparent in both liberal democratic polities and state socialist systems, thus allowing a characterisation of the 'postmodern condition' as one of coincidence between 'crises of representation' in the fine arts, philosophy, the social sciences and 'modern' political institutions.[1]

One of the arguments in this chapter will be that the intensity of the modernity/postmodernity exchange among left intellectuals has signalled the depth of the crisis in neo-Marxist thinking on culture, and has acted as a kind of warranty, freeing Marxist critics, even if temporarily, from some of their earlier theoretical obligations. The reasons for this crisis and its implications for cultural studies have not as yet been argued through. Nor has the reductionist return to Marxism, as advocated by Fredric Jameson, been held up to scrutiny. It is critics like Jameson and David Harvey, each of whom in the course of their respective analyses *re-states* a case for a more conventional mode of neo-Marxist or historical materialist analysis, who none the less benefit most from the theoretical 'loosening up' which postmodernity seems to offer them.[2] Their writing brings greater breadth to cultural theory. The enormous number of critical responses there have been to Jameson's milestone article on postmodernism is a measure of the scope it has provided for stimulating debate.[3] But one of the questions which remains unasked, is precisely that of the status and the future of Marxism in the study of culture in the 1990s; or, more brusquely, where now?

The purpose of this chapter will be to take stock of the contribution of postmodernity to cultural analysis, and also to consider one of those permutations which has emerged from this same set of conceptual sea-changes, bearing with it a more immediately political project. 'New Times' is a term coined by contributors to the highly respected monthly journal of the Communist Party, *Marxism Today*.[4] British rather than international in its connotations, the term signals something of the diversity of social and political upheavals in Britain over the last ten years including the success of 'Thatcherism', the decline of traditional working-class politics, the emergence of a politics of identity and consumption, and most importantly the challenge these present to the left. Despite being linked originally with the Communist Party, New Times has moved into the wider vocabulary of cultural intellectuals, providing them with a means of finding common ground with political activists. It has also entered the political agenda of the weekly magazine, the *New Statesman and Society*, and, to an extent, of the Labour Party.[5]

New Times might be seen as a take on postmodernity, a means of drawing from it a viable left politics. The ghost of Marxism also lies behind New Times, though for the moment it is very dormant. One of the important things about New Times is its tone. While it hardly offers an invitation to party ('like it's 1999') and thus is not wholly open to attack from those critics of postmodernity who detect there a kind of funhouse of nihilism and meaninglessness, New Times politics emerges, none the less, on the upbeat.[6] It is enthusiastic rather than defeatist about new alliances and new identities, and it is determined to recapture lost ground by taking popular pleasures seriously.

The settling of accounts which follows will outline a number of problems raised, not so much by postmodern writing per se – it is not my intention to offer another critique of Baudrillard – but rather by its cultural studies critics. A number of worrying strands within New Times thinking will be considered, and this will be followed by a set of proposals about how cultural studies, or more generally how the study of culture, might usefully advance into the 1990s. The form that the critique will take comprises two broad platforms. Of postmodernity it will be suggested that this remains most useful, not as an anti-foundationalist philosophical concept whose basis lies in the disavowal of truth-seeking in intellectual inquiry, and which thus differentiates itself from the project of modernity, but as an analytical/descriptive category whose momentum derives from its cutting free from the long legacy of meanings associated with modernity. The term postmodernity indicates something of the scope and the scale of the new global and local social relations and identities set up between individuals, groups and populations as they interact with and are formed by the multiplicity of texts, images and representations which are a constitutive part of contemporary reality and experience.

This notion of postmodernity is most usefully deployed in the study of the mass media, where it has encouraged a shift away from textual analysis towards considering more fully the broad interconnections between different media forms, not just at the level of the patterns of ownership and control of global communications, but also in the cross-cutting of interlocking generic devices and effects, and in the constant use of trailers of narratives, in advertising, in pop videos and in TV mini-dramas. Postmodern media criticism has recognized that it is as important theoretically to 'flick across' the media, as it is to linger over the single image in search of its 'preferred meaning'. But much of the tone of the earlier postmodern voices in media studies has been proclamatory or declarative in the style of Baudrillard.[7] Perhaps what is now required is a more subdued, and more cautious, mode, grounded in the recognition that there are no quick answers to the questions thrown up by contemporary culture even when it seems to move as quickly as it does.

New Times will be considered more specifically in terms of its concern with a new politics of consumerism and the debates this has provoked in cultural studies. It will be argued that the study of consumerism is still at a stage of underdevelopment. Those who have recently rescued the

26

pleasures of consumerism for serious academic consideration have failed to contextualize it in the practices of everyday life. They have also conveniently forgotten those feminist analyses of the late 1970s which saw consumerism as a labour of love and which also, while recognizing the pleasures of domesticity, insisted on the home as the site of reproduction.[8] Like the postmodernists, the enthusiastic New Timers tend to provide a minimum of detailed empirical material, or indeed of concrete examples, to illustrate or give weight to their arguments.

If anything is needed in the field of cultural analysis now, it is a return to the phenomenological/empirical field (with all the complexity that this involves). The contributions to the New Times debate which I will be dealing with below have performed an important function. But the interest in consumerism, for example, has led to an extrapolation of cultural objects out of the context of their usefulness (or their materiality); they have been prised away from their place in history and from their role in social relations, and have been posited instead in a kind of vacuum of aesthetic pleasure and personal style. The lived experience which breathes life into such inanimate objects is noticeable by its absence. Despite the commitment to restore the consumer to his or her rightful place as a discerning 'politician' of everyday purchases rather than a cultural dupe of advertising and life-style, there are none the less very few voices to be heard in these debates other than those of the cultural intellectuals who first initiated them.

TWO PROBLEMS WITH POSTMODERNISM

The first problem comes into focus around the meaning of the term fragmentation. This too is a word which, through over-usage in recent cultural debates, has become shorn of meaning. Postmodernity has been associated by Fredric Jameson with the emergence of a broken, fractured shadow of a 'man'.[9] The tinny shallowness of mass culture is, he argues, directly reflected in the schizophrenic subject of contemporary mass consciousness.

Against Jameson, Stuart Hall has recently said that it is just this de-centring of consciousness which allows him, as a black person, to emerge, divided, yes, but now fully foregrounded on the postmodern stage. 'So one of the fascinating things about this discussion is to find myself centred at last. Now that, in the postmodern age, you all feel so dispersed I become centred. What I've thought of as dispersed and fragmented comes, paradoxically, to be the representative modern condition! This is coming home with a vengeance.'[10]

These are, then, two perspectives on the problem of postmodern fragmentation. There is Jameson, who looks back nostalgically to the notion of unity or totality and who sees in this a kind of prerequisite for radical

27

politics, a goal to be striven for. And there is Hall, who sees in fragmentation something more reflective of the ongoing and historical condition of subaltern groups. Jameson's unified 'man' could be taken to be a pre-Freudian, Enlightenment subject, and thus be discredited by those who have paid attention to Lacan's notion of the fragmented subject.[11] But the endorsement of postmodern fragmentation is equally not without its own problems. Have 'we' become more fragmented than before? Can we specifically name a time and a place for the moment of fragmentation? Is fragmentation the 'other' of 'humanity'? Or is the *representation* of fragmentation coincidental with political empowerment and liberation? (I feel broken but in expressing this feeling, and in others feeling it with me, I become more whole.)

Feminists have used the notion of fragmentation both sociologically and psychoanalytically to describe that state of distraction created by 'women's time'.[12] This degree of distraction was identified in those forms of popular culture associated with women, such as soap operas, long before fragmentation came, in the late 1980s, to be couched in terms of postmodernity.[13] Is postmodern fragmentation therefore a rather vague term for describing aspects of the subaltern experience as it is lived in contemporary culture? Or must we find a more precise definition for fragmentation in order for it to be capable of describing more than just a contemporary state of mind?

Christopher Norris has argued that postmodernity (and postmodern fragmentation) stands at the end of the long line of intellectual inquiry which starts with Saussure, works its way through poststructuralism and Lacanian psychoanalysis and ends with Baudrillard.[14] In Norris's terms fragmentation is to be understood as marking an absolute and irreparable break with the unified subject, a break which is now writ large in culture. Present-day fragmented subjectivity is captured and expressed in postmodern cultural forms, a kind of superficial pick-and-mix of styles. According to Jameson, however, unfragmented subjectivity, by contrast, produced great works of uncluttered 'heroic' modernism. There is a degree of slippage in the connections being made here. The problem lies, at least partly, in the imprecise use of the word 'fragmentation'. There is a vacillation between the 'high' psychoanalytical use of Lacan and a much looser notion, one which seems to sum up unsatisfactory aspects of contemporary cultural experience. Modernists, however, *also* felt confused and fragmented. Fragmentation, as a kind of 'structure of feeling', is by no means the sole property of those living under the shadow of the postmodern condition.[15] Bewilderment, anxiety, panic: such expressions can be attributed to any historical moment as it is transposed into cultural and artistic expression over the last a hundred and fifty years. The category of fragmentation seems to have become either too technical to be of general use (i.e. in Lacan's work) or too vague to mean anything more than torn apart.

The more important issue might be the one of who gets to be able to express their fragmentation, and who is able to put into words or images or sounds, the language of their private, broken subjectivities. In short who can contest, who can represent and who gets to be listened to? In this sense fragmentation can be linked with the politics of empowerment, with finding a way of mounting a challenge. A unity of sorts emanates from the tumult of fragmented voices. But for Jameson (and for white middle-class masculinity?) it means disempowerment, silence, or schizophrenic 'cries and whispers'.

The second question which might be asked of neo-Marxist critics of postmodernity, concerns determination, and the return to a form of economic reductionism in cultural theory. Fredric Jameson argues that postmodernism is the cultural logic of capital, but his argument, as Paul Hirst writing about trends in both New Times and postmodern writing, has suggested, 'slips from a rigid causal determinism into casual metaphor'.[16] Jameson, going back to Mandel's *Late Capitalism*, has argued that the kinds of cultural phenomena which might be described as postmodern form part of the logic of advanced or late capitalism.[17] This does away, at a sweep, with the difficult issue of explaining the *precise nature* of the social and ideological relationships which mediate between the economy and the sphere of culture and it simultaneously restores a rather old-fashioned notion of determination to that place it had occupied prior to Althusser's 'relative autonomy' and his idea of determination 'in the last instance'.[18] David Harvey's *The Condition of Postmodernity* has taken this mode of analysis even further.[19] Quoting Lyotard, Harvey takes up the notion of the temporary contract as the hallmark of postmodern social relations.[20] What he sees prevailing in production, in the guise of new forms of work, he also sees prevailing in emotional life and in culture, in the temporary contract of love and sexuality. Like Jameson he decries this state and looks forward to something more robust and more reliable, something from which a less fractured sense of self and community might emerge. He views postmodern culture disparagingly, as aesthetic rather than ethical, reflecting an avoidance of politics rather than a rising to the challenge of a politics posed by new or changing conditions of production.

But it is the vocabulary of postmodernism which seems to allow both these writers to return to broader questions of politics and culture and to the idea that what is happening in production has consequences for changes in culture. There is a postmodern warranty which provides both Jameson and Harvey with a wonderfully wide analytical sweep. Cultural analysis has become more versatile, more engaged across the whole field of representation. Harvey moves effortlessly from describing

29

global money markets, represented on flickering green screens, to considering *Bladerunner* and *Wings of Desire* as reflective of a postmodern aesthetic. The critique of postmodernism simultaneously allows these writers a kind of breathing space from what were the conventional rigours (or the rigidities) of Marxist cultural analysis, and at the same time brings them back to a simpler and more direct notion of determination. What happens in the economy has a direct effect on what happens in culture.

Jameson and Harvey both see more of value to left critics in modernist rather than in postmodern cultural expression. In attributing to works of modernism more depth (Jameson) or a stronger ethics (Harvey) they fail, however, to include in their analyses the historical conditions of modern production which also marked out the long moment of modernism. Would they trace modernism to an origin in the alienating conditions of production which were, surely, the precondition of modernity, in the same way as post-Fordist flexible specialization is the precondition of the culture of postmodernity? Or is this an irrelevant connection? Surely not, if their central arguments which connect culture with the economy so directly, are to prevail.

Despite their sweeping rejection of postmodern writing, both Jameson and Harvey take advantage of the conceptual and methodological breadth found in these theories to circumvent (or short-circuit) the key problems which have arisen in cultural studies in the attempt to specify and understand the social relations which connect culture to the conditions of its production. Their conceptual leap into a critique of postmodernism allows these writers to avoid confronting more directly the place of Marxism in cultural studies from the late 1980s into the 1990s, a moment at which Marxism cannot be seen in terms other than those of eclipse or decline. Postmodernism exists, therefore, as something of a convenient *bête noire*. It allows for the evasion of the *logic* of cultural studies, if we take that logic to be the problematizing of the relations between culture and the economy and between culture and politics, in an age where the field of culture appears to be increasingly expansive and where both politics and economics might even be seen, at one level, as being conducted in and through culture.[21]

SOME DOUBTS ABOUT NEW TIMES

New Times is a phrase coined by a number of regular contributors to *Marxism Today* and has since become something of a political catchphrase, by no means the exclusive property of the Communist Party, but a phrase which none the less points back in the direction of the magazine, if not the party. A collection of articles drawing on this work, as well as a number of pieces which take issue with New Times, has recently appeared in book form.[22] It is not my intention here to provide a detailed critique of the articles included in this volume.[23] Instead I will first raise a few general points about the New Times approach to consumption and I will then pick out two issues addressed, not in this case in *Marxism Today* (though similar pieces have also appeared there), but in a pair of articles carried in one edition of the weekly magazine *New Statesman and Society*, once again under the heading of New Times. The issues focused on here are those of consumerism and the end of work. I choose to look at them in more detail because they so strongly articulate the key *political* questions posed by New Times thinking, and because many of the ideas expressed in these pieces are now being absorbed into the mainstream of cultural studies.

The current place on the political agenda of consumerism is the product of a dawning awareness on the left of the need for fresh thinking in this arena of social activity. The demise of town hall socialism in the mid-1980s, the changes taking place in the urban landscape, the expansion of leisure culture and the seemingly unrelenting popularity of Thatcherism, forced the left and the women's movement to take a long hard look at the appeal of the consumer culture celebrated by the Tories. This also involved facing up to the recomposition of the working class, as traditional manufacturing declined, creating instead an expanded service sector, a variety of new 'clean' microchip technologies, a smattering of creative jobs in the new leisure and media industries and a shift in manufacturing towards what has recently become known as post-Fordism.

The issue of pleasure, intricately connected with consumerism, had by this time already been drawn into a political vocabulary as feminists and gay men attempted to theorize those experiences which they enjoyed even though orthodox left opinion seemed to disapprove. In both cases consumer goods had a role to play in the insistence that 'guilty pleasure' could be used as part of a process of self- and collective empowerment. Subcultural theory, particularly that developed by Dick Hebdige, gave further credence to this argument, by pointing to the way in which commodities could be invested, particularly by working-class youth, with new, bizarre, or oppositional meanings, and from a feminist perspective Erica Carter, for example, showed that a pair of nylon stockings could, in the context of postwar West Germany, bestow upon their proud owner the confidence she needed to define herself as an independent and modern young woman, able to stand up for herself against a strict and coercive family.[24]

New Times writers more recently have moved a long way beyond the careful rehearsal of the processes of subversive consumption outlined by Hebdige and Carter. They have expanded the category of consumerism so that at points it overwhelms and dominates all the practices of everyday life. At the same time these writers have removed from the notion of consumerism many of the more onerous circumstances of everyday life which accompany it. Thus shopping, for instance – the process of consumption – is conceived simply as buying. But shopping covers a diversity of activities and experiences, including, for example, deciding not to buy, but to return home empty-handed. Shopping also takes place in different contexts. What is a pleasant shop one day, can the next day, in the company of two tired children, be unpleasant or exhausting. The continuing emphasis on consumer pleasure among the New Times writers, fails to raise the question of displeasure or disappointment in consumption, the acquisition of something which fails to please.

The most important absence in the debates on consumerism which straddle *Marxism Today* and the *New Statesman and Society* is the lack of any recognition that most, if not all, consumerism takes place not so much in the sphere of pure leisure as in the sphere of necessary reproduction. This term is simply missing from the vocabulary. Perhaps it is too potent a reminder of the 1970s-style Althusserian Marxism/feminism which New Times politics is anxious to move away from. But turning away from the issue of reproduction suppresses any recognition that as well as being an often pleasant and relaxing activity, most daily shopping is carried out in order to feed or clothe the self or the family unit. It is therefore part of domestic labour and part of the work of reproduction, the sustaining of the self and others, in preparation for the return to work the following day. The term reproduction still proves useful in understanding the relationship between work and leisure, and identifying the way in which the ideology of consumerism mediates between these, endowing the work of leisure with more pleasurable connotations.

As Jane Gaines has pointed out, the notion of consuming currently found in cultural and media studies has focused exclusively on 'meaning-making'. Gaines indicates some of the problems which emerge from this usage.

> Does 'consuming' mean buying, having, or using? In some ways buying is the epitome of the bourgeois signifying act, since we all 'buy in' to a degree, as we pay, even if we snub conventional use-values by turning safety pins into nose-rings and shoes into hats. To what degree, however, would we want to see every act of consumption as an act of meaning-making . . .? Today, the analysis of culture as commodity may have lost its explanatory potency since we are left with so few examples of uncommodified relations.[25]

In current usage of the term, we find consumerism individualized and reduced in meaning. There is no mention of the work of consumption, where shopping is domestic labour. At the same time consumption is inflated in meaning, so that each and every transaction or acquisition becomes a grand gesture of will, an act of opposition or an expression of identity. The meanings in the objects, activated, uncovered, or indeed created by the consumer, quite overshadow the social or interactive dimensions of consumption. Consuming regains its place in cultural theory, after being eclipsed for so long, as central, majestic, dominant. As Susan Sontag has said, the 'freedom to consume has come to be equated with freedom itself'.[26] But so also is reproduction central, dominant, if not majestic. The swing in political and intellectual life towards a focus on consumerism reflects the rejection of the old model of consumption as an illusory (or ideological) relation (commodity fetishism) under which the real relations of production or reproduction lie. The present emphasis on consumption is part of that process of reinstating the consuming subject in a role other than that of passive dupe to 'the magic system'.[27] But reproduction and consumption are integrally linked. Without reproduction, consumption remains suspended in an asocial, ahistorical space, given over to meaning-making but at the same time quite unconnected to other meanings and to the world of social relationships.

Take, for example, the act of going for a swim in the public baths, having bought a £1 ticket. Is this an act of consumption, or of reproduction, or, in the presence of children, is it part of the burden of childcare or of domestic labour? Is it a subsidized service, provided by the local council, in the hope that the population will become healthier and thus be less of a drain on the health services? Or is it a more personal activity, part of the work of reproducing the self as a healthy, efficient and aesthetically pleasing body? Swimming might be pleasurable and it might be part of leisure culture but it is not generally conceived of as an act of consumption. Even though you buy a ticket, you do not buy a swim the way you buy a can of coke after you have dried your hair. Swimming enters into consumer culture through, for example, the swimwear fashion industry, the cosmetics industry and the world of women's magazines. But it is primarily understood as an energetic activity which services, reproduces, or, in situations of danger, saves the physical body. In this context, then, reproduction becomes a term which still merits critical and analytical attention, not in isolation from but in conjunction with consumerism. Emphasis on reproduction does not deny the pleasures of consumerism by replacing them with drudgery, but it registers the intersection of social control, state intervention and leisure culture with the requirement for a body whose beauty is at least partly the expression of its health and efficiency.

In the 1970s, reproduction was seen by left critics as part of labour discipline, a social requirement of capital. Reproduction was made palatable or even desirable with the help of ideology, in women's magazines, on TV and in consumer culture. Now, however, there has been a dramatic shift away from this kind of thinking which, it is generally agreed, overemphasized the victim-like positioning of the consumer. Instead the emphasis

33

is on the meanings which can be drawn from the choice of objects of consumption and which in turn creates for the consumer a new or different and potentially mobilizing identity, the new you.

Thus, when working-class lads in the 1980s go to Armani to buy expensive cashmere jumpers, this is seen by one New Times commentator, Frank Mort, as evidence of consumerism not being a mindless passive activity indicative of social conformity, but instead reflecting a shift in perception on the part of these lads as they resist some of the demands of a conventional working-class masculinity which insists that they renounce the cissy or classy meanings associated with such jumpers.[28] Through consumerism, the meanings of working-class masculinity are undergoing a transition, a renegotiation and perhaps even a feminization. (The fact that these boys are buying their own jumpers rather than having their mothers or their girlfriends buy them, is also perhaps reflective of the changing division of labour in the home, though this returns us to the field of reproduction and domestic labour.)

Cashmere jumpers have traditionally been available to a luxury market. High prices have been justified on the grounds of quality fabric. But this exclusive consumer space has been invaded by a foreign force from the opposite end of the social spectrum. And the market has run the risk of either losing its original clientele or else of losing the chances of a higher profit margin by finding some means of resisting the advances of the popular consumer. Mort's argument points to the power, in this case, of the young working-class consumer who can destabilize the fashion market by utilizing his consumer freedom in an unexpected or unanticipated way – a mode of consumption which brings into play new unsettling ideas about his gender and class identity.

But the excess of meanings found in consumerism, sometimes at the expense of an analysis of the social relations of shopping, can lead to consumerism being celebrated *per se*. It is, then, often with the voice of the born-again shopper that many of the New Times writers can testify to the unadulterated pleasures of visiting, for example, the IKEA furniture warehouse on the North Circular Road in London, or indeed the Armani Emporium in Knightsbridge, without attempting to put those pleasures in their social or historical context.[29]

NEW TIMES, WORK AND LEISURE: MORT AND GORZ

In an article published in *New Statesman and Society* (25 May 1989), Frank Mort considers the pleasures of the home and home consumption.[30] Drawing on the findings of one market research company Mort examines the consequences of a shorter working week and a higher standard of living for the British people in the 1980s. His conclusion is that the old politics of civics is dead and that people now prefer to spend their free time at home, as Zygmunt Bauman has put it, 'freed from the burden of politics'.[31] They derive an important part of their identities from buying and consuming. Thatcherism has harnessed these goals and values to its own political agenda, leaving the left confused and in disarray.

Mort attempts to rescue this embracing of domesticity from charges of apolitical individualism by pointing to the political possibilities which have recently emerged from within the heartland of domestic consumerism: eco-consumer politics, for example, or the global charity events carried out on TV and addressed to people at home. These, he suggests, might create 'a new relation that can form the basis for a future common sense'.[32] It is in and around the home, therefore, that we can see new, more expressive identities being forged. It is here that people really feel themselves to be 'at home'.

Despite the emphasis on the domestic, however, Mort's new politics of consumption is technicist, masculinist and bereft of the mediating power of the social relations which ultimately underpin, activate and bring to life the world of commodities. From his standpoint the sphere of domesticity is equated with individualized leisure epitomized in Do-It-Yourself (DIY) home improvements. It is also the space of time free from capitalist control and labour discipline. There is no understanding of the work carried out in the household, or of the interactive and emotional ties which hold this unit together and which also, under patriarchy (a word rarely used these days), legitimate the individualized leisure of the male breadwinner for the very reason that he has earned his right to real leisure – unlike his wife. Quite missing from this account are the economic realities of family life, where DIY is often a necessity. Mort fails to consider, for example, what has been called the 'new underclass' for whom the free time of unemployment allows no opportunity to buy the tools and the equipment for DIY. He also ignores the fact that family structure in the UK is no longer the stable unit it used to be. Single-parent families, whose household budgets hardly extend to leisure culture, are not the only social grouping which does not conform to his model. There are also divorced and remarried units, struggling to bring up children and stepchildren. There is still the significant fact that women across the social class spectrum earn less than their male counterparts. In the married unit they make up for this economic debit by carrying out domestic tasks. In the single-parent family they struggle to stay above the poverty line.[33]

Where Mort paints a picture of a nation at leisure, in their own back gardens, the French sociologist, André Gorz, in an interview in the same issue of the *New Statesman and Society*, focuses more on the new conditions of work and on how post-Fordist means of production will free more and more people for leisure.[34] Like Mort he assesses the possible political potential for the left of this liberation. Gorz draws on European

35

research which suggests that the dwindling sections of the working class still employed in manufacture, identify less with the workplace and more with the community in the form of the local neighbourhood, or with the home.

Gorz offers no understanding of a feminist perspective on this new leisure. Nor is there an assessment of what the consequences of short-time or part-time work are, or might be, in the UK. It may well be that in this country the disadvantages of the new forms of work will quickly outweigh the advantages of working for oneself or being able to work from home. For example, for many young people in the UK, the appeal of self-employment has been further enhanced by government-sponsored initiatives like the Enterprise Allowance Scheme. (This pays young people £40 a week for their first year of self-employment.) The sustainability of these enterprises has not as yet been examined, nor has the full cost of the self-exploitation which it entails. But judging from Ruggiero's recent analysis of the new small-scale industrial units of northern Italy, many self-employed young workers are unable to pay their own insurance stamp, or to contribute to a pension fund. They cannot afford an annual holiday, are entitled to no sickness benefit and could not afford maternity pay, should they want to start a family. New work in this context signals the 'end of work' only in so far as it is a disguise for long-term unemployment.[35]

Post-Fordism differentiates between the relatively well-off core workers and those employed on the periphery. There are now suggestions, however, that this latter grouping will slowly outnumber the core workers. Soon there will be no rigid line between the two, as it becomes normal to start off in one category and end up in the other, or vice versa. Core workers are an almost exclusively male grouping, and in the UK at least, the evidence is emerging that many will in fact use their 'free time' to find other forms of part-time employment.[36] Even if they do spend more time in the home there are no grounds for assuming that this is spent entirely at leisure. If their wives are doing shift-work or part-time work then these men will also be participating in domestic labour and childcare.

Gorz happily embraces an anti-work position on the assumption that most work is unrewarding, routine and requires little creative endeavour. But it is perhaps telling that at the very moment when he and Mort are suggesting a return to the home, more women in greater numbers than at any time since the war are moving back into the institutionalized space of the workplace, even if the work on offer is indeed repetitive and boring. For married women returning to work, it is not simply the money which is the attraction but the company at work, the shopfloor culture, and the escape from the isolation of the home. Both Mort and Gorz emphasize technology or objects of consumption at the expense of the social relationships which entwine themselves around these forms, whether at work or in the home. In Mort there is the image of the man, surrounded by gadgetry, in his garage or greenhouse. In Gorz there is technological determinism which will set the working class free from the burden of labour. Home and leisure replace work and party politics and these come to represent new arenas for political contestation.

The point of New Times politics might be seen, then, to lie in the valorization of the domestic, and in the recognition of identities and involvements other than those of class and traditional party affiliation as being important, particularly those connections that develop in the home, the neighbourhood, the community, or for that matter the shopping mall. We might add to these the role of the caring parent, the responsible citizen, or the environmentalist. But in one sense none of these is an entirely new proposition. For many years, after all, feminists, the libertarian left and the gay movement have been arguing precisely for a politicization of the domestic, the personal sphere and the local environment. What the contributions by Mort and Gorz have done is to add to these concerns the gloss of consumerism and the appeal of popular pleasures. They both paint a convincing picture. But what is lost, ironically, is the pleasure and reward of work, as often as not a product of the social relations of work, as an outcome of the task itself. Likewise the home is not all pleasure and relaxation. At a more general level it is extremely debatable whether the claims of these New Timers to have identified deep-rooted historical shifts in economic and cultural relations are indeed correct. A good deal more work in this area remains to be done before such conclusions can be reached.

FORWARD TO THE FUTURE

The neo-Marxist critics of postmodernity have endorsed an economistic Marxism, where culture is seen to reflect, or express, or exist in a mimetic relation to, 'the base'. What is happening in the economy allows an incredible flowering of culture in late capitalism. Culture is consistently understood as texts, images and representations rather than as social relationships. And it is new technology which brings more texts, images and representations to people on a global scale and particularly in the form of television.

The New Timers are similarly concerned with culture. Although they consider culture as lived, in the home environment, in the urban environment and in leisure, for the purposes of their argument culture is condensed into items and objects of consumption. Gestures are made to trends in popular consumption, but it is the individual's relation to and experience of the objects and the commodities which fuel the analysis. The New Timers are more interested in work than the cultural critics of postmodernity are in the economy. But rather than concentrate on the social and cultural consequences of the changes in work as a result of flexible specialization, computer technology and the growth of the service sector, the New Timers use this as a base from which they can make cultural forecasts as a result of the freeing of labour from the old constraints of work, the recomposition of class and the simultaneous eclipsing of class by other social identifications.

One strand in the postmodernist debate, therefore, moves us back to a reductionist Marxism, while the New Times writers, in contrast, seem to move away from Marx altogether.[37] There are two ways of accounting for the erasure from the vocabulary of cultural studies of key words from earlier Marxist analysis. First we could point to issues internal to the development of the discipline, including what Stuart Hall refers to as the culturalist and the structuralist paradigms.[38] Within structuralism ideology came to signal too strongly the notion of a systematized and coherent set of ideas and practices which were packaged and presented to a population of more or less passive subjects. Stuart Hall's other paradigm, that of culturalism, also produced difficulties for the theorists of contemporary culture. Culturalism, in so far as it was concerned with the active experience of culture by subordinate groups and classes, fell foul of its own complexity. It looked for class or gender or racial coherence on the part of its subjects, but rarely found it. Instead it found slippages and inconsistencies and contradictions in consciousness. The founding categories of class, gender and race were invariably cut across by other, often stronger, points of identification such as region, religion, or nationality. And there were other problems. Culturalism emphasized agency and the active engagement of the group or individual in creating their own cultural space. This was often stressed at the expense of other acts of conformity or quiescence.

The second force for moving cultural studies away from the Marxism it embraced throughout the early years has come from the broader sociopolitical stage. As the communist world has dissolved itself from within, Marxism has been dropped as a primary frame of reference. There were very few cultural intellectuals in the west who linked their Marxist-feminist theory with what did or did not exist in Eastern Europe. But the disintegration, literal and metaphorical, of the images and representations of repressive totalitarian Marxism (the renaming of streets to their original pre-Marxist titles, the dismantling of statues and street decorations bearing 'his' name) has, not surprisingly, discouraged theorists of contemporary culture from representing themselves in this now old-fashioned language.

However, since Marx was if nothing else the most sophisticated critic of capital, and since capital is simultaneously in crisis and globally dominant, the abandonment of what Marxist cultural theory has taught us about, for example, the meaning and the modalities of the mass media, would be nonsensical. In so far as the urgency which has fuelled the establishment of culture as a field of political inquiry has come from a concern to understand the dynamics of social and cultural inequality and the ways in which these are lived in and through a variety of social categories and ideological identifications, some of which are mobilizing, others of which might be seen as immobilizing, then the very rationale for cultural studies disappears when this critical and analytical imperative is lifted. The question then might be, why bother?

Dick Hebdige has argued in this context for a 'Marxism without guarantees' and Stuart Hall, in a recent piece in the American journal *October*, remembers the profoundly political impulse which motivated him into the field of cultural analysis in the early 1960s.[39] He is fearful that, as cultural studies emerges into the staple of interdisciplinary studies, this kind of impulse will be forgotten. What I have attempted to do here is to demonstrate the dangers in using existing neo-Marxist analyses of postmodern culture as a means of returning eventually to a crude and mechanical base-superstructure model, and also the dangers of pursuing a kind of cultural populism to a point at which anything which is consumed and is popular is also seen as oppositional. What is missing in both these models is analytical work which is 'structural, historical and ethnographic'.[40] It was this integrative approach which gave body and substance to those areas of analysis opened up by cultural studies in the 1970s. In *Policing the Crisis*, for example, Gramsci's concept of hegemony was used to analyse a particular moment in postwar British society, and a particular sociocultural phenomenon, the emergence of a moral panic around the figure of the young black male in the UK during the 1970s.[41] Equally, it is in those studies where consumerism has been demonstrated to be oppositional through concrete reference to a particular instance and a particular moment in time, that the argument has been most convincing.[42]

What I have been arguing for here is a holding on to the middle ground: for an extension of Gramscian cultural analysis into newly emerging fields of study such as popular consumerism. This would entail a return to an integrative mode of analysis and would avoid the temptations of the 'textual trap'. In a sense it was the appeal of textual analysis in media and cultural studies in the early 1980s which allowed the neo-Marxist critics to appear to be providing all the answers when they entered the field of debate on postmodern culture. In conclusion I will set out a five-point summary.

(1) What is now required, in other words, is the development of a paradigm for analysing consumption in everyday life. There are problems with trying to think about everyday life analytically: what to exclude, what to discard? The dilemmas posed by such a project might be

avoided by suggesting in the first instance, a return to the terrain of 'lived experience' such as that marked out by Paul Willis in *Learning to Labour*.[43] Instead of moving from the objects, texts, or media messages back to the individual reader, viewer, shopper, or consumer (as has been the tendency of late in media studies), it might be more wise to start at the opposite end of the spectrum, to begin with the social group, the family, the peer group, the community. Studies of this sort would enable us to develop a clearer picture of what exactly we mean by consumption.

(2) To understand the compulsion to consume we must also return to pleasure, and to what Žižek has called 'the undergrowth of enjoyment'.[44] Each of us has an enormous capacity for pleasure, leisure and enjoyment. For the left and for cultural intellectuals in the past this was a source of guilt, a private, stolen experience in an otherwise gloomy and unhappy world. At best it was understood as prefigurative, a glimpse of the future. But what happens when it seems as though the entire global population, and particularly those peoples liberated from forty years of East European or Soviet communism, derive the utmost pleasure from the glossy objects provided only by consumer capitalism, and further, when the self-restraint described above begins to seem politically like an unnecessary sacrifice? Do we go down the road of enjoying consumer life to the full, though within the constraints of our personal budgets? Is the new politics of consumption one which requires that we exercise restraint only on grounds of morality, ecology and physical health, or must we move towards a deeper understanding of our social and historical relationships to the world of commodities?

(3) A further imperative is an examination of what we mean by identity, and what value this concept has for cultural analysis in a world where the mass media creates global homogeneity yet where in this global village people and populations are increasingly differentiated. As Morley and Robbins suggest, 'we must grasp how these identities, in Saussure's terms, are originally constructed in and through their relations with each other. . . . Thus, difference is constitutive of identity . . . identity is as much about exclusion as it is about inclusion.'[45]

(4) We need a more detailed engagement with the culture of the workplace and the extent to which New Times do indeed prevail in work; we must investigate the sustainability of self-employment, the appeal and the costs of working in the self-expressive fields of the mass media, i.e. in the culture industries. This would also entail

taking a much closer look at what has loosely been labelled the 'aestheticization of culture'.

(5) Finally we need a mode of analysis which is connective and integrative and which tracks the social and ideological relations which prevail at every level between cultural production and consumption. This would involve reintroducing to the field of cultural analysis more institutional voices, more ethnography, more participant observation. It would also mean turning away from the temptation to read more and more from the cultural products and objects of consumption, readings which invariably are of most enjoyment to our own interpretive communities. Such a turning-away does not mean being against interpretation, rather it means examining all of those processes which accompany the production of meaning in culture, not just the end-product: from where it is socially constructed to where it is socially deconstructed and contested, in the institutions, practices and relationships of everyday life around us.

This article first appeared in *New Formations* 13 (Spring 1991): 1–16.

NOTES

1 See the introduction to R. Boyne and A. Rattansi (eds) *Postmodernism and Society*, London, Macmillan, 1990, p. 12.
2 F. Jameson, 'Postmodernism, or the cultural logic of capital', *New Left Review* July–August 1984, vol. 146, pp. 53–92; and D. Harvey, *The Condition of Postmodernity*, Oxford, Blackwell, 1989.
3 D. Kellner (ed.) *Postmodernism-Jameson-Critique*, Washington, DC, Maisonneuve Press, 1989.
4 A special New Times issue of *Marxism Today* was published in October 1988.
5 When he was opposition spokesman for consumer affairs Bryan Gould contributed to several New Times events organized by both *Marxism Today* and the *New Statesman and Society*.
6 C. Norris, 'Lost in the funhouse: Baudrillard and the politics of postmodernism', in R. Boyne and A. Rattansi (eds) *Postmodernism and Society*, London, Macmillan, 1990, pp. 119–34.
7 ibid.
8 See, for example, L. Bland et al., 'Women "inside and outside" the relations of production', in Women's Studies Group (eds) *Women Take Issue*, London, Hutchinson, 1978, pp. 35–79.
9 Jameson, op. cit.
10 S. Hall, 'Minimal selves', in *Identity*, ICA Documents 6, ed. Lisa Appignanesi, London: Institute of Contemporary Arts, 1987.
11 J. Lacan, *The Four Fundamental Concepts of Psycho-analysis*, London, Hogarth Press, 1977.
12 See, for example, J. Kristeva, 'Women's time', in N. O. Keohan, M. Z. Rosaldo and B. C. Gelpi (eds) *Feminist Theory: A Critique of Ideology*, New York; Harvester Press, 1982, pp. 31–55.

13 T. Modleski, *Loving With a Vengeance: Mass-Produced Fantasies for Women*, New York; Methuen, 1982.
14 Norris, op. cit.
15 This phrase belongs of course to Raymond Williams in *The Long Revolution*, Harmondsworth, Mx, Penguin, 1965.
16 P. Hirst, 'After Henry', in S. Hall and M. Jacques (eds) *New Times: The Changing Face of Politics in the 1990s*, London, Lawrence & Wishart, 1989, pp. 321–9.
17 E. Mandel, *Late Capitalism*, London, New Left Books, 1975.
18 L. Althusser, *Lenin and Philosophy and Other Essays*, London, New Left Books, 1971.
19 Harvey, op. cit.
20 Quoted in ibid.
21 C. Mouffe, 'Hegemony and ideology in Gramsci', in T. Bennett (ed.) *Culture, Ideology and Social Process*, London, Batsford, 1982, pp. 219–35.
22 S. Hall and M. Jacques (eds) *New Times: The Changing Face of Politics in the 1990s*, London, Lawrence & Wishart, 1989.
23 See, for example, A. McRobbie's review of Hall and Jacques (eds) *New Times, Feminist Review*, Autumn 1990, 36, pp. 127–31.
24 D. Hebdige, *Subculture: The Meaning of Style*, London, Methuen, 1979; and E. Carter, 'Alice in the consumer wonderland', in A. McRobbie and M. Nava (eds) *Gender and Generation*, London, Macmillan, 1984, pp. 185–214.
25 J. Gaines, 'Introduction', in J. Gaines (ed.) *Fabrication: Costume and the Female Body*, New York, Routledge, 1990, quoting from p. 15.
26 S. Sontag, *On Photography*, Harmondsworth, Mx, Penguin, 1979.
27 R. Williams, 'The magic system', in R. Williams, *Culture and Materialism*, London, Verso, 1986, pp. 170–96.
28 F. Mort, 'The politics of consumption', in S. Hall and M. Jacques (eds) *New Times: The Changing Face of Politics in the 1990s*, London, Lawrence & Wishart, 1989, pp. 160–73.
29 Hall and Jacques (eds), op. cit.
30 F. Mort, 'The writing on the wall', *New Statesman and Society*, May 1989.
31 Quoted in ibid.
32 ibid.
33 See, for example, Hilary Land, 'Being poor', in J. Brannen and G. Wilson (eds) *Give and Take in Families*, London, Longman, 1987, pp. 38–54.
34 Interview with A. Gorz titled 'In the land of Cockayne?', *New Statesman and Society*, May 1989.
35 V. Ruggiero, 'Turin today: premodern society or postindustrial bazaar?', *Capital and Class*, Spring, 1987, vol. 31, pp. 25–39.
36 A series of figures released by the Department of Employment from 1987 onwards has shown that in the UK the average male wage is buoyed up by overtime payments to a greater extent than in any other European country. Regular earnings within the hidden economy are, for obvious reasons, more difficult to assess. However, it has been suggested that such earnings are frequently a supplement to wages rather than, as is often assumed, an illegal addition to unemployment benefit.
37 The *New Times* collection cited above (note 22) makes no mention whatsoever, across thirty-two articles, of those neo-Marxist concepts which so dominated political and cultural analysis throughout the 1980s.
38 S. Hall, 'Two paradigms in cultural studies', in T. Bennett (ed.) *Culture, Ideology and Social Process*, London, Batsford, 1989, pp. 19–39.

39 See D. Hebdige, *Hiding in the Light*, London, Routledge/Comedia, 1988, p. 207; and S. Hall, 'Cultural studies and the crisis of the humanities', *October*, Summer 1990, pp. 11–23.
40 In S. Hall and T. Jefferson (eds) *Resistance through Rituals*, London, Hutchinson, 1977, these three levels are specified as necessary in developing a full understanding of the phenomena of UK postwar youth subcultures.
41 S. Hall *et al.* (eds) *Policing the Crisis: Mugging, the State and Law and Order*, London, Macmillan, 1978.
42 See references to Hebdige and Carter above.
43 P. Willis, *Learning to Labour*, London, Saxon House, 1977.
44 S. Žižek, 'The undergrowth of enjoyment: how popular culture can serve as an introduction to Lacan', *New Formations*, Winter, 1989, vol. 9, pp. 7–31.
45 D. Morley and K. Robbins, 'Spaces of identity', *Screen*, Autumn, 1989, no. 30, pp. 32–59.

3

POST-MARXISM AND CULTURAL STUDIES

The word crisis is one which appears with alarming regularity in the discourses of cultural studies. In *Cultural Studies*, the recent (1992) collection edited by Grossberg, Nelson and Treichler, Lidia Curti (1992) uses it to refer not just to the ever-increasing marginality of intellectuals from political life, but to the collapse of many of the intellectual frames of reference which have fuelled the development of cultural studies. From structuralism to post-structuralism, from Marxism to feminism, there has been, she argues, an erosion of belief, a decline in the centrality of 'strong narratives', a turning away from binary relations in favour of what Derrida describes as 'an indefinite series of differences'.

But there are additional difficulties strewn in the path of cultural studies which might make panic a more appropriate word to describe its current condition. Marxism, a major point of reference for the whole cultural studies project in the UK, has been undermined not just from the viewpoint of the postmodern critics who attack its teleological propositions, meta-narrative status, essentialism, economism, Eurocentrism, and its place within the whole Enlightenment project, but also, of course, as a result of the events in Eastern Europe, with the discrediting of much of the socialist project and with the bewildering changes in the Soviet Union which leave the western critic at a loss as to what is now meant by right- or left-wing politics.

As I have argued elsewhere in this book, the kind of Marxism which cultural studies can retain in these very different circumstances is as yet unclear. What does seem certain is that the return to a pre-postmodern Marxism as marked out by critics like Fredric Jameson (1984) and David Harvey (1989) is untenable because the terms of that return are predicated on prioritizing economic relations and economic determinations over cultural and political relations by positioning these latter in a mechanical and reflectionist role. The debate about the future of Marxism in cultural studies has not yet taken place. Instead the great debate around modernity and postmodernity has quite conveniently leapt in and filled that space. Stuart Hall begins to open up such a dialogue in *Cultural*

44

Studies (1992). Of course in one sense he is right, that Marxism was one problematic among many in the history of British cultural studies. For the likes of Raymond Williams and E. P. Thompson and, indeed, Richard Hoggart it was not just a problematic but a real problem. All three writers have displayed a difficult and unresolved relationship to Marxism.

None the less it would be wrong to underestimate the extent to which neo-Marxist theory informed a good deal of cultural analysis in the 10-year period between 1975 and 1985. Admittedly, both the culturalist and the structuralist paradigms described by Stuart Hall (1989) as at that time informing the field of cultural studies drew on traditions well beyond that of Marxism. Yet a touchstone in both paradigms remained the early Marx of the *1844 Manuscripts* as a critical influence on culturalism, and the later scientific Marxism of *Capital* as read by Althusser as a form of structuralist neo-Marxism. The absolute pre-eminence of Gramsci's (neo-Marxist) notion of hegemony gave a tighter political focus to the field in the conjunctural analyses developed by Stuart Hall (*et al.* 1978) in another seminal text, *Policing the Crisis*, and in his later work on Thatcherism. The complexities and historical specificities of the means by which consent is secured have, by drawing on Gramsci, enabled us to understand the force and political effectiveness of the Thatcher years, the success of the new right and equally the lack of success on the part of the left even to begin to compete with this ideological radicalism.

Now the place of Gramsci is no longer so certain. Lidia Curti discusses Bill Schwartz's description of his work as the 'last bulwark of totalizing theory' and while Stuart Hall recognizes Gramsci's contribution to an understanding of the formation of social blocs and ensembles and class relations as well as the need for alliances and solidarities, it is Gramsci's 'displacement of Marxism' which is now emphasized (Curti, 1992; Schwartz, 1985; Hall, 1992). Also problematized is the role of the organic intellectual and the politics of knowledge inscribed in that role. In the era of post-Marxism who will be leading whom? If the notion of a unified class whose historic role was that of agency and emancipation disappears, then what role is now to be allocated to the organic intellectual? On whose behalf is he or she acting?

It is not just textuality, difference, identity politics, and Derrida's insistence on the relational and unfixed nature of meaning (the 'floating signifier'), nor is it the 'interruptions' of feminism and race which have wrought the crisis of Marxism in cultural studies. Stuart Hall is quite right to remind us that from the start cultural studies emerged as a form of radical inquiry which went against reductionism and economism, which went against the base and superstructure metaphor, and which resisted the notion of false consciousness. However, no matter how far removed cultural theory became from political economy, it did retain a sense of political urgency.

But what has now gone, with Marxism, and partly in response to the political bewilderment and disempowerment of the left, is that sense of urgency. This has not been helped by the way in which postmodernism has been construed in the UK, as either playful or conservative. The deferral of meaning in Derridean deconstruction has not necessarily helped matters in this respect. Intellectually, deconstruction is dazzling. Politically, it is enabling. But in the name of deconstruction there can also be produced a series of tasteful and elegant forays into the field of culture, dipping into it in the absence of the need to be constrained by materialism (a requirement or obligation which itself would be subject to deconstruction), or held to account by a political agenda. Hall reminds us that deconstruction can 'formalize out of existence the critical questions of power, history, and politics' (Hall, 1992).

Where there remains a political urgency, as there does in the field of race (and also in feminism and in the battle against AIDS), then that elegance does not become merely skilful, that simultaneous pursuit and deferral of meaning does not become totally formalized. I am not, therefore, talking about the kind of deconstruction practised by Gayatri Spivak [see the interview reprinted in chapter 7] who uses it as a tool of conceptual interrogation which ensures political vigilance and who also talks about the 'strategic use of essentialism'. Nor am I casting aspersions on the kind of deconstruction found in the writing of Homi Bhabha. When he talks about 'affective writing' and when he encourages us to 'think outside the certainty of the sententious', he remains within both theory and politics. Rephrasing Lacan, he wants us to understand politics as 'structured like a language' (Bhabha, 1992). It, too, is relational, deferred, and continually within what Chantal Mouffe describes as a wider 'chain of equivalences' (Laclau and Mouffe, 1985).

Deconstruction and the move away from binary oppositions, including those of absolute beginnings and absolute endings, can here be seen as opening up a new way of conceptualizing the political field and creating a new set of methods for cultural studies. This is manifest in recent work on race, and most forcibly in Kobena Mercer's (1992) analysis of race as a major signifier across the postwar years on both sides of the Atlantic. Likewise, Paul Gilroy (1992) shows how, far from being on the outside of political meaning and cultural formation, race has been right in there, at the heart of English debates on what is meant by national culture, and on the nature and value of European culture and European aesthetics. Gilroy skilfully connects nineteenth-century debates with the formative moments of cultural studies. He parts company with that aspect of Gramscian Marxism which considered the political potential of the 'national popular'. Nationalism has meant repudiation and exclusion, the drawing up of borders and boundaries which keep out, but which by virtue of their very existence also define a population negatively, and so keep them within, but in relations of exclusion and subordination. Gilroy invents a transnational perspective, the black Atlantic world, as a better way of conceptualizing the space of black political and cultural dissent.

Here theoretical developments combine with a sense of political urgency bringing to cultural studies what we might still expect of it, a mode of study which is engaged and which seeks not the truth, but knowledge and understanding as a practical and material means of communicating with and helping to empower subordinate social groups and movements. Theory need not always lead so directly to politics. But what has worried me recently in cultural studies is when the theoretical detours become literary and textual excursions and when I begin to lose a sense of why the object of study is constituted as the object of study in the first place. Why do it? What is the point? Who is it for? On my first reading of the collection *Cultural Studies*, a volume which has since become known as the 'blockbuster', I was gripped by panic. Where have I been for the last five years? Much of this kind of cultural studies does not at all tally with what I teach, with what I find useful in understanding the everyday world and everyday culture around me. I was struck by a number of absences. Cultural policy is addressed in only one of the papers included in the volume. Likewise, 'lived experience' and the culture of everyday life is considered only by John Fiske. There is relatively little direct engagement with the role of cultural intellectuals in the UK, in the USA, in the new Europe, or, indeed, in any of the emergent global sociopolitical formations of the 1990s.

And yet this is our very own terrain. As part of the '68-educated radical professionals, our everyday lives at work, especially in teaching and in education, but also at home and in the community, comprise endless political interventions conducted at every level, from simple acts of communication and pedagogy to high-level policy-making decisions. Postmodernity has not stopped us from functioning in this hyperactive way. The totalizing field of Marxist theory may have been discredited, but it has not meant the end of politics. Academics working in media studies, cultural studies and sociology have found ample opportunity to become involved in educational and cultural policy-making. This in itself is evidence of the impact which work in these fields has had outside as well as inside the academy.

This intense intellectual and political activity finds only a partial expression in *Cultural Studies*. The multi-disciplinarity is shaken off (evident in the decline of a sociological presence, found in only two contributions, one by Simon Frith and the other by Janet Wolff), and a much purer and sometimes less colourful discipline emerges. At the very moment at which cultural studies begins to gain institutional recognition, it seems that not only is it shorn of its interdisciplinary character, but its foundations are shaken by the critique of Marxism and by the decentring of class relations which in the early years gave cultural studies much of its distinctive identity.

What remains is a sophisticated but virtually unrecognizable mode of inquiry. Why unrecognizable? Because, in my view, cultural studies was always messy. Characterized by intense internal theoretical conflict, it was also a messy amalgam of sociology, social history and literature, rewritten as it were into the language of contemporary culture. Not only did these disciplines feed into and sustain cultural studies (many of us got jobs teaching sociology, after all) but they also came in for heavy criticism from within cultural studies. In the first instance it was part of the cultural studies project to subject sociology, history and literature to critique, then later these same subject areas as well as cultural studies itself were shown to be heavily Anglocentric and blind to the perspective of the colonial or postcolonial subject.

The ferocity of this critique has, ironically, brought back to cultural studies what has been missing from it, the notion of its being a contested terrain of study. Not only contested but also resistant to disciplinary purity. Precisely because it is so embedded in contemporary social and political processes, because, for example, the recent changes in Europe affect how we think about culture, because class diminishes as a site of identification before our very eyes, cultural studies must continue to argue against its incorporation into what is conventionally recognized as a 'subject area'. For cultural studies to survive it cannot afford to lose this disciplinary looseness, this feeling that, like other radical areas of inquiry, such as psychoanalysis, its authors are making it up as they go along.

CONTINGENCY, HISTORICITY AND IDENTITY

> I haven't rejected Marxism. Something different has occurred. It is Marxism that has broken up and I believe I am holding on to its best fragments.
>
> (Laclau, 1991: 85)

The intention here is to draw the preceding section together with the critique which follows by exploring in more detail what the meaning of post-Marxism might be for cultural studies. So far it has been suggested that, apart from the continuing centrality of 'textuality', there is a hesitancy about where the theoretical future of the field might lie. There is no shortage of critical terms or political ideas, but to grasp them and their potential it seems we have to dig beneath the surface. For example, Kobena Mercer (1992) refers to the idea of the 'democratic antagonism', and also draws on and makes use of other key terms found in recent work by Ernesto Laclau and Chantal Mouffe (1985). However, the emphasis in

Kobena Mercer's piece is, of course, on his own chosen object of study, the place of race as a 'floating signifier' in postwar political and cultural discourse, and so this underlying theoretical frame of reference remains cryptic or assumed rather than fully explicated. Kobena Mercer also rejects any notion of a binary relation (signifier/signified) as having a validity in the analysis of cultural meaning. Instead, he talks about relations of equivalence. In addition, there is the question of identity and identity politics which runs right through a number of papers, especially those which deal with race. But what exactly is meant by identity? Is it a term which implies the psychic processes of acquiring identity as theorized by Lacan? Is it a term which somehow suggests the political shift away from class? Or does class identity constitute one among many identities of equal validity in the struggle for a pluralist radical democracy? Through what processes has identity in cultural studies come to replace the more psychoanalytical notion of the subject?

In a recent interview, Ernesto Laclau (1991) explains that his is not a rejection of Marxism *tout court* so much as a process of moving on beyond the theoretical vocabulary of the various Marxisms and neo-Marxisms. It is no longer useful to retain the word Marxism to characterize the current mode of inquiry. Post-Marxism suggests taking the radical political project further, and at the same time using what has been called the crisis of Marxism as an opportunity to go back and deconstruct, in Derridean terms, the Marxist canon.

What is Laclau's starting-point? That the emancipation of society through the agency of one united class no longer stands as a model for understanding or anticipating social change. That class struggle is not inevitable, that this was a theoretically flawed argument based on the misapplication of the Hegelian concept of 'contradiction' to the processes of capital accumulation and the wage labour relation, that antagonism is not inherent to capital, but based around external, contingent and historical processes. It is, therefore, the conditions outside capital which contribute to social antagonisms – the inability of the worker, for example, to participate in the broader society as a consumer. The 'constitutive outside' is necessary in what Laclau calls antagonism.

We are here entering a very different kind of sociopolitical universe from that understood by Marxism. 'What we find is not an interaction or determination between fully constituted areas of the social, but a field of relational semi-identities in which "political", "ideological", and "economic" elements will enter into unstable relations of imbrication without ever managing to constitute themselves as separate objects' (Laclau, 1991). This begs several questions. What of the subject? What are the mechanics of identification? Laclau seems to be drawing on Lacan and extending his psychoanalytical vocabulary to incorporate a more sociopolitical perspective. Full identity is never achieved, just as the subject of

49

Lacan is defined through lack. Identity requires acts of identification, and this, in turn, implies agency and process. The social subject can take responsibility for his or her own history, though not to achieve 'fullness'. It is this incompleteness which creates the 'social imaginary', which, in turn, is the sphere of representation. 'The imaginary is a horizon ... as modes of representation of the very form of fullness, they are located beyond the precariousness and dislocations typical of the world of objects' (Laclau, 1991).

Incompleteness, fragmentation and the pluralities of emergent identities need not mean loss of political capacity. Instead, they can point the way to new forms of struggle, they can create conditions which are 'more difficult to manipulate and control'. As the subject of social control disperses, the strategies of social control are, in a sense, thrown off guard. This means that techniques of evasion can be more easily realized. What de Certeau (1984) would call 'ruses' can, for Laclau, mean an avoidance of the 'dictatorship by market, state, or direct producers'.

There is a certain obfuscation about the actual processes of acquiring identity in Laclau's recent work which remains unresolved. He is on more solid ground in his critique of Gramsci. Following his abandonment of Marx's reliance on the notion of a fundamental class, which bears within it emancipatory capacities as inherent and therefore 'outside political struggle', Laclau extends this argument to key elements in Gramsci's writing. While the great value of Gramsci's thinking is that it brings Marxist theories down to the level of 'concrete social contexts', the very notion of hegemony depends, none the less, on a 'privileged' class which by necessity will emerge, and which will be led to a dominant position by those organic intellectuals whose role it is to 'know ... the underlying movement of history'. It is this logic of necessity which, argues Laclau, binds Gramsci to an essentially authoritarian notion of leadership. For a more democratic conception of social change to emerge, a logic of contingency would need to prevail. When contingency is combined with equivalence and when no social group is granted a privileged place as an emancipatory agent, then a form of relational hegemony can extend the sequence of democratic antagonisms through a series of social displacements. Laclau gives as an example the trade union organization set up in a neighbourhood and able to stretch its interests to engage with gay struggles and thus to let slip the centrality of class from the trade union identity. When this happens then a hegemonic centre can be said to exist. 'The radicality of a conflict depends on the extent to which the differences are re-articulated in chains of equivalence' (Laclau, 1991).

What we have to expect is not the growing simplification of the class structure as predicted by Marx, nor the inevitability of a universal class subject emerging, but rather the development of a multiplicity of partial and fragmented identities, each with its own role to play in the pursuit of radical democracy. The collapse of Marxism need not be construed as signalling the end of socialist politics; indeed the beginning of a new era, where the opportunities for a pluralist democracy are strengthened rather than weakened, is now within reach. What is inconceivable, however, is a society without conflict, a harmonious entity like the post-revolutionary utopia envisaged by Marx. This is impossible because 'power is the condition for society to be possible'.

It would seem, then, that if Laclau is correct we have little option but to work within the confines of the contingent and historically specific processes which are constitutive of our positioning and of our identities. There is no longer a pressure to rank identities in some kind of grand universal order of ascending political importance, since the road to radical democracy lies both in the incommensurability of such struggles and also in the possibility of forming chains of connection and articulation across different interest groups. Laclau's analysis remains focused around the political. Radical democracy suggests an alternative to capital, but, we are reminded, democratic freedom need not imply greater state intervention in public life; it might involve less. Likewise, the free market offers opportunities for new emergent identities; besides which, capital in the homogeneous absolutist way in which we on the left have tended to refer to it, is itself a more fractured and fragile entity.

Laclau's recent writings raise a number of questions of key importance to cultural intellectuals. In one sense he is providing the theoretical underpinning for what has already happened in cultural studies. There is a greater degree of openness than would have been the case some years ago, when the pressure to bring the chosen object of study firmly into the conceptual landmarks, provided first by Althusser and then by Gramsci, imposed on cultural studies a degree of rigidity. This new discursiveness allows or permits a speculative 'writerly' approach, the dangers of which I have already outlined, but the advantages of which can be seen in the broader, reflective and insightful mode which the absence of the tyranny of theory, as it was once understood, makes possible. This is most evident in Lidia Curti's commentary on soap opera as a mode of continually articulating the practices of identification and the anxieties around identity. She draws attention to the staple of narrative strategies in soap, the sudden loss of memory prompting the question 'Who am I?' The adopted child's search for the real mother or father is a bid once again to find out who s/he is; the split identity of the heroine who is mysteriously replaced by a double; the close-ups, as women viewers lose themselves in the subjects whose innermost feelings they identify with: all of these acts comprise forms of self-interrogation about who I am and how I want to be, or how I expect to be.

What remains underdeveloped in Laclau's analysis is the place and role of culture, in the process of 'building a new left' (the title of one of the

51

pieces). When this question was put to him, Laclau agreed that hegemony was indeed a type of articulation working through culture and not just in the field of politics (Laclau, 1991). It is also in culture that identity is most thoroughly shaped, and it is the task of culture in the post-Marxist period to 'transform the forms of identification and the construction of subjectivity that exist in our civilization'. But the direction of the movement that this process must now take is not towards some universal subjectivity but towards an identity which maintains the 'dignity of the specific'. It is his commitment to the historically specific which allows Laclau not to be specific. He cannot spell out the practices of, or the mechanics of, identity formation, for the very reason that they are, like their subjects, produced within particular social and historical conditions. This permits a consistently high level of abstraction in his political philosophy. But the work of transformation which is implicit in his analysis is exactly concurrent with the kind of critical work found in the contributions on race in the *Cultural Studies* collection.

GHOSTS, AIDS AND MOBY DICK

In her article in *Cultural Studies*, 'Representing whiteness in the black imagination', bell hooks describes the way in which black people who did not live in the 'bush of ghosts' represented white people and whiteness in their own everyday experience and in black popular culture. These white ghosts combined the strange with the terrible. From the child's point of view white people were a source of terror. In the article hooks remembers her own trips across town to get to her grandmother's house in a predominantly white neighbourhood. Her image of whites as potentially violent, with the capacity to terrorize her, was drawn partly from their stares of hate as she passed by. As a child, she had to learn that in order to be safe she must recognize 'the power of whiteness, even to fear it and avoid encountering it'. Living in a black neighbourhood, her only experience of white men was the insurance salesmen who 'terrorized by economic exploitation'. This constant fear is something white people learn about 'secondhand', but it is formative in the development of black identity, and it accompanies black people as they move through different states, countries and social situations. The suspicious glances of the airport immigration officers staring down at her passport are not so different from the antagonistic stares of the white people looking at the young bell hooks from their porches as she ran towards the safety of her grandmother's house.

The experience of travel in the formation of black identity remains a critical example in the history of racial subordination, but as Paul Gilroy argues in his contribution to the same collection, it is also something which can be turned to political advantage in the reconceptualization of the world map to create a transnationalism expressive of the historical mobility of black people. The aim is not to achieve a black oneness, an absolute ethnicity, but rather to allow a plurality of black identities to emerge. The specificities of black settlement in any one place will produce a particularly nuanced identity. But this coexists with the reality of the dislocated map, the articulations across and beyond the barriers and boundaries set by the nation-states. Thus there are set in place, in Laclau's terms, the conditions for a much longer chain of equivalences which preclude reductionism or essentialism and which give rise to both a common and an uncommon culture emerging. This is not simply cultural diversity in the liberal sense. As Homi Bhabha argues, such a notion slides too easily into ideas of difference as reflective of tolerance. What is really at stake is the nature and form of the relationships which bind these differences together and from which they accrue their meaning. It is in relation to each other that identity is formed. If meaning is relational, so too is identity.

Kobena Mercer understands the new politics of identity as partly emerging from a deep rupture within the traditional sites of consciousness, including those of class, party, nation and state. It is not enough, however, to fill the theoretical gap opened up by this social de-alignment by acknowledging or citing what he calls the cultural studies 'mantra' of race, sex and class identities. When sex and race are mechanistically added to class there is a tendency to slide back into seeing them as intact and absolute categories, which is, of course, exactly what Mercer, Gilroy and, some years previously, a number of feminist theorists including Denise Riley (1988) have argued they are not.

Mercer also suggests that the new right has been much more successful than the left at mobilizing around the 'signifiers' of identity by forging radical meanings on to the pre-existing meanings of race. These are political struggles over the 'multi-accentuality' of the sign.[1] If representation remains a site of power and regulation as well as a source of identity, then cultural academics working in the fields of representation have a critical job to do in attempting to recast these terms by inflecting new meanings and by prising apart and disentangling old ones – as, for example, Kobena Mercer himself does in his invoking of the place of race in the events of 1968, in the hippy underground and the counter-culture, and even in the notion of the Woodstock nation. As he shows, racial signifiers were not just adopted by white youth, but were constructive in creating the actual subcultural discourses of those sectors of postwar white youth who 'disidentified with racism'. Black expressive culture provided a language for the new social movements which emerged in the early 1970s; black pride re-emerged as gay pride; and black liberation struggles helped create 'gay lib' and, indeed, 'women's lib'.

In the last ten years it has been the right which has managed most successfully to intervene and shape the 'imaginary and symbolic dimensions of hegemonic politics' (Mercer, 1992). The importance of the fields of the symbolic and the imaginary should not be underestimated. These are also, of course, the fields of culture and of the mass media. How might they be more successfully reinflected or cathected by the left, by black intellectuals, by feminists? If there was a simple answer to this question then we would not spend so much time worrying about it. But the power of representation, the seduction of received rhetoric, the ease with which the self dissolves into the image on the screen, the appeal of easy pleasures and the occasional desire to relinquish responsibility, gives to the ever-ready radical right a clear advantage over and above the political and material advantages they already have at their disposal. With these adversaries in mind, Stuart Hall reminds us of the difference between academic and intellectual work. He urges intellectual modesty and, at the same time, insists on the urgency of politics on the intellectual agenda of cultural studies. This is like saying: 'Look here, as marginal intellectuals there is not a great deal which we can do, so let's not kid ourselves. On the other hand, the critical attention which we can pay to the field of dominant culture and to the world of representation, and the extent to which we can show how meanings are constructed and how they are neither inevitable or natural or God-given, is an important task. What is more, it is increasingly in culture that politics itself is constructed as a discourse; it is here that popular assent in a democratic society is sought. While we should not overestimate our social effectivity, neither should we wallow in our own marginality and leave the field of forging cultural meanings to those who already take it as their preordained right.'

In his essay in *Cultural Studies* (1992) Stuart Hall considers the disparity between the intense political activity which has emerged around AIDS and the too-leisurely mode of the deconstructive voice in cultural studies. His fear is also that the dominant language through which AIDS is understood will eventually spell the death of desire itself. This threat is at the very heart of Douglas Crimp's important contribution on this subject, because what he shows is how intent the media and the powers of representation are to de-sexualize the gay community in the light of AIDS. This strategy has been pursued with relentless force, with great brutality, and with a callous disregard for people's privacy and for their suffering. The value of Crimp's study is as follows: first, it charts with historical specificity the unfolding and developmental chain of images and narratives through which the US media interprets and makes sense of AIDS for the general public (i.e. for white middle-class heterosexuals); second, it shows how in the guise of sensitivity and realism the liberal arts, and in particular the work of one art photographer, Nicholas Nixon, merely reinforce the pathologization of the gay community; third, it records the views of the art critics who, with only one exception, William Olander, the curator of New

York's New Museum of Contemporary Arts, congratulate the photographer for managing to get his subjects, many of them in advanced states of illness, to 'hold nothing back'. What, in contrast, Olander and Crimp see in the pictures is loneliness, lack of help and community, no sign of work or activity, no names and no identities.

In a particularly exploitative and sensationalized piece of reportage which Crimp describes, a TV programme tracks down a disadvantaged young gay black AIDS sufferer as he is moved on from town to town by family and by local authorities anxious to get rid of him. The media portray him, poor and still hustling, as a kind of sexual terrorist, a walking time-bomb. He, in his misery and like so many other millions of would-be TV celebrities, revels momentarily in this brief moment of fame and notoriety. Crimp ends his piece with a discussion of an independently produced videotape titled 'Danny'. The film-maker, Stashu Kybartas, who is documenting Danny's experience of AIDS, breaks the rules which have implicitly established themselves around the treatment of this subject in the arts and the visual media by attributing to Danny, despite his skin lesions, an active sexuality to which he himself is drawn. As Crimp points out, Danny is 'nevertheless still fully sexualized'.

Nothing could be further apart from this erotic moment recorded on the voiceover ('It was suddenly very quiet in the studio, and my heart was beating fast') described by Crimp than the current 'phobic' representations of sexual desire found in the commercial cinema. Fear of AIDS has created a structural problem about how to represent sex in a visual medium which, since the late 1960s, has depended on what might be called a never-ending stream of promiscuous narratives. While, at one level, heterosexual culture has defined itself as safely removed from the immediate threat of AIDS, at a much deeper level there is a recognition of how wrong this is. Through a tangled web of anxieties there emerges a set of narrative solutions: monogamy replaces promiscuity, the baby replaces the penis, the couple at home replaces the singles bar, parenthood becomes a subject worthy of narrative investigation. In the surprise blockbuster *Ghost*, we find race and sex brought together as critical 'floating signifiers' in contemporary urban discourse. *Ghost* might be seen, then, as one of those moments in popular culture where there is a vast over-investment in meaning. Its popularity is partly dependent on its ability as a cinematic narrative to transcend and overcome social fears and anxieties within the framework of comedy and entertainment. While it has been condemned by critics like Judith Williamson (1990) writing in the *Guardian* as particularly pernicious in its use of moral absolutes (good people who die go to heaven in a cloud of light, bad people are dragged by screaming hags downwards to hell), it is precisely the assertion of absolutes in what is a much murkier and unclear landscape of contemporary urban society which adds to its appeal.

Ghost is a modern fairy tale/horror film predicated on a supernatural device which allows a young white man, beaten to death on the streets of Manhattan while his girlfriend looks on helplessly, to return to earth as an invisible observer/protector. Race is a necessary counterpoint to the narrative. The yuppie couple are just settling into their loft apartment when tragedy strikes. Their environment is middle-class. She is a potter, he works on Wall Street. They are surrounded by art objects; they go out one evening to the theatre; they are confronted by a non-white assailant and the young man, Sam, dies in a violent struggle.

The young mixed-race audience in the Holloway cinema where I saw the film holds its breath, puzzled. Is it possible that a blockbuster movie made in 1990 could conceivably rely on such negative stereotypes for its narrative action? But wait a minute. Sigh of relief. The narrative slowly unfolds. Their assailant is Hispanic. And he is set up by the white yuppie business partner of the dead man. For some complicated reason the business partner has to get rid of Sam in order to complete the fraudulent dealings he has got involved with as a means of paying off his cocaine debts. Thus he hires José. As a ghost, Sam manages to establish contact with a black woman, Oda Mae Brown (played by Whoopi Goldberg), who makes a living as a medium. Only through her can Sam alert his girlfriend Molly to the danger she is in as the owner of a vital computer code left among his personal belongings. The humour and fun in the film derive partly through the culture clash between Sam and Oda Mae. This is expressed in language and in the contrast between sophisticated white consumer culture and black folk culture and superstition. The partnership which emerges in the end is, however, between the two unpartnered women. Mixed-race female friendship triumphs, presenting itself both as a narrative solution (in the light of the death of the male lover) and as a metaphorical bonding process which overcomes the problem of urban race conflict and the threat to whites posed by the poor black underclass.

What is counterposed in the film is black and white urban culture. *Ghost* is a mixed-race 'women's film' as viewed from a white perspective. Blacks are poor but not, as it originally seems, criminalized and angry. Black and white cultures are geographically separate, coming together only under extremely unusual circumstances. Oda Mae Brown rarely goes uptown and overdresses for the occasion. Molly hardly moves out of her loft for the duration of the film. Apart from José there are no other significant non-white male figures, and it is, therefore, a black woman who takes on the role of the racial 'other'. She can survive living in poverty without resorting to either drugs or crime, and she is able to turn her personal talents, including her wit and good humour, to her advantage by working as a medium.

Oda Mae is given no particular sexual identity. Sex in *Ghost* is wholly focused around the glamorous couple Sam and Molly (played by Patrick

Swayze and Demi Moore). Their love ends tragically in Sam's premature death. In what has become one of the most celebrated sex scenes in recent cinematic history, sex-in-love in *Ghost* is celebrated symbolically as an erotic exchange of bodily fluids. The sex scene lasts for the entire duration of the classic pop song by the Righteous Brothers, 'Unchained Melody' (subsequently re-released as a chart-topping single). It begins with Molly at her potter's wheel. She is sculpting a clay piece which increasingly takes on phallic proportions. She moulds and caresses the emergent penis/pot. The clay suddenly melts and crumbles and she starts again. It is a comic moment of detumescence. Then she is joined by Sam and the rising clay becomes part of their sexual foreplay. It collapses again and this time the soft liquid clay takes on an erotic charge of its own. Both partners begin to play with it, letting it run through their fingers, smearing it on to their hands, and rubbing it on to each other's bodies.

In this scene of highly romanticized sex between a monogamous young couple, sex is so safe that it is able to incorporate into its momentum the symbolic equivalent of unsafe sex. It acts as a reply to those who would urge the universal adoption of safe sex. The exchange of body fluids is made safe, as long as it takes place within the monogamous partnership. It is the erotic moment.

I was encouraged to see this film by my 14-year-old daughter who had already seen it several times. She came to see it with me again and warned me that there was a 'naughty' scene in it. But, she added afterwards, 'It was very nice, wasn't it, because they really loved each other.' The 'naughtiness' was the 'sight' of the erect penis as a flesh-coloured clay form, Demi's active sexual pleasure in caressing this penis/pot, and finally the couple's shared pleasure in touching each other's bodies with the soft running clay.

The centrality of this scene in the film represents a defiant statement about sex and eroticism in the 1990s. There is no question of using a condom, there are no questions about each partner's sexual past. There is no need for the new vigilance around sex. The running clay has a literary precedent, in Melville's classic novel *Moby Dick*, when the sperm and fluid remains of the trawl of fish are discovered as a source of strong erotic charge by the narrator who immerses his hands in the cloudy semen-like discharges and finds himself losing his whole sense of being. In the novel, the scene acts as a centrepoint. Sexuality is about lubrication, dissolution and the polymorphously perverse infantile pleasures of smearing, touching and rubbing.

Why conclude this chapter with such an example of the power of popular culture to encode popular anxieties into the language of desire and social conformity, and to treat race from the assumed viewpoint of the white spectator (the popular audience) as a gendered category, an urban experience and a folk culture? The answer to this question must be that my sketchy account of the film and its audience reflects a number of themes which have informed this chapter. Race is a floating signifier in *Ghost* rather than an absolute category. It travels across the city which is, at one level, racially divided, but at another, through the currency of drugs and, then, through the forces of good, connected. *Ghost* also shows how deeply internalized the fear of AIDS has been and how at a symbolic level even heterosexual monogamy (in the context of physical beauty, youth, wealth and cultural capital) is threatened by a malevolent external force. Sam, after all, dies in horrible and unexpected circumstances. Finally, *Ghost* addresses and gives a place to new emergent identities. Its women, one black and funny, the other, white and an artist, are the survivors. They embody integrity, good sense and racial goodwill. Their single status at the end of the film also says something significant about changes in sexual culture.

What remains problematic in this new terrain of cultural studies where identity plays such an important role is the actual process of identity acquisition. It is unclear as to how this important process is actually being conceptualized. On the one hand, it is fluid, never completely secured and continually being remade, reconstructed afresh. On the other hand, it only exists in relation to what it is not, to the other identities which are its 'other'. Identity is not the 'bourgeois' individual, nor is it the personality, the unique person, but neither is it the psychoanalytical subject. As it is used in current cultural discourse it implies a combative sense of self, but one which makes sense in terms of a broader overarching category, such as race or sexuality or, indeed, class. Identity, therefore, is predicated on social identity, on social groups or populations with some sense of a shared experience and history. And yet it is also a category doomed to dispersal and to fragmentation, committed to anti-essentialism, to anti-absolutism.

Identity could be seen as dragging cultural studies into the 1990s by acting as a kind of guide to how people see themselves, not as class subjects, not as psychoanalytical subjects, not as subjects of ideology, not as textual subjects, but as active agents whose sense of self is projected on to and expressed in an expansive range of cultural practices, including texts, images and commodities. If this is the case, then the problem in cultural studies today is the absence of reference to real existing identities in the ethnographic sense. The identities being discussed, and I am as guilty of this myself as anybody else, are textual or discursive identities. The site of identity formation in cultural studies remains implicitly in and through cultural commodities and texts rather than in and through the cultural practices of everyday life. This, then, is where I want to end, with a plea for identity ethnography in cultural studies, with a plea for carrying out interactive research on groups and individuals who are more than just audiences for texts. In this sense, I am with John Fiske in his desire to find the right theoretical vocabulary to understand everyday life in its fleeting, fluid and volatile formations (Fiske, 1992). Looked at in this way, identity becomes submerged into and virtually indistinguishable from everyday life in all its contingency and with all its historical specificity. For it to re-emerge at the other end, it is necessary that we somehow move away from the binary opposition which still haunts cultural studies, that is, the distinction between text and lived experience, between media and reality, between culture and society. What is now required is a methodology, a new paradigm for conceptualizing identity-in-culture, an ethnographic approach which takes as its starting-point the relational interactive quality of everyday life and which brings a renewed rigour to this kind of work by integrating into it a keen sense of history and contingency.

This article first appeared in L. Grossberg, C. Nelson and P. Treichler (eds) (1992) *Cultural Studies*, London: Routledge, pp. 719–30.

NOTE

1 A phrase borrowed from Volosinov/Bahktin and used by Stuart Hall and Kobena Mercer in their contributions to *Cultural Studies*.

REFERENCES

Bhabha, H. (1992) 'Postcolonial authority and postmodern guilt', in L. Grossberg, C. Nelson and P. Treichler (eds) *Cultural Studies*, London: Routledge, pp. 56–69.
Crimp, D. (1992) 'Portraits of people with AIDS', in L. Grossberg, C. Nelson and P. Treichler (eds) *Cultural Studies*, London: Routledge, pp. 117–34.
Curti, L. (1992) 'What is real and what is not: female fabulations in cultural analysis', in L. Grossberg, C. Nelson and P. Treichler (eds) *Cultural Studies*, London: Routledge, pp. 134–54.
de Certeau, M. (1984) *The Practice of Everyday Life*, Berkeley, CA: University of California Press.
Fiske, J. (1992) 'Cultural studies and the culture of everyday life', in L. Grossberg, C. Nelson, and P. Treichler (eds) *Cultural Studies*, London: Routledge, pp. 154–74.
Frith, S. (1992) 'The cultural study of popular music', in L. Grossberg. C. Nelson and P. Treichler (eds) *Cultural Studies*, London: Routledge, pp. 174–87.
Gilroy, P. (1992) 'Against ethnic absolutism', in L. Grossberg, C. Nelson and P. Treichler (eds) *Cultural Studies*, London: Routledge, pp. 188–99.
Grossberg, L., Nelson, C. and Treichler, P. (eds) *Cultural Studies*, London: Routledge.
Hall, S. (1989) 'Cultural studies: two paradigms in cultural studies', in T. Bennett (ed.) *Culture, Ideology and Social Process*, London: Batsford, pp. 19–39.
Hall, S. (1992) 'Cultural studies and its theoretical legacies', in L. Grossberg, C. Nelson and P. Treichler (eds) *Cultural Studies*, London: Routledge, pp. 277–95.
Hall, S. *et al.* (1978) *Policing the Crisis: Mugging, the State and Law and Order*, London: Macmillan.

Harvey D. (1989) *The Condition of Postmodernity*, Oxford: Blackwell.

hooks, b. (1992) 'Representing whiteness in the black imagination', in L. Grossberg, C. Nelson and P. Treichler (eds) *Cultural Studies*, London: Routledge, pp. 338–47.

Jameson, F. (1984) 'Postmodernism, or the cultural logic of capital', *New Left Review* 146, (July–August 1984): 53–92.

Laclau, E. (1991) *Reflections on the New Revolutions of Our Times*, London: Verso.

Laclau, E. and Mouffe, C. (1985) *Hegemony and Socialist Strategy: Towards a Radical Democratic Politics*, London: Verso.

Mercer, K. (1992) ' "1968": periodizing postmodern politics and identity', in L. Grossberg, C. Nelson and P. Treichler (eds) *Cultural Studies*, London: Routledge, pp. 424–50.

Riley, D. (1988) *'Am I That Name?': Feminism and the Category of 'Women' in History*, Minneapolis, MN: University of Minnesota Press.

Schwartz, B. (1985) 'Gramsci goes to Disneyland: postmodernism and the popular', *Anglistica* (Naples).

Williamson, J. (1990) 'Arts Dairy', the *Guardian*, October.

Wolff, J. (1992) 'Excess and inhibition: interdisciplinarity in the study of art', in L. Grossberg, C. Nelson and P. Treichler (eds) *Cultural Studies*, London: Routledge, pp. 706–19.

4

FEMINISM, POSTMODERNISM AND THE 'REAL ME'

A three-way split has developed recently around postmodernism. There are those who refuse to admit that postmodernism engages with anything that modernism is not better able to explain and who also defend the values of modernism as they relate to both intellectual work and political analysis. This grouping has established itself as a counterbalance to those others who from such a 'reasonable' standpoint display what are viewed as the excesses of postmodernism. Allowing even for predictable negative typecasting in a debate which has become as heated as this, the image of these postmodernists remains particularly flimsy and marked by what Butler (1992) describes as a kind of slur of infantilism or at least youthful aberration. The third path is occupied by the postcolonialists and there is in this work both a notion of what Gilroy (1993), drawing on Bauman, labels 'the counter-cultures of modernity' and at the same time a remorseless critique of modernity and a looking to those accounts of postmodernity as a way of finding a place from which to speak and a space from which to develop that critique of the places and the spaces of exclusion inside modernity.

The question which will be asked in this chapter is what does this three-way divide mean for women? And how does feminism define itself in an intellectual world now characterized by shifting borders, boundaries and identities? To begin to answer this question it is necessary to look first at how two strands of this debate, the pro-modernist and the postcolonialist, put on the agenda quite separate issues as central to our understanding of contemporary society. These usefully set a framework for going on to consider the place of feminism in this new conceptualization of the social. But in engaging with the feminists who have taken up a strongly postmodernist position, the reader should be warned that these writers have been criticized for 'taking leave of their senses'. To enter their discourse is therefore to display a willingness to consciously explore the other side, the under-side of contemporary critical theory, a realm of thinking which is frequently charged with the abandonment not just of reason, but also of the subject, good sense and politics. In this process of searching around in the landscape of post-feminism, as well as postmodernism and postcoloniality, the question of who 'we' intellectuals are these days and what role we have to play in feminist politics is constantly forced into prominence.

POSTMODERNISTS: GUILTY OF PLAYING WITH POLITICS

My starting-point is to suggest that the provocative stance adopted in language by a figure like Lyotard (1984), which results in his being charged with playfulness, is a deliberate strategy, a way of positioning himself within a certain kind of rhetorical mode which allows him to develop his critique. Gregor McLennan (1992a: 18) has recently expressed his antipathy to this way of thinking as follows: 'The contemporary world, in spite of patches of surface civilisation, remains too ravaged by oppression, ignorance and malnutrition for privileged intellectuals to trade in seriousness for the sparkling interplay of language games.' Contrary to this position it can be argued that postmodernism represents neither an absence of seriousness, nor a kind of political immorality or irresponsibility. It works as a critique because it forces precisely this kind of response, either urgently (and perhaps defensively) to redefine and defend the political and intellectual formation of modernity, or else, having subjected to scrutiny the great pillars of thinking which have supported the project of modernity, to stand back and ask 'What's going on?' (as the great soul singer Marvin Gaye put it).

Postmodernism is a concept for understanding social change. It seems feeble to suggest it, but maybe the reason for the hostility to the concept in Britain lies at least partly in the abysmal fate of social science research and intellectual work in general in the UK during and after the Thatcher years, where the nature of these constraints inevitably produced defensive political and intellectual responses. Sociology as well as 'society' itself became such redundant categories that there was little opportunity to investigate what the new theoretical vocabulary might look like in practice. Thus while there has been a debate about 'new ways of living' and about post-Fordism as well as one on fragmentation and identity, there has been little opportunity to examine in any depth the lived 'condition of postmodernity'. As a result the really engaged debate on how best to understand this refiguring of society was never able to take place. What happened instead was either a rejection and retrenchment which none the less involved re-examining the premises and the assumptions upon which the intellectual edifice of modernity was based, or else a process of translating some of the categories of French or American postmodernism into the cultural politics of contemporary Britain. This latter can best be seen in the emergence of 'New Times' (Hall and Jacques, 1989) politics in the late 1980s and early 1990s with its interest in consumerism, identity, ethnicity, and with the critique of essentialism, be it in relation to gender (Riley, 1988), class (Laclau, 1991) or ethnicity (McRobbie, 1985; Bhabha, 1990).

FINDING THE 'REAL ME'

The notion of the 'real me' suggests the fictive unity of the self and the essentialism entailed in the search for such a person. What is being questioned in this phrase as used by Stuart Hall (1992) is the possibility of ever finding a 'real me'. One of the issues that will be explored here is what remains when we do away with the real me. How do we construct what I would define as a sufficiently focused 'social self' in order to be effective in politics? And who can such a politics now claim to represent? Who, therefore, is the discursive 'I' which speaks or writes, to whom and with what purpose? This question will be returned to in the final part of this chapter. But, for the moment, I would want to signal postmodernity as marking a convergence of a number of discourses each of which opens up new possibilities for positioning the self. Many would argue that feelings of dislocation or turbulence, and experiences of fragmentation and crises of identity were as much part of the experience of modernity as they now are of postmodernity (Berman, 1984). But what is distinctive about the discourses considered in the following pages is the respect for difference which they display, not, as some might see it, a 'simple' celebration of difference, but rather a rigorous thinking through of what 'living with difference' (Mercer, 1990) might entail. In addition I think there is a brave and necessary inclusion in the new intellectual agenda of difference, a different kind of language, one which insists on the interplay between intellectual boundaries and borders and also one which recognizes the importance of what have been the hidden dimensions of subjectivity, those which arise from positionalities which, within modernism, had no legitimate place, i.e. that of the black woman, that of the mother, the daughter, that of the feminist intellectual, the feminist teacher.

This kind of work is reflected in Carolyn Steedman's *Landscape for a Good Woman* (1985) which pulls together strands of social history and personal psychoanalysis producing a remarkable text where the oblique search for the 'real me' through the joint guidance of history and psychoanalysis produces instead a layered, mysterious, unresolved self, a fictive daughter, whose positionality as daughter within a particular configuration of class, culture and family, has required that 'she' produce 'this' book. Feminism, in Steedman's case, also requires a necessary interdisciplinarity of intellectual work which problematizes its own foundations. It may well be that it is this which makes such work, as well as that produced by postcolonialist writers including Trinh T. Min-ha (1989), Homi Bhabha (1990) and Gayatri Chakravorty Spivak (1992), appear unruly and truculent and poetically disrespectful of the boundaries which have guarded and guaranteed the old rules of academia. It is partly this 'game' of academic convention and the defence of disciplinary boundaries as guarantors of academic authorship and identity, which underpins recent altercations between those who defend modernity and those who move in some 'other' direction.

In the recent volume which is part of the new Open University social science course, *Modernity and Its Futures*, we find an interesting version of the debate for and against postmodernism being played out by Gregor McLennan (1992b) and Stuart Hall (1992). Neither author wholly defends one against the other. But as McLennan veers towards modernity, Stuart Hall leans towards the exploration of fragmented subjectivity. In the following pages a reading of these debates will be suggested as a means of establishing a framework for considering recent work in feminist theory.

CRITICAL EMBRACE: MODERNITY AND ITS CRITIQUE

In some ways the embracing of modernity as a critical concept in contemporary political thinking is a way of decentring Marxism by showing it to belong to a broader philosophical project. Thus, while Stuart Hall shows how modernity and its focus on 'man' and the unified subject was itself undermined by Freud (the unconscious), by Marx himself (production and labour rather than exchange, the market and free will), later by structuralism (which opposed the transparency of meaning) and more recently by the social movements (including those of gender, sexual identity and ethnicity), so also could we say that the interest in modernity can be seen as a way of both relocating Marx in a less universalistic mode (a kind of process of downgrading or relativizing) and of looking to find something in modernity which can be used to ward off the encroaching chaos of postmodernity. Feminist intellectuals (with a few exceptions) have tended either to argue for the necessity of some of those great modernist values: truth, objectivity, reason (Nicholson, 1990), or else they have argued against the assumed invisibility of women found in much of the recent writing on modernity (Bowlby, 1992; Nava, 1992).

Gregor McLennan reminds us that the Enlightenment gave rise to the idea of social betterment, of improving and making better the society in which we live. The development of the social sciences was part of this project. Are these 'foundations of modern thought' now obsolete? Or do they only need to be revised? The first of these questions implies that postmodernity blows everything away, the second that the existing vocabulary merely needs updating. McLennan opts for modifying modernity. He pitches the 'overhauling' Lyotard against the more 'reasonable' Habermas (1985). For Lyotard the Enlightenment promised science as pure knowledge and as narrative-free practice, but that picture of pure knowledge was in itself part of a very powerful story which helped legitimize capitalist exploitation. Therefore, beware of the meta-narratives. Knowledge is not pure or in the mind but moves in a game. Habermas, in contrast, sees the Enlightenment as an ideal not a reality. It poses questions of morality, science and art as separate from myth and primitivity. To abandon the commitment to reason and rationality is to embrace despair and conservatism. We can retain hope of objectivity in universals (the good life, the better society) without having 'naive expectations'. Enter the theory of communicative action/reason.

For McLennan relativism is the issue. Does cultural relativism lead to cognitive relativism, that is, we cannot understand therefore we give up and go home? Relativism encourages indifference, he suggests. It means that arguments about what is good and true cannot be engaged in and across cultures. Critics of this position (the rest, the others) would, McLennan agrees, say that what is being defended here 'is the culture and society of western science and philosophy'. He says in defence of this position that some values can be shared cross-culturally. And if this is not possible and if knowledge has such little import then why carry on doing academic work at all? Modernity did not promise one kind of progress but many. There was always a radicalized strand within modernity.

McLennan argues his position on the grounds that there is communicative action across cultures. There are still universals; for example, the possibility of democracy. One problem is that he takes the postmodernity critique as a kind of intellectual earthquake. He responds truculently. It is one or the other. If there is no logic, no reason, then we all shut up shop or embrace mysticism or unreason or madness. But this mode of argumentation based on pitching two binary opposites against each other need not always be the most useful way of proceeding. The tendency is to feel the necessity of coming down strongly in favour of one or the other, or, as McLennan does in a later piece, more measuredly, to bring together the 'better elements of Enlightenment sociology' with 'the undoubted insights of "post" currents. Not ... in order to form some bland and convenient theoretical convergence but rather to generate a series of productive and taxing tensions' (McLennan, 1992a: 20). What this restrained mode cannot afford to do is to look beyond the 'reasonable' frame of reference within which the debate is conducted. Why not? What happens when we challenge this kind of management of reason, when we suggest that the tensions are more usefully explored when they remain aggressively outside and deeply uncomfortable with this kind of 'convergence'?

STUART HALL: WORKING IN A WORLD OF SHIFTING BOUNDARIES

Stuart Hall travels down a different road. What he is interested in exploring are the new worldly identities which have come into being, sweeping away, as capitalism itself does, the old nation-states which were the bearers of modernity and the givers of identity and 'nationality'. Instead we live in a world of moving boundaries, a world in which borders are crossed, new sub-nationalisms and transnationalisms are embraced. For Hall it is the struggle to explain which is important. What he turns his attention to are those aspects of modernity which incorporated subjection and subordination in the language of social advance, exploration, development, civilization. This more open-ended approach avoids the either/ors which define the terms of McLennan's argument. Instead it adopts a strategy of unsettlement and an embracing of the idea of difference and hybridity. What is also unsettled and differentiated is the 'real me'. This approach is also quite different from Jameson's (1984) and Harvey's (1989), as well as McLennan's, in that we see no sign of a return to the values or ethics of modernism being proposed. It is focused around the 'new ethnicities' and it looks out for the connections among subjugated people which emerge from within the tracks of the meta-communications networks of the new global order.

Hall's contribution is significant also in that it does not prioritize an exclusively academic mode as the means of producing knowledge and understanding. Postcolonialist writing acknowledges the work found in and produced by the intersection of art and popular culture. Culture is a broad site of learning, and perhaps we learn best and are most open to ideas when the barriers between the discipline and the academy and the experiences of everyday life are broken down. There is a sense in which Stuart Hall is here speaking from the other side, from the space of difference. Where those who espoused modernity and its ideals saw vision and order and reason and achievement he sees turbulence and savagery. Included in Hall's essay is a quote from Salman Rushdie responding to the review of his book *The Satanic Verses*, 'A bit of this and a bit of that is how newness enters the world. It is the great possibility that mass migration gives the world' (Hall, 1992: 311; quoting Rushdie). If, therefore, postcolonialist experience shares anything in common with the postmodern experience, then it must be a postmodernism which is much more than an overstylized posture adopted by those who can afford to abandon politics. Instead it is a way of marking out a new set of convergences and divergences round certain critical questions about the society in which we live.

TOWARDS A FEMINIST POSTMODERNISM

In her contribution to *Beyond Equality and Difference*, Rosi Braidotti (1992) rejects the defence of theoretical reason, the unity of the subject and even of equality (equal to whom, she asks?) as 'domination', Enlightenment concepts, which have been part of an apparatus of regulation and subordination hidden under the great achievements of rationality and knowledge. This marks her out immediately as a postmodern feminist. The question that has to be asked, she suggests, is that of how we think, what is it to think? What does it mean if reason and truth are unsettled from their secure places in the foundationalist discipline of philosophy? She thus opens up for debate not only the possibility of other ways of thinking, but also the question of on whose behalf do we think as critical feminist intellectuals? What is the responsibility of the feminist intellectual? Is it not, in part, to think about thinking and thus to unveil some of the power relations caught up in the category of knowledge?

These questions which she is asking from a feminist viewpoint, happen to coincide with the critique of western thinking by subaltern discourses. So the whole status of thinking and of thought is called into question. Let us move out of a dualistic logic, she continues: male versus female, women equal to men. 'Feminists propose that reason does not sum up the totality of or even what is best in the human capacity for thinking' (Braidotti, 1992: 181). Do we therefore learn to think differently as a 'female feminist subject'? The postmodern subject, argues Braidotti, is a subject in process, organized by a will to know and a desire to speak. The crisis of subjectivity produced by postmodernity 'offers many positive openings' (Braidotti, 1992: 183). This crisis emerged in the dying moments of modernity through Freud, for example, with his insistence of the non-coincidence of the subject with consciousness, and then later with Foucault's account of the self as the product of discourse. Much thought, she reminds us, following Freud, is pre-rational, unconscious matter. Rationality rests on premises about thinking which are themselves non-rational. And desire 'is that which being the a-priori condition for thinking is in excess of the thinking process itself' (Braidotti, 1992: 184). For Braidotti the enunciation of a philosophical stance rests, therefore, on a non-philosophical disposition to represent the self, to inscribe the subject in language. How then do we rethink subjectivity and the body as an 'interface of will with desire', that is, the will to know and the desire to say?

Such an emphasis on desire inevitably runs the risk of positing desire as the source of a new essentialism. This is particularly the case when desire coincides not just with language but also with sexuality which is then taken, as Foucault (1984) has pointed out, as representing the truth of the body and of the self. Or is it rather, as Braidotti argues, that in western culture the sexed body dominates over the other levels of

67

experience? It is how we are known, how we come to know. In language we are sexed and this process of being sexed is one of the key modalities of power inscribed in each of our bodies: 'Sexuality is the dominant discourse of power in the West' (Braidotti, 1992: 185).

It is therefore a point of contestation. What, the feminist critic might ask, *is* the female body, what is it for, for whom? And to follow in this vein the feminist cultural critic might ask, is it because Madonna constructs herself exactly along this axis of *all body* that she unnerves and disrupts the axis of power which prefers to remain hidden? She pulls it all off the top shelf of the newsagent's, brings it – sex, power, pornography, the body – to the surface and leaves us to respond. It could be suggested that by placing her body on precisely those lines of classification, for example, as the site of sex, as the truth of femininity, and also as the property of the female self, something that can and does give pleasure quite autonomously from the regulative discourses within which it is more traditionally placed, the image of Madonna is disruptive. It is too much about sexuality to exist comfortably within the commercial machine, even where that machine is already linked with excessive sexual imagery (i.e. pop), or where it is licensed to shock. Instead of simply rejecting the essentialism which equates woman with body, Braidotti argues that (like Madonna) we must revisit the sites of assumed essentialism and work through them. We should explore the boundaries by going back to them.

But if we no longer know what woman is, if we are all good anti-essentialists, and if we take into account the critique by black feminists of white feminism's universalism, how do we move from analysing the implications for power of the borders and boundaries, to actively redefining the bonds through which a politics remains viable? Like all of the postmodern feminists being considered here, Braidotti puts the possibility of a communicative bond between women as the basis for politics on the agenda. This takes the form for feminist intellectuals of a kind of accountability, a recognition of the relations of responsibility between a writer and her readers and, it could be added, between a teacher and her students. Feminist thinking should, then, attempt to represent and analyse what it is to be female. In one decisive way, this breaks down the barriers between art, fiction, culture and the academic disciplines in much the way that Stuart Hall suggests (Hall, 1992). By far the most visible example of this force for breaking down barriers is the success and achievement of black women's writing over the last few years, not just for the community of women it brings into being as readers, but also because it *is* simultaneously art, history, literature, sociology, politics, biography, autobiography and also popular culture. At the opposite end of the same spectrum but 'doing' in her own theoretical work very much the same kind of thing, we could also place Gayatri Chakravorty Spivak. Coming from the high end of deconstruction, and bringing to this practice a feminist postcolonialist critique, Spivak works within the discourse of theory but so transforms it as to make it an entirely different kind of practice. It becomes an interrogative, interweaving, reflective poetics. For Spivak the community of women can only come after the recognition of difference between women, and after the raising of some key questions about who is talking to whom, and why, all points which she returns to in her contribution to *Feminists Theorise the Political* (Spivak, 1992).

This is a similar position to that described by Judith Butler, who also engages with a notion of the community of women. In articulating women, from a feminist perspective, such a category is immediately broken and it is the breaking that is the important point (Butler, 1992). Who is not spoken to in feminism? In addition, who was the 'subject' of feminism, but is no more? How has feminism opened itself out to speak to many female subjects and yet still engages with only a few? Butler sees these as crucial questions and illustrates them by referring to the old centrality of the mother as one of the primary stable subjects of feminist discourse. But this figure of the mother is not a biologically defined and stable category. She herself shifts and changes, just as feminism also does. As her children grow up and move away she no longer defines herself primarily through that particular mode of subjectivity. So the subjects of feminism change, feminism itself changes, particularly as it becomes subject to criticism by black women and, as the society within which feminism exists also undergoes quite dramatic changes, this too has an impact on what feminism is and can be. We could also add to Butler's questions the important one of how under such conditions feminism, or what remains of it, can hope to reproduce itself among a generation of younger women? What space away from feminism do young women need in order to disconnect from the historical experience of their mothers or their teachers and then find their own way towards feminism, redefining it in the process for themselves? These questions of how feminism continues and seeks to extend itself while recognizing different histories, experiences and identities are therefore crucial. Can it continue, can it still call itself feminism? What must it do to be able to legitimately address women?

As well as laying the ground for developing post-feminism theoretically, Judith Butler also takes issue with the slightly ridiculing tones frequently adopted to make light of postmodernism. As though in direct engagement with Gregor McLennan she disputes the assumption that there 'must' be a foundation and a stable subject to have a politics. She sees this as authoritarian, the use of the 'must' clause. Postmodernism does not mean that we have to do away with the subject but rather we ask after the process of its construction. The value of postmodernism therefore is that, like deconstuction, it shows clearly how arguments bury opposition. Its disorderly force is rude and impertinent in that it shows where power resides, hidden and quiet and displeased at being exposed. Demonstrating these ruses does not mean descending into unruly chaos. Rather it allows for open debate and dispute about boundaries and disciplines and what constitutes a study, what is knowledge. 'A social theory committed to democratic contestation within a post-colonialist horizon needs to find a way to bring into question the foundations it is compelled to lay down' (Butler, 1992: 8).

Thus even minimal foundations need scrutinizing. Within feminism there is a need to speak as and for women but no sooner is this done than it is objected to. This is the point at which things move. Women then become 'an undesignatable field of wills'. The dispute *is* the ground of feminist theory. The category of women has to be released from the anchoring which feminism felt it needed. 'What women signify has been taken for granted too long. . . . We have to instead break from the list of meanings and expand the possibilities of what it is to be a woman' (Butler, 1992: 16). Sex imposes a uniformity on bodies for the purposes of reproductive sexuality. This is also an act of violence. Therefore there must be a redefining, an invention of new categories. (We could add to this the question of whether this is already happening, with the emergence of the 'single mother' as a sign of these expanded possibilities of being female, a category which marks a changed society and a changed mode of familial organization.)

Jane Flax (1992a) completes the assault on the male modernists who defend reason by saying how comforting it is to believe that reason will triumph and bail us all out. How often has it? Admittedly, it is frightening to think that without truth, pure power might prevail. Feminists are as prone to this wishful thinking that reason will win through as anybody else. But, says Flax, this failure to face up to the limits of reason, truth and knowledge is predicated on fear of letting go and of thinking outside the safety of inherited assumptions about thought. 'They fear what will emerge in disrupted places if they are not in feminist control. They believe innocent clean knowledge is available somewhere for our discovery and use' (Flax, 1992b: 457). Flax prefers desire, fantasy and power. 'What we really want is power in the world not an innocent truth' (1992b: 458). Many feminists are fearful of losing what they have gained by embracing or being seen to embrace postmodernity. But this being made insecure is productive and it coincides with being made insecure by the critique of women of colour. 'At its best postmodernity invites us to engage in a continual process of dis-illusionment with the grandiose fantasies that have brought us to the brink of annihilation' (Flax, 1992b: 460). Feminist postmodernism does not eliminate the subject or the self but finds it in operation as a series of bit parts in the concrete field of social relations. Politics must therefore imply subjectivities in process, interacting and debating.

This idea of, as Stuart Hall puts it, becoming rather than being, continues the mode of argument that all of these feminist writers adopt, that is, to avoid binary oppositions and to dispute the value of terms like equality, and relativism, as the other of a discourse of absolutism (men, universalism) which they are committed to questioning. What emerges from this work is a desire to hold on to the notion of a meaningful feminist politics by interrogating rather than assuming the relations between who is talking to whom. In subjecting some of the big questions and concepts to critical scrutiny these feminist writers are not taking leave of their senses but rather are asking questions about how we learn, how we think and write. This has the effect of realigning the disciplines, rearranging the furniture of intellectual life. It allows for a certain interdisciplinary licence.

In the absence of a 'real me', what I would describe as a social self (the female feminist subject as Braidotti labels her) none the less emerges, marked by a set of constraints and dispositions. This social self participates in intimacy, in communality and communication. She also uses desire and will in order to understand the process of subjection. The feminist social self, it might be suggested, is an amalgam of fragmented identities formed in discourse and history and called into being both by the experiences of femininity and by the existence and availability of a feminist discourse whether that comes in the form of books, education, mass media, or through friends, politics and community. This, I think, is what Butler and the other feminist writers discussed here mean by the communicative aspect of female experience.

UNMASKING THE 'REAL ME'

But while little work has been done on what is left behind when the myth of the 'real me' is revealed, deconstructing the 'real me' has involved showing it to be a social and political requirement, a form of enforcement, a means of regulating legitimate ways of being, legitimate ways of understanding the self and the world. The 'real "respectable" me' is also the product of a certain kind of psychoanalytical violence where desire is also constrained and endlessly defined in culture around the tropes of heterosexuality. Not being at one with this 'real me' has produced much pain and suffering and has required, on the part of gay men and lesbian women, enormous effort to construct different kinds of subjectivity. But if the 'real me' is a mask, a fiction which transcends discourse as an essence, how then, once we have dislodged this kind of self, can we talk about women, about identity, or indeed of feminism as mobilizing political categories? Once again Gayatri Spivak shows how, for white western feminists, there is still instant recourse to a language where feminism is pursued unalert to the limits of its efficacy and unwilling to be constantly

71

interrogating who is the subject of its address. It is her attentiveness to the consequences of being designated a subaltern subject as she moves with her passport through the boundaries and barriers of nation-states and is inevitably questioned as to her professional status as teacher, as a person 'here' to give a paper, that makes her ever alert to the question of power. In her contribution to *Feminists Theorise the Political* Spivak 1992: 56) asks, 'What is it to write for you? What is it to teach? What is it to learn? What is it to assume that one already knows the meaning of the words "something is taught by me and something is learned by others"?'

The value of the work of these feminist writers lies in their interrogating of the ground rules, the boundaries and the barriers which define feminist theory and politics and which simultaneously have to be broken, have to be trespassed on. In this postmodern field what we find is not, however, a scene of catastrophe, the cost of questioning reason, the punishment for risking rationality. The riposte to white feminists that they were not speaking and could not speak on behalf of 'all women', has prompted a reassessment of the feminist self and who she is, and is speaking to and about. At the same time this particular fragmentation of the feminist subject is confirmed through the global and postmodern critique of the European Enlightenment. It is not so much a question of what is left behind, what fragments of the disassembled self can be picked up and put together again, but rather how might the continual process of putting oneself together be transformed to produce the empowerment of subordinate groups and social categories. This might mean living with fragmentation, with the reality of inventing the self rather than endlessly searching for the self. But abandoning the 'real me' need not mean resignation, despair, or simply being reconciled to the loss of wholeness.

Living along the fault-lines of the postmodern condition might also give us some reasons to feel cheerful. We might modestly be aware of our limited successes, in putting feminism (with all the limits that word implies) into the webs of popular discourses about gender and sexuality. The appearance of new feminist discourses, not just in the academy but also in women's magazines, for example, and in some other spaces within the commercial mass media, tells us that feminism now has some control over constructions of the feminine, as Charlotte Brunsdon has recently suggested (1992). But this fact should not be viewed as unproblematic success. There remains the question of what sort of feminism is found in these spaces and to whom is it speaking?

This kind of question challenges, by necessity, the process of reproducing feminism. Just as a feminist 'real me' was perhaps a necessary fiction in the early 1970s, so also was it necessary then to believe in the reproduction of feminism as part of the process of politicization. That such an attempt can backfire is not just about 'backlash' but more productively about other younger women (like black women) disputing their being represented by feminists, just as much as they might take issue with their being represented in advertising, or in popular culture, or in the tabloid press. Thus, once again, politics occurs in the act of breaking away from the claim to be represented. New, emergent or otherwise excluded identities emerge from this discourse of rejection and repudiation. 'This is not us', they are saying. And in saying so there is also a question of who indeed 'they' are.

While this might create a crisis for the (white) feminist movement and for the feminist intellectuals who came into being in the 1970s, such a crisis is no bad thing. In the process of being challenged, older feminist identities are also revised. And what remains is remembered, perhaps even in a 'passion of remembrance' (Blackwood and Julien, 1985).

The passage of feminism into the 1990s should not be seen, in conclusion, as a process of political dismemberment, leaving behind a sadly dispersed band of individuals dotted about the globe but found mostly in the universities of the western world and defining themselves as 'feminist writers' or 'feminist intellectuals'. Nor should it be understood, after postmodernism, as a politics of difference based simply on pluralism, on everyone going their own way. In short the strength of feminism lies in its ability to create discourse, to dispute, to negotiate the boundaries and the barriers, and also to take issue with the various feminisms which have sprung into being. The value of the contribution to new feminist theory by Butler and Scott in *Feminists Theorise the Political*, Bock and James in *Beyond Equality and Difference*, and Hall, Held and McGrew in *Modernity and Its Futures* (all 1992) lies first in their rejection that there could be or should be 'one voice', second in their willingness to take risks by exploring the relatively unnavigated political continent which lies 'beyond equality and difference', third in their engagement with the politics of difference as characterized not by pluralism but by lines of connection and of disconnection, and fourth by their abandonment of the search for the 'real me' in favour, to use Judith Butler's words again, 'of expanding the possiblities of what it means to be a woman'.

This article first appeared in *Theory, Culture & Society* 10 (1993): 127–42.

REFERENCES

Berman, Marshall (1984) *All That Is Solid Melts into Air: The Experience of Modernity*, London: Verso.

Bhabha, Homi (1990) 'DissemiNation: time, narrative and the margins of the modern nation', in H. Bhabha (ed.) *Nation and Narration*, London: Routledge, pp. 15–48.

Blackwood, Maureen and Julien, Isaac (dirs) (1985) *The Passion of Remembrance*, Sankofa Films.

Bowlby, Rachel (1992) *Still Crazy After All These Years*, London: Routledge.
Braidotti, Rosi (1992) 'On the feminist female subject or from she-self to she-other', in G. Bock and S. James (eds) *Beyond Equality and Difference: Citizenship, Feminist Politics and Female Subjectivity*, London: Routledge, pp. 176–92.
Brunsdon, Charlotte (1992) 'Pedagogies of the feminine: feminist teaching and women's genres', *Screen* 32, 4: 364–82.
Butler, Judith (1992) 'Contingent foundations: feminism and the question of "postmodernism"', in J. Butler and J. W. Scott (eds) *Feminists Theorise the Political*, London: Routledge, pp. 3–22.
Flax, Jane (1992a) 'Beyond equality: gender, justice and difference', in G. Bock and S. James (eds) *Beyond Equality and Difference: Citizenship, Feminist Politics and Female Subjectivity*, London: Routledge, pp. 192–209.
Flax, Jane, (1992b) 'The end of innocence', in J. Butler and J. W. Scott (eds) *Feminists Theorise the Political*, London: Routledge, pp. 445–64.
Foucault, Michel (1984) *The History of Sexuality*, Vol. 1, Harmondsworth, Mx: Penguin.
Gilroy, Paul (1993) *The Black Atlantic*, London: Verso.
Habermas, Jürgen (1985) 'Modernity: an incomplete project', in H. Foster (ed.) *Postmodern Culture*, London: Pluto Press, pp. 3–15.
Hall, Stuart (1992) 'The question of cultural identity', in S. Hall, D. Held and D. McGrew (eds) *Modernity and Its Futures*, Oxford: Polity Press, pp. 273–327.
Hall, Stuart and Jacques, Martin (1989) *New Times: The Changing Face of Politics in the 1990s*, London: Lawrence & Wishart.
Harvey, David (1989) *The Condition of Postmodernity*, Oxford: Blackwell.
Jameson, Fredric (1984) 'Postmodernism, or the cultural logic of capital', *New Left Review* 146: 53–92.
Laclau, Ernesto (1991) *Reflections on the New Revolutions of Our Times*, London: Verso.
Lyotard, Jean-François (1984) *The Postmodern Condition*, Manchester: Manchester University Press.
McLennan, Gregor (1992a) 'Sociology after postmodernism', inaugural address, Faculty of Social Sciences Occasional Papers, Massey University, Palmers Bag, New Zealand, pp. 1–22.
McLennan, Gregor (1992b) 'The Enlightenment project, revisited', in S. Hall, D. Held and D. McGrew (eds) *Modernity and Its Futures*, Oxford: Polity Press, pp. 327–79.
McRobbie, Angela (1985) 'Strategies of vigilance: an interview with Gayatri Chakravorty Spivak', *Block* 10: 5–9 (reprinted in chapter 7 of this book).
Mercer, Kobena (1990) 'Welcome to the jungle', in J. Rutherford (ed.) *Identity*, London: Lawrence & Wishart, pp. 43–71.
Min-ha, Trinh T. (1989) *Woman, Native, Other*, Bloomington, IN: Indiana University Press.
Nava, Mica (1992) *Changing Cultures: Feminism, Youth, Consumerism*, London: Sage.
Nicholson, Linda J. (ed.) (1990) *Feminism/Postmodernism*, New York: Routledge.
Riley, Denise (1988) *'Am I That Name?': Feminism and the Category of 'Women' in History*, London: Macmillan.
Spivak, Gayatri Chakravorty (1992) 'French feminism revisited', in J. Butler and J. W. Scott (eds) *Feminists Theorise the Political*, London: Routledge, pp. 54–86.
Steedman, Carolyn (1985) *Landscape for a Good Woman*, London: Virago.

Part II

KEY FIGURES IN CULTURAL THEORY

5

THE MODERNIST STYLE OF
SUSAN SONTAG

SITUATING SONTAG

Who is Susan Sontag? Feminist and cultural analysis today suggests that
we scrutinize the image, examine the photograph on the book jacket, in
order that we can make some putative connection between the woman
and the work. Sontag has done this herself, in her well-known essay on
Walter Benjamin, 'Under the sign of Saturn', where she fondly compares
the photographic image of Benjamin as a younger man ('the downward
look through his glasses – the soft daydreamer's gaze of the myopic')
with that of him older, corpulent, weary ('The look is opaque, or just
more inward: he could be thinking – or listening') (1983). These sentences
also indicate the extent to which we look to the image and to the physical
appearance of figures from the past with a kind of sensual back projection.
It is that degree of desire, or simply of sentiment, which provides the
additional momentum to the critical and analytical task. The image of
Susan Sontag is, like that of Walter Benjamin, cerebral. It is an image
formed in the early 1960s, immune to and perhaps beyond, fashion (no
ear-rings, no hair-styles) and sustained twenty, almost thirty years later.
The picture is invariably in black and white. It too conveys something of
the dreamer. It is an image which combines sinewy female strength with
casual elegance. Thick dark hair, same style at varying lengths, dark eyes,
olive complexion, square jaw, virtually no makeup. On the cover of the
collection of short stories *I, etcetera* (1978a) she is shown full length, in
black trousers, black polo-neck and wearing cowboy boots. She is
stretched out on a window-sill with a pile of books and papers under her
arm. The seriousness is lightened by the faint flicker of pleasure: this is
an image which pleases the author. At home, with books, wearing black.

Sontag is an American critic who has consistently looked to Europe,
but not to England, for her subject-matter and who therefore occupies
an uncertain place in British intellectual life. She is respectfully quoted.
By the literary establishment she is credited with great intelligence. She
is almost too highbrow. Many of the writers and artists she discusses

Figure 1 Cover picture of Susan Sontag by Thomas Victor, for *I, etcetera*, published by Farrar, Strauss, Giroux, New York, 1978. Reproduced by permission of Farrar, Strauss, Giroux and Thomas Victor

remain virtually unknown in the UK even though they are familiar names in France and Germany. This means that her readership in the UK is more specifically academic than might be the case elsewhere. Sontag is unusual in that, as an American cultural critic, she rarely if ever considers American art. Nor has she turned her attention to the all-pervasive force of American popular culture.

Eminently quotable, lines from her two best-known works, *Illness as Metaphor* (1979) and *On Photography* (1978b), can be found in feminist criticism, in women's studies, in cultural studies and in media studies. It is in these new and interdisciplinary fields that her work has been most avidly read. It is read, however, without being debated. It remains strangely set apart from academic discussion. Sontag has only rarely written about women artists or writers. The intellectual space which she has defined as her own is one in which gender does not figure. As Sontag said herself in many earlier interviews, there should be no need of a different criterion for women. The problems in pursuing this 'no difference' line of argument are by now familiar. As feminist scholarship has shown, there may well be no essentially female experience in art or in writing, but there is a long shared experience of exclusion from or marginalization in art. Reconstituting another tradition altogether by uncovering this lost history, or else by theorizing the terms of the exclusion, have provided the basis for much feminist criticism. Despite writing extensively on modern literature, drama, cinema and art, Sontag has kept herself entirely apart from this kind of project. Such principled avoidance of these more recent questions, which have, after all, broken out from the narrow confines of the scholarly journals and have entered into and informed the arts pages of the quality press on both sides of the Atlantic, and which have also generated a great mountain of research and a vast library of scholarly publications, begs some consideration. What this distance between Sontag's work and the question of gender indicates is, I think, the extent to which in high or late European modernism – the broad conceptual umbrella for Sontag's work – there was no critical place for women unless they demonstrably transcended gender. There was no available space to speak as a woman.

Sontag's side-stepping of gender could also be seen as a product of her own commitment to a perhaps lofty critical style, which is far removed from gossip, personality, or the more popular modes of writing and reviewing (the literary biography/autobiography, the in-depth interview, the personal account) which have come to prominence in the last twenty years. Sontag's achievement is partly that she engages with difficult works with great clarity making them available to wider audiences. She does this, however, from within the framework of formalism. Her repudiation of content is paralleled with a refusal to speculate on the writer's intent or on any biographical details which other critics might see as contributing to the meaning of the work.

Sontag is more than an exponent of high modernism. She has written on aspects of popular culture and she has also written a definitive work on the meanings which have attached themselves to illness. This puts her within the field of discursive analysis marked out by other major figures such as Walter Benjamin in the 1930s, and more recently Roland Barthes, Umberto Eco and Michel Foucault.

The purpose of this chapter is to re-examine Sontag's work from the viewpoint of both feminist criticism and contemporary cultural analysis, that is, from within the intellectual world which I myself inhabit. The predicament most immediately posed by Sontag's work is that on one level it is about value, discrimination and the construction of a high modernist or avant-gardist canon. In this sense Sontag can be seen as someone who confers value, and who bestows a seal of approval on a few chosen works. Given that so few of these works are by women, and given also that this kind of approach clearly goes against the grain in recent feminist cultural analysis to challenge established values and to develop an alternative critical language, the question might be: why bother going back to Sontag's work at all?

I think the answer to this question must be partly curiosity, partly the desire to understand so singular an intellectual project as Sontag's, and the unswerving lack of interest, as America's best-known woman intellectual, in all of those debates which have fuelled the establishment of feminist criticism in the last quarter of a century. It is not so much that this weakens Sontag's work, or that it constitutes some kind of great omission. It represents rather a peculiar and idiosyncratic disavowal. Since intellectual debate and criticism feed into and sustain the kind of culture and art which is produced, since there is, in fact, a dialogue continually going on between critics, artists and writers, Sontag's distance from these feminist debates means that she is also removed from much of the artistic practice which has prevailed during this period. Her own critical style of writing can be seen as modernist and her work is historically located in the moment of late, perhaps fading European modernism and the avant-garde. This puts her in the same kind of relationship to those figures who remain in her canon (Pina Bausch, Heiner Muller, Hans Jurgen Syberberg) as feminist art critics like Janet Wolff, for example, or Griselda Pollock are to feminist artists like Barbara Kruger or Nancy Spiro in the USA or in the UK to Therese Oulton or Rosa Lee.

The commitment to high culture and to what Sontag herself has more recently labelled international modernism creates, in the age of postmodern culture, problems for Sontag in terms of responding to the more hybrid forms which so freely cross the barriers between high and popular art, and which so self-consciously play with these divisions. Sontag has only been able to engage with what, in 1964, she herself called the 'popular arts' within limits (Sontag, 1967). Some of these new forms are not only worthy of sustained critical attention but can also, with approval, be welcomed into the world of the arts. This is Sontag's 'take' on pop culture, that it can be selectively accredited with some importance. As I shall be arguing, this not only sets Sontag apart from recent cultural scholarship, it also traps her in an unworkable paradigm whereby art generously volunteers to open up its doors to a few select popular texts. The problem is that the available canonical vocabulary is simply not appropriate for developing a fuller understanding of these popular texts. Feminist work has pursued an entirely different pathway by looking to non-canonical works, and by developing a critical language aimed at understanding their meaning rather than assessing their value. In this respect Sontag's approach is diametrically opposed to feminist critical practice.

This is one reason why Sontag's work occupies an uneasy place in the new radical humanities; another reason for her marginalization has been her consistent shying away from Marxism. Throughout her work there has been a demonstrated conviction that art should not be accountable to politics, though it may well choose to engage with politics on its own terms. There is no trace of a neo-Marxist influence in Sontag's work, although a thread of structuralism runs right through her writing from the earliest pieces on style, to the mid-1970s essays in *On Photography* (1978b). Nor is there any mention whatsoever of feminism. Neither of these absences is, however, sufficient reason to dismiss Sontag, as many on the left have recently done, as a writer who flirted with radicalism in the 1960s and withdrew thereafter, moving to the new right along with many of her intellectual colleagues in New York in the 1980s. It is true that she has been vociferously anti-communist in recent years, earning condemnation from the activist left in New York, but this anti-communism is the result of her involvement with persecuted Soviet writers such as Joseph Brodsky, and her championing of artistic freedom in her work as chairperson of PEN (Poets, Playwrights, Editors, Essayists, Novelists). Sontag has always been a liberal democrat which, in American terms, has on occasion cast her further to the left than in reality she was.

It will be my contention that to understand Sontag's work it is necessary to temporarily bracket off these left/feminist disappointments and to place her writing at that end moment of high modernism where it is looking uncertainly towards the future. Postmodernism is on the horizon, but it is as yet unclear whether it will emerge smoothly from the modernist movement or whether it will be locked in battle against it. It is this uncertainty which is reflected in Sontag's criticism of the 1970s. She is a committed anti-realist and a spokesperson for high modernism, but she is also a critic who witnesses the ascendancy of pop culture, who welcomes its vitality, who recognizes its intellectual forcefulness, yet who invariably holds back on the breaking down of the barriers between high and low culture. This is not to say that Sontag eschews pop culture. Several of her best-known essays, including 'Notes on "camp" ' (1967), 'Fascinating fascism' (1983) and those pieces collected together in *On Photography* (1978b) display an acute grasp of the power of the popular image. Likewise, some of her best work is on cinema, whose popularity she instinctively seizes upon and welcomes.

What Sontag turns away from are those artistic and cultural forms identified directly with postmodernity, and also those fields of popular representation which, viewed conventionally, have no formal aesthetic value and which exist outside the category of art and inside the province of commercial mass culture. This includes all those forms of popular culture whose roots and orientation remain firmly within the landscape of 'the masses' or 'the people'. Unlike Eco she has not looked to the cultural meaning of James Bond. Unlike Barthes she has shied away from advertising or fashion. Unlike most contemporary female critics she has shown no particular interest in female genres of popular culture. Her task instead has been threefold. First and foremost, to introduce to English-speaking audiences the work of great European writers, dramatists and essayists; second, to extend the boundaries of art so that they open themselves up to and embrace new emergent, and *more* popular forms; and third, to reflect on some of the wider cultural currents of the moment, such as the clusters of metaphors which have gathered around illnesses like cancer and more recently AIDS. If the first of these is a formidable and esoteric project, the second and indeed the third are by no means without their own difficulties. In relation to bestowing on popular forms the label of art, there are particular conceptual problems, since, as Charlotte Brunsdon has perceptively argued, 'the recalcitrance of these media (also apparent, of course, with photography) to traditional aesthetic discourse means that any canons are peculiarly hybrid' (1990).

In contrast, then, with many of her European counterparts, especially with that generation of postwar cultural intellectuals, including Barthes, Eco, and in the UK, Raymond Williams and Stuart Hall, Sontag steers clear of low (or mass) culture. She is an unwilling critic of American writing, of art, or, for that matter, of Hollywood cinema. This in itself poses problems for her as a culture critic. It is as though she is resisting or arguing against what many *émigré* and mostly Jewish intellectuals from Europe, living in America in the 1950s under the spectre of McCarthyism, resisted so strenuously: the total Americanization of culture through the universality of the commodity form and the mass culture which went with it. However, this becomes a more difficult task when from the late 1960s onwards, a generation of younger artists reject what they see as the élitism of modernism and the avant-garde and identify with and draw on popular mass culture. Sontag herself witnesses the decline of modernism but attributes this to its being pulled into the mainstream of American corporate culture. The implication is that the further 'out' art is, the better. The increasing prominence of the popular arts, and the decision by younger artists to embrace this new field, contributes, I think, to the melancholy, slightly defensive tone of Sontag's more recent cultural criticism. If her favourite artists and film-makers were themselves responding to the world of the mass-produced image (Godard in the 1960s and early 1970s and Syberberg in the late 1970s and early 1980s), the dominance of mass culture and the extent to which, from the late 1960s onwards, art seems to have taken up almost permanent residence in the house of pop, has had the effect of casting Sontag adrift. Against the decanonization of art by literary theorists, the relativism of cultural values by the new generation of black intellectuals, and the rediscovery of a huge stock of women's art and women's writing by feminist intellectuals, Sontag holds out in favour of what she perceives as the great, the good and the (seriously) terrible.

In the following pages I will consider in some detail that work for which Sontag is best known. (I will leave to the side her fiction and the three films she has directed.) This task would have no purpose if it were not my feeling that it is time that Sontag's contribution to cultural analysis was more fully recognized. The difficulty remains, however, in making a case for this impressive body of work from the standpoint of feminism. Sontag presents a sexually ambiguous image and has spent most of her writing career looking at works produced by men. What, if any, conclusions can be drawn? Sontag is the sole woman alongside a generation of great Jewish intellectuals including John Berger, Jonathan Miller and George Steiner. Many of her themes are theirs too: the holocaust, the condition of modernity as being one of homelessness and often hopelessness, the role of art in giving voice to the void of experience, the isolation of the intellectual, the passion for learning. Despite the impersonal voice, Sontag's identification with Walter Benjamin and with Elias Canetti is palpable and resonates through her essays on their work. The nature of this identification is the job of the psychoanalyst, not the feminist critic. I will therefore concentrate here on the defence of high modernism as a defence of the role of the intellectual in a world which seems dangerously anti-intellectual, on the over-reliance on a conceptual framework born out of that historical moment of high modernism which is ill-equipped to understand the new, more plastic forms of popular culture (with their emphasis on enjoyment), on the shying away from those notions of a politically engaged art which emerged throughout the 1970s, on the image of a woman writer, for whom distance has been central, but whose distance from the intellectual community of the last twenty years, including the community of feminist intellectuals, cannot be construed as anything other than a loss.

AGAINST INTERPRETATION/STYLES OF RADICAL WILL

The numerous essays included in the two collections *Against Interpretation* and *Styles of Radical Will* were written between 1964 and 1968. Within a space of four years Sontag wrote at length on theatre, literature, anthropology, cinema, pornography, aesthetics and politics. She was the only woman critic of her generation to achieve such a high profile right across the world of the arts. The two introductory essays in *Against Interpretation* (1967) can be taken as a manifesto for anti-realism and for the construction of a more fully grounded formalist aesthetic. Sontag is disputing the value of the search for the statement in art, the search for what it is 'trying to say'. She endorses what has been taken as a founding premise of structuralist criticism, that 'the interpreter is altering the text'. The rewriting that the critic does, however, fails to enhance the value of the work. According to Sontag, in most cases it detracts from it, desensualizing the work of art. This is what she means by setting herself against interpretation.

Sontag therefore sides with those artists and writers who resist the attempts of the critics to render completely transparent the meaning of the work. One strategy adopted to counter this search for meaning is to move towards abstraction. And in film-making, a popular form at that time unencumbered by the label of serious art, it was possible to escape this reductive tendency by using a quite different ruse, a misleadingly superficial content, as Sternberg does, in order to confound the search on the part of the critics for a statement. Sontag pursues a formalist path by arguing that to have content is already to be within the confines of style. By implication she is suggesting that realism, so favoured by literary critics of the moment, is a specific generic construct, a means of producing certain kinds of meaning as a result of manipulating a variety of stylistic devices.

While this argument is now commonplace to students of the mass media, or indeed of literature, the two essays, 'Against interpretation' (1967) and 'On style' (1967) were possibly the first accessible accounts of such ideas to be available in the USA, almost twenty years before they eventually became respectable and institutionalized in academia. As she says in 'On style', 'Nonetheless the notion of style-less, transparent art is one of the most tenacious fantasies of modern culture' (1967: 18).

The meaning of modernity forms an equally important strand in these two volumes. Modernity as a condition is equated with loss of feeling, alienation, loneliness, suffering and madness. It is a largely male condition, though not spelt out as such. The sensibility of literary modernity which

Sontag explores, enters into and shapes her own critical style of writing. So deeply impersonal is this mode that Sontag's enthusiasm is always tempered and constrained. There is hardly a trace of her own personal voice, not a trace of gender, of place, or of preference. Sontag's modernity is stripped bare. It is associated neither with Walter Benjamin's urbanism, for example, nor with his modernist interest in technology and consumer goods (Buck-Morss, 1990). It is a modernity of the mind, for which, to quote the title of Christa Wolf's novel, there is '*No Place on Earth*' (1983). It is from within this viewpoint that Sontag praises Lévi-Strauss's remarkable anthropological work *Tristes tropiques*. In an essay titled 'The anthropologist as hero' (1967), Sontag sees in Lévi-Strauss's melancholy tones, as he witnesses the decimation of history wrought by the West's ravaging of what remains of the pre-modern civilizations, a fine expression of modernist feeling.

Sontag also emphasizes the significance of Lévi-Strauss's structural anthropology. By showing the arbitrariness of kinship rules, the extent to which they make sense only in connection with each other, and the extent to which rites and customs are meaningless in themselves, Lévi-Strauss is showing how structuralist principles of analysis are as appropriate for the analysis of so-called 'primitive' societies, as they are for contemporary urban society. This is, suggests Sontag, a radical proposition. In reality there is no such thing as primitivism, *they* are not so *other*.

Sontag sees a great deal that is admirable in the ex-Marxist Lévi-Strauss, but she takes issue with Lukács, the Marxist critic who decries the modern movement in its projection of alienation and de-humanization (1967). To side so decisively with the realist tradition, as Lukács does, is, argues Sontag, to refuse the autonomy of form in art, and to expect that all art is reducible to a strictly historical interpretation. Sontag is here insisting on the relatively detached status of form. Her objection to the orthodox Marxist criticism of the time was that it denied this autonomy. The enthusiasm with which Marxist critics were later to seize upon structuralism is in some ways a measure of the importance of Sontag's repudiation of Lukács.

Alongside and within modernity, in both these volumes there is also the question of popular culture or the popular arts. It is the two essays 'Notes on "camp"' (1967) and 'The pornographic imagination' (1969) which give Sontag ample opportunity to make sense of her own pleasure (albeit stiffly expressed) in pop. 'One cheats oneself, as a human being, if one has respect only for the style of high culture, whatever else one may do or feel on the sly' (1967: 287). The 'aura' of art is definitively broken as modern scientific advances find ways of producing the image or text for a mass audience. Drawing on Walter Benjamin (Benjamin, 1973) Sontag recognizes that art/non-art boundaries are breaking down. Science has had the effect of displacing sentimentality from art and replacing it with a new 'coolness'. This more measured mode, this impersonality, then becomes a hallmark of modernism and a benchmark for Sontag's own critical writing. However, such a sensibility should not blind the critic to the pleasure and the hedonism with which younger intellectuals and artists respond to 'pop'. 'I feel for the popular arts', says Sontag in 'One culture and the new sensibility' (1967: 303) with the endearing awkwardness of somebody who has spent too much time with her elders.

'Notes on "camp" ' (1967) is generally recognized as one of Sontag's most impressive pieces of writing. Despite the abbreviated note form, Sontag departs somewhat from her own 'cool' style and displays a real enthusiasm for camp. It appeals to her both for the pleasure with which it pronounces good taste in bad taste, and for its self-conscious artificiality. Perhaps what also appeals to Sontag is the aestheticism of camp, the idea of living 'art', and of transforming the self into a kind of 'living work of art'. She sees this as a modern dandyism and she applauds the exaggeration, the anti-realism. Camp exists as an aesthetic sensibility, even if it trails behind in third place after modernism with its high moralism, and after the avant-garde with its extremities of feeling. Camp is the light relief to be enjoyed alongside the more serious project of modernity. The task at hand in 'Notes on "camp" ' is therefore to confer value on this hitherto ignored cultural phenomenon through acknowledging its 'generous' aestheticism (the 'love for human nature ... the love that has gone into certain objects and personal styles' [1967: 291]). The staginess of camp creates a simultaneous feeling of immediacy and disengagement. Camp can never be confused with realism or with the search for authenticity.

Because everything is said or done with a nuance, an edge or, as Sontag puts it, 'in quotation marks', there is always a suggestion that something is not what it seems. Camp 'sponsors playfulness'. Camp is the other of modernism. But its artfulness, its artifice and its delicate touch are sufficient reasons to evaluate such an aesthetic mode positively. The drift of this essay therefore is to reward camp, for all its striving, with the seal of approval, from the 'high ground'. The irony, however, is that at the very moment at which Sontag was writing this essay, camp was seeking a new and more secure home for itself in pop culture, notably in pop music, from which it has never since re-emerged. Pop music history, from Cliff Richard to Barry Manilow, from Gary Glitter to Marc Almond, could simultaneously be written as a history of camp within the camp, as it were, of popular culture. Sontag's aim is that we should enjoy camp but also take it seriously. To do this it must be elevated so that it can take its place as a lesser art, but an art no less.

This is certainly one way of seeing it, but since the mid-1960s camp has also provided a momentum for the creation of postmodern culture, where the boundaries of high and low art are irrevocably blurred, and where camp detaches itself from the subcultural world of the gay scene and enters into mainstream, roaming free in the field of popular entertainment, while retaining an affectionate attachment to gay culture. Sontag's main choices of pop culture, camp and pornography, both of which she draws into an expanded notion of 'the arts', have in a sense defected, and more comfortably re-established themselves within mass culture, on television, in pop music, in fashion, in 'trash culture'.

A similar desire to instate pornography into the canons of intellectual respectability fuels 'The pornographic imagination' (1969) ('What makes a work of pornography part of the history of art rather than of trash is not distance . . . it is the originality . . . and power of that deranged consciousness itself' [Sontag, 1969: 47]). It is a certain genre of erotic writing which attracts Sontag's attention ('a minor but interesting modality or convention within the arts' [ibid.: 35]). The task at hand is to break down the petty prejudices of the critics who see cardboard characters and stock scenes designed only to arouse and with a minimum of psychology, and to argue not only that it is precisely in these stock sets that the interest lies, but that in adapting such stripped-down tableau situations in the service of sexual arousal, the writers of erotica, including Bataille and Pauline Reage, are indeed departing from the bourgeois satisfactions of the conventional novel form and are instead embarking on an experimental journey which brings them close to the project of literary modernity. Sontag applauds the anti-realism, the descent into sexual madness ('The exemplary modern artist is a broker in madness' [ibid.: 65]). Pornography is a genre of writing which taps into the quintessentially modern condition. Addressing itself exclusively to individual desire and appetite, it finds itself, by necessity, pursuing varieties of 'impersonal – or pure-sexual encounter(s)'. Its dominant tone is parody, a language far removed from realism and from authenticity, a style which embodies a deathliness.

Once again, however, the same argument could just as easily justify keeping pornography in its place within the broader culture, not of modernity but in the undifferentiated (or less differentiated) terrain of postmodernity. Since the early 1960s pornography has slid up and down the scale marking out the gradations of high and low culture with remarkable dexterity. Its reliance on pastiche, parody and an abundance of familiar second-hand styles, its wallowing in tackiness, and its deathly superficiality reflect exactly those aspects of postmodernity recently documented by Fredric Jameson (1984). What Sontag draws upwards into the field of art can also be considered from within mainstream mass culture. In fact, pornography could be taken as a kind of cultural barometer, whose multipurpose nature, as raw material, as a touchstone of controversy for artists as diverse as David Hockney and Robert Mapplethorpe (on whom Sontag has recently written [1985]) and as a potent resource for the shock tactics of the punk subculture in the mid-1970s, renders it a particularly plastic and mobile form. If there is any one overriding characteristic of pornography it is its anonymity, its reliance on pseudonyms. Sontag recognizes this, seizes upon it as another mark of its modernity but none the less also seizes on its better-known authors, de Sade and Bataille, in her attempt to bestow on it status and meaning. But pornography is deeply resistant to *auteurism*. The flamboyant, tacky, or simply offensive styles of pornography are everywhere in evidence, but its authors, its producers, its artists, its models and its consumers are content to remain in the shadows, unless they are already artists employing the anonymous conventions of pornography to make a particular point. This is not to suggest that Sontag's aim in this 1969 essay was entirely mistaken. After all, popular culture only really blossomed and became dominant later in the decade. It is more a question of method. The desire to confer value, the analysis of popular forms from the viewpoint of art or the modernist canon, makes it difficult for Sontag to develop this interest in popular culture in her later work.

UNDER THE SIGN OF SATURN

The essays brought together under the title of Sontag's introduction to Walter Benjamin (1983), in *Under the Sign of Saturn*, are possibly the most unified example of her writing. In this collection Sontag's major concerns are finally knitted together to great effect. Her enthusiasm for, and sadness at the death of, two of her favourite writers and mentors produce the pieces 'On Paul Goodman', one of the few American voices on whom she has written, and 'Remembering Barthes', a short summary of the achievement of France's best-known semiologist. The essays on Artaud ('Approaching Artaud') and Elias Canetti ('Mind as passion') demonstrate Sontag's interest in the presence of an impersonal voice in art, but also her interest in madness and suffering, and in strategies in art for avoiding co-optation into conventional 'modern' society. Both writers are loners who revel in their sense of apartness. Canetti's stated desire 'to show how complex selfishness is' reveals his unsociable demeanour, but it is his commitment to learning which most impresses Sontag, his desire at sixteen 'to learn everything', as well as his mode of writing which remains quite beyond the forces of co-optation. Canetti is an off-beat and reluctant modernist. Like Walter Benjamin, he luxuriates in his own melancholy, he is avowedly alone. This permeates his writing style and becomes a personal philosophy – such extraordinary bookishness, such memories of a lonely childhood buried in books and anxious to please an absent mother.

With Walter Benjamin, however, Sontag's sense of identification is almost palpable. He is marked by a profound sadness, he showed himself incapable of sustaining marriage or parenthood with any success, he said 'solitude appeared to me as the only fit state of man'. It is Benjamin's writing which holds the greatest attraction for Sontag – the aphoristic style, the density and deep impersonality, the erudition, the ambivalent passion for modernity, for urban life, for objects and images and for things rather than people. Benjamin reveals himself even in his diaries as somebody who only fleetingly connects with other individuals but who inhabits a not entirely unhappy world of his own construction. This is the city for which, as a *flâneur*, Benjamin creates his own personal map. The modern city, earlier described by the famous German sociologist Simmel as the space of personal anomie, provides an ideal setting for impersonal exchanges. For Benjamin (as for many other modernist writers) the figure who epitomizes these exchanges is the prostitute.

Death is a continual presence in Benjamin's writings. Suicidal thoughts give shape to his urban reveries, his childhood memories, his endless walks through Paris, Berlin and even post-revolutionary Moscow, where he went in pursuit of an elusive and seemingly uninterested lover. Like Sontag, Benjamin perfects the essay form. He makes fleeting attempts at fiction but remains throughout his life the essayist and 'freelance intellectual'. From Sontag's perspective, one of the marks of the modernist writer is this pervading sense of isolation which finds expression in an inner voice of fragmentation or despair and which is unfailingly broken, disjointed and anti-realist. Sometimes, however, it veers towards the personal or even the autobiographical by way of an unexpectedly circuitous route. That route is through the inner maps of childhood, never revealing, never narrativized, never confessional. Instead these are opaque, elliptical, melancholic images, fragments and memories. This is true for Benjamin. It is true for Canetti, and also for Barthes in his later writing on photography.

Sontag's introduction to Syberberg's third major film, *Hitler The Film*, demonstrates her abilities as a critic and also reveals her, finally, as an enthusiast, a fan, though with characteristic reserve she says the film is 'tonic'. Syberberg reflects all those qualities as a film-maker which Sontag so greatly admires. He is, like so many of her heroes, relatively unknown outside Germany and France, and she writes about him with a sense of mission, to enhance his reputation and to introduce him to an English-speaking audience. Even within the ranks of the 'highbrow' press, however, Syberberg is condemned as difficult if not incomprehensible. His films are three times as long as the average feature film. He is likely to inspire both boredom and bewilderment on the part of at least sections of his audience, and he is profoundly and determinedly anti-realist in his cinematic approach to history.

European history and in particular German history are Syberberg's subject. In *Hitler*, Sontag sees Syberberg evading that strand of modernism which had by the mid-1970s become stale, predictable and co-opted into the mainstream of consumer culture. Syberberg does this by staging an idiosyncratic and at times bizarre mixed-media spectacle. He dramatizes history by playing with it. He does this in recognition that the documentary form has already done its work exhaustively. Sontag welcomes his avoidance of familiar concentration-camp footage. Instead, Syberberg 'ruminates', he discourses alongside his chosen images and his selection of voices.

Syberberg develops a sophisticated set of cinematic ruses. As Sontag shows, he circumvents the complexity of Nazism by drawing in his 9-year-old daughter as witness to his bedtime 'story'. He moves past Nazism to the three decades of postwar German culture drawing on pornography and on rampant consumerism as evidence of the German 'inability to mourn'. Nazism is part and parcel of modernity and *Hitler The Film* makes this charge by drawing into its vision the goods and the gadgetry we have come to associate with the postwar democracy of consumer culture. Syberberg's visual inventiveness and the ironic sense of fun which also runs through his work makes him an 'exalte' rather than a melancholic, according to Sontag. But this fevered imagination might also be understood as a temporary relief, she suggests, a febrile moment, which only masks a deeper sadness and despair.

A case can also be made, however, for Syberberg the postmodernist; for example, in his parodies of history, his playfulness, his refusal to seek the reality of history (because in the age of the mass media there can be no real history), the absence of one voice in his cinema, the distortion of sound so that it comes to the viewer refracted, cathected, a cacophony, the replacement of narrative with a set of 'small stories' with no beginning and no apparent end. All of these put Syberberg much more firmly within a postmodern aesthetic. Indeed it might even be argued that Syberberg directly utilizes a self-consciously postmodern aesthetic to settle the accounts with those who retain a heroic vision of modernity, by staging Nazism as one of its most tragic and most memorable products.

ON PHOTOGRAPHY

On Photography (1978b) is simply the most lucid, the most comprehensive and the most informed introduction to the cultural meaning of photography to date. The organization of the book continues Sontag's preference for the essay form. Each of these essays can be read as a quite distinct set-piece. Most were published, like so many of Sontag's other essays, in the *New York Review of Books*. These pieces display a keen interest in many of the themes already present in her work and are further evidence of continuity and development. Almost every argument which has emerged from within the field of photographic theory over the last fifteen years exists in embryonic form, often as throwaway comment, or a sentence, in this book. Sontag's preference for the broader overview, for the whole picture, allows her to view photography from a variety of perspectives. Most important is the anti-realist strand, the assertion that even when they appear to reflect reality – for example, in the documentary photograph – such images are social constructs, cut, cropped, or manipulated for a desired effect. The first essay, 'In Plato's cave', and the last, 'The image-world', are the most useful to the student of contemporary culture. 'In Plato's cave' documents the various uses of photography as evidence, as memory, as entertainment, as embellishment, as a means of 'certifying experience'. The essay also describes photography as an 'elegaic art', a means of creating nostalgia. Following Barthes, the influence of whose work runs through this volume, Sontag also points to the polysemy of the image and the consequent need for it to be 'named', the need for an attached linguistic message to anchor the meaning of the image and stop it from straying off in the wrong direction. Thus we see already the seductively easy transparency of meaning in photography, itself the effect of the codes of realism, being challenged and interrupted by Sontag's emphasis on style, effect and form. We also see in this essay, photography as a means of social control, made possible through the apparent ability to capture the truth.

The critical assessment of Diane Arbus's studies in 'America, darkly' shows Sontag at her most successful as a critic, capturing in words exactly the discomfort the viewer experiences in looking at Arbus's work. She understands Arbus to be voyeuristically identifying with the amoral free-for-all of the 1960s by having her unfortunate subjects (freaks, grotesques) 'amiably' surrender to the camera. Arbus's style combines a pop mentality ('terrific') with a kind of impertinent childish naivety. Yet Arbus is also an urban sophisticate in 'the familiar modernist way', her chosen subjects constitute a 'programme of despair'. Later in the book Sontag comments on the role of photography in creating a kind of national inventory. And in 'America' this means taking pictures of everyday items, things which have in their very ordinariness the power to become iconic objects. 'The true modernism is not austerity but garbage strewn plenitude' (Sontag, 1978b: 46).

Although there are more frequent references to the popular uses of photography in this volume than elsewhere in Sontag's work (in tourism, at leisure, at home) the emphasis remains on the ambivalent relation to art. Photographic realism releases the artist to explore abstraction. The artist is no longer obliged to report. Photography 'freed painting for great modernist abstraction', while it in turn followed suit and became increasingly abstract itself. Here Sontag is thinking of great art photographers like Edward Weston, whose 'heroic vitalism' she compares to D. H. Lawrence's writing.

There is a sense in which Sontag credits photography with catapulting us into modernity, and in so doing retaining something of the magical, the pre-modern. This is the importance of photography. The moment of its invention corresponds with that great lurch forward. It is not surprising then that photography should retain within it the hint of the past, the need for sentimentality, the inevitability of death and thus also something of the meaning of change and loss. 'The image-world', one of the later essays in the book, propels us into the postmodern world where 'reality is more like what we are shown by cameras' (Sontag, 1978b: 168), and where current cultural obsessions with images of stars and celebrities come to compensate for, and indeed eclipse, the need for personal power, control, success ('the injuries of class, race and sex'). Images are now a central part of leisure culture, their free availability 'is equated with freedom itself' (ibid.: 178). The photographic image accompanies not just the vital stages in the life-cycle but also the cycle of capital itself, particularly as the product is processed through advertising to become the object of consumption and of desire. If photography acted as a forerunner for modernity, it could now be seen as providing us with a foretaste of postmodernity, where the image is primary and referential, where it is an index of reality, and where the event is conducted not for and in itself but with a sharper, more poignant and urgent sense of the anticipated images it will produce. The enjoyment of the event is delayed and displaced into the projected enjoyment of the image of the event.

ILLNESS/AIDS

What compels Sontag to write *Illness as Metaphor* (1979) is the shame which cancer sufferers feel as a result of the range of cultural meanings which have gathered over the years around the disease from which they suffer. These meanings have stigmatized the patient, and have cast their shadow over the whole person. Such a way of thinking sees the cancer victim as having partly brought about the disease upon her- or himself. Too much stress, too much repression, too few outlets for emotional release. The answer, argues Sontag, then becomes one of cajoling the victims to cure themselves, to rally round and take responsibility for their own return to health. This denies the physiology of disease, the reality of death, and it further weakens the individual who is made to feel that she or he is almost wholly responsible for their own ill health. The shame which is attached to cancer does not extend to other common and often fatal diseases like heart disease. Cancer has replaced TB as being synonymous with some kind of lurking horror, in the atmosphere, in the food we eat, or in the flawed individuals we are. Unlike TB, cancer has never been romanticized, only vilified.

The greater part of the essay is given over to describing and illustrating the kind of metaphors, in literature and in everyday life, which have developed around these two illnesses. This writing shows Sontag at her most erudite (the literary references span the centuries) and at her most impassioned. The essay was prompted by a cancer diagnosis. It was the attitudes Sontag perceived on the part of those who came into contact with her during this period which sent her off on this cultural journey.

One of the problems with Sontag's more recent book *AIDS and Its Metaphors* (1989) is that the emergence of AIDS has coincided with an instant politicizing of the disease, from every side and with such intensity that any similarities with the slow stigmatization of cancer and the shaming of cancer victims pale in comparison. Thus, although AIDS appears to fit neatly with Sontag's earlier argument, particularly the extent to which the metaphors further intensify the distress of the sufferer, the much greater social response and the mobilizations by the professionals, the new moral majority, the gay lobby, the left, the art establishment in America, and governments themselves, has meant that there is a lot more at stake in making sense of AIDS. Its meanings are more heightened and more closely connected to the body politic because, unlike cancer, AIDS can be transmitted throughout the population as a whole. It is therefore much more discursively crowded. As usual, Sontag's writing displays impeccable reason. She always prefers the cool dry tones of the thinker who seeks to remove a complex social phenomenon from its immediate and emotive context and view it more objectively. The criticism of Sontag in this respect, coming from right across the spectrum of gay activists, the left, feminists and those involved in the culture industries, is that, as metaphors abound, people continue to die. As wider cultural meanings and explanations proliferate, governments delay on giving support to sufferers.

Sontag's purpose is precisely to challenge this kind of metaphor-making, but it is her careful, cautious disentangling of meaning which angers her critics. Sontag not only evades confronting the extent to which the cultural meanings and metaphors which come into play around AIDS are inextricably connected with the politics of AIDS, she also suggests that one response to AIDS will indeed be a reduction or slowing down of sexual appetite. This, argues her critics, shows the extent to which she herself is caught within the web of misleading and homophobic myths about AIDS, that perhaps *they* got AIDS because *they* had too much sex.

CONCLUSION

For all of the reasons outlined above, from her apparent disinterest in feminist criticism and scholarship, from her defensive attachment to the literary and artistic canon, from her limited view of popular culture, her angry anti-communist retorts at political rallies, her depiction of gay sex in the AIDS book as potentially 'suicidal', Sontag has not of late won many friends from within a younger generation of cultural intellectuals. Indeed, it might be true to say that in many circles she is viewed with suspicion as at best an élitist, Eurocentric aesthete. A more damning criticism is difficult to imagine. There is no doubt that Sontag has courted controversy in the last few years from within the ranks of exactly that stratum of people who it might be imagined would be most interested in and predisposed to her work. I do not think it is necessary to dismiss Sontag on the grounds marked out above. She can be allowed the liberty of contradictory political ideas. Some would argue that on politics Sontag has always displayed an ambivalence and a lack of direction. More relevant to my concerns here is Sontag's insistence on the importance of art and of aesthetic value.

I want to conclude by suggesting that there exists a degree of bad faith on this issue in contemporary cultural theory and in feminist intellectual debate. We have gone so far down the road of the popular (where there is no art/non-art, no good/bad) that we are in danger of choosing out our own canon for analysis and being able to justify this only on the grounds that it has mass appeal. Worse still, we now run the risk of entering into a meaninglessly pluralist paradigm for studying the popular, where everything goes, where only in the popular does there lie the possibility of resistance, and where unpopular questions like the value to young people of reading literary classics rather than teen magazines are simply no longer asked. There is also a degree of disingenuousness here since, as Judith Williamson has recently pointed out, in our own critical practice we actually choose out with a fine degree of discrimination one text for analysis over another (Williamson, 1990). We produce our own inverted canon. As she puts it, 'Why *Bladerunner*?' There is the additional point that while we deconstruct the canon we also teach in art schools where students will graduate with ambitions of making it in the art world. We encourage our students to develop their literary talents, we would probably rather see them writing a novel than writing a soap-opera script. Despite the breaking down of the old distinctions between high art and low culture, we have not entirely abandoned the notion of art even when it does not come with a prefix certifying the authenticity of its cultural origins. There may be no going back to the old days where art was art and pop was pop, but that does not mean we need not continually interrogate the principles by which we order and categorize the world of culture as the first stage in trying to understand it.

Sontag's continual presence in the field of arts and cultural policy in the USA, and in international organizations like PEN, where issues around censorship increasingly dominate discussion, is not just important but vital. Sontag's preference for difficult or obscure works cannot be regarded as a sign of cultural snobbishness. To assign her to this camp would be to assign ourselves to the camp of anti-intellectualism. In the end there remains the figure of Sontag, a mysterious woman, standing alone alongside a gallery of the great male philosophers and writers of the century. Her own heroic vision, formed by her embracing of European modernism, was one which freed her from the constraints of gender. It granted her access to a privileged world. Unlike other women of equal intellectual stature (one thinks of de Beauvoir), she has spurned the personal and the feminine as the object of study, or even as points of connection with other objects of study. If she has become something of an intellectual star, she has, none the less, resisted the pressure to conform to that mode, and drop the mantle of intellectualism in favour of the 'chat show' milieu. The erudite mode she adheres to as a point of principle as well as a mark of personal style, serves the function of reminding us of the value of 'mind as passion'. However, history, art and culture have moved far beyond that moment when women had to forget gender to be taken seriously, when art had to be clean, cool and heroic, and when culture had to differentiate itself from pop. There is a sense in which, for Sontag, modernism became a strait-jacket. Its over-stated principles of confidence and vigour, of innovatory technique, of style, abstraction and clean, fluid lines, uncluttered by the detail and messiness of everyday life, were soon swallowed up, not by corporate culture, but by a dawning recognition that it was increasingly the messiness of everyday life which provided the richest source of raw materials for art and pop alike.

This article first appeared in *Feminist Review* 38 (Summer 1991).

REFERENCES

Benjamin, Walter (1973) 'The work of art in the age of mechanical reproduction', in *Illuminations*, London: Fontana, pp. 219–55.
Brunsdon, Charlotte (1990) 'Problems with quality', *Screen* 31, 1: 67–91.
Buck-Morss, Susan (1990) *The Dialectics of Seeing: Walter Benjamin and the Arcades Project*, Cambridge, MA: MIT Press.
Jameson, Fredric (1984) 'Postmodernism, or the cultural logic of late capitalism', *New Left Review* 146: 53–92.
Sontag, Susan (1967) *Against Interpretation*, London: Eyre & Spottiswode.
Sontag, Susan (1969) *Styles of Radical Will*, London: Secker & Warburg.
Sontag, Susan (1978a) *I, etcetera*, New York: Farrar, Strauss, Giroux.
Sontag, Susan (1978b) *On Photography*, London: Allen Lane.
Sontag, Susan (1979) *Illness as Metaphor*, London: Allen Lane.
Sontag, Susan (1983) *Under the Sign of Saturn*, London: Writers and Readers.
Sontag, Susan (1985) 'Sontag on Mapplethorpe', *Vanity Fair* 47, 5, July.
Sontag, Susan (1989) *AIDS and Its Metaphors* London: Allen Lane.
Williamson, Judith (1990) unpublished paper presented at the Futures conference, Tate Gallery, November.
Wolf, Christa (1983) *No Place on Earth*, London: Virago.

6

THE *PASSAGENWERK* AND THE PLACE OF WALTER BENJAMIN IN CULTURAL STUDIES

Walter Benjamin has occupied an ambivalent place in cultural studies since the early 1970s when his two seminal essays written in the 1930s, 'The artist as producer' (Benjamin, 1970a) and 'The work of art in the age of mechanical reproduction' (Benjamin, 1970b), were first published in English. They were rightly hailed as key contributions to the development of Marxist theories of art, as well as to what has since become known as cultural politics. The influence of Brecht is particularly noticeable in 'The artist as producer'; and in cultural studies generally, as well as in journals like the *New Left Review*, the names of Brecht and Benjamin were frequently mentioned together. Both writers were looked to for their committed but unaligned Marxism which was far removed from that of the official Marxism of the communist parties of the 1930s and later of the Stalinist era. Both Benjamin and Brecht recognized, with some urgency, the need to extend the role of the intellectual in order to engage with the people and to do this through transforming the existing mass media while simultaneously making use of their technological advances. While this might seem commonplace now in the 1990s, the simple insistence by Benjamin (who was writing against the backdrop of Nazism with all that entailed politically and culturally) that 'The rigid, isolated object (of art) . . . is of no use whatsoever. It must be inserted into the context of living social relations' (Benjamin, 1970a: 52) was a remarkably radical statement even in the early 1970s when in the British university system there were almost no interdisciplinary studies in the humanities, where politics was still something which rarely if ever entered the seminar room or lecture theatre, where the social sciences were narrowly positivistic and empirical, and where theory was equated with the history of ideas.

That moment in the 1970s when Benjamin's writings were warmly embraced, albeit in the marginalized enclaves of cultural studies in Birmingham, did not last long (Working Papers in Cultural Studies, 1972). What was available of Benjamin's other work was too obscure and mystical, or else too literary to be of much use to those areas of study such as film or television which were rapidly developing and which found instead in Althusser's writing a much more useful set of concepts, particularly ideology. This was followed, a couple of years later, by the interest in Gramsci's work and in the concept of hegemony. It was left to the Marxist literary critic Terry Eagleton (1981) to explore in greater depth Benjamin's less accessible writings and at the same time to reclaim him as an impeccable Marxist theorist, despite the Messianic threads running through much of his work. Apart from Eagleton's book, the bulk of Benjamin scholarship has been carried out in Germany and in the USA. With the exception of Dick Hebdige (1979, 1988) and Iain Chambers (1985a, 1985b), both of whom have consistently looked to Benjamin for the exceptionally lucid, even poetic flashes of insight found in many of his less well-known essays, and who have also perhaps empathized with Benjamin's intellectual sadness, his despair at the outcome of events around him, Walter Benjamin had throughout the 1980s been more or less laid to rest in cultural studies.

Recently, in the last two or three years, there has, however, been a flicker of renewed interest. This has involved returning to Benjamin through a highly circuitous route. Two things have happened at once. There has been a shift away from the kind of foundational vocabulary established in cultural studies in the 1970s and summarized under the twin headings of *culturalism* and/or *structuralism* (Hall, 1981) and with this there has been a critique of the assumptions which underpinned the Marxism which played such a key role in cultural studies during that time, including the working class as an emancipatory force, the notion of history as moving inexorably to socialism, the belief in social progress and the leadership role of the organic intellectual. In place of these there has emerged (also under the influence of poststructuralist critiques of meaning) a much looser, even literary vocabulary. Cultural studies has shown itself able to read across the signs of everyday life without having to restrict itself to the search for pure or perfect meaning (Grossberg, Nelson and Treichler, 1991). At the same time, as I have argued at length elsewhere (McRobbie, 1991, 1992), the loss of faith in Marxism has been replaced by a concern for the previously uninvestigated broad cultural setting for the texts and images whose analysis took up so much time precisely because they were seen as being the privileged sites of ideology. The two terms modernity and postmodernity have been taken up as supplying the framework for this broader context. Whether or not they are opposing or interrelated concepts, they have each insisted on the integrated experience of everyday life including the urban environment, architecture, consumer culture and the 'passage' of the individual at whatever precise historical moment in time through these forms, whether he or she, for example, is the *flâneur* of urban modernity, or the insulated walkman of postmodernity.

To the extent that Walter Benjamin can be understood as responding to modernity as it moved towards social catastrophe, and where some of his work other than the two essays mentioned above can be seen as feeding directly into the documentation of urban modernity, it is not surprising that cultural studies might now look back to *One Way Street* (Benjamin, 1979) or *Illuminations* (Benjamin, 1970b). What interest there has been in the UK is also very much thanks to the cultural sociology of the journal *Theory, Culture and Society* (Featherstone, 1980–) which has been responsible for the renewed theoretical interest in figures like Georg Simmel, Norbert Elias and Siegfried Kracauer as well as Walter Benjamin. Finally, it should be remembered that it was feminism which insisted on the place of biography and autobiography in cultural studies. This too has accounted for a different kind of object of study emerging in the field of culture, one which makes it possible to incorporate into the field a piece of autobiographical writing like 'A Berlin chronicle' (published in *One Way Street*; Benjamin, 1979).

In Germany we find an unbroken interest in Benjamin since the late 1960s, including the publication of letters, manuscripts and catalogue material to accompany exhibitions drawing on his life and work (Puttnies and Smith, 1991). In German scholarship, particularly in social history, we find the continual influence of Benjamin's writings on historiography and on the practice of history. And in both Germany and the USA there is a great interest in Benjamin's contribution to 'modern Jewish Messianism' (Rabinbach, 1985). Alongside this, for those working in the field of German Studies on both sides of the Atlantic, there is Benjamin's work itself as a literary and historical object of study. *One Way Street*, for example, is generally seen as a kind of literary montage strongly influenced by the visual work of John Heartfield rather than a critical essay in the traditional sense. There is also Benjamin's critical writing, on Baudelaire, Kafka and Proust, on the historian and collector Edward Fuchs, on Karl Krauss, as well as the essays on literary and cultural practices and pursuits such as translating, collecting books, and telling stories (Benjamin, 1970a, 1970b, 1979). Finally there are the few fragments of autobiographical material, of which two stand out. The *Moscow Diary* published by the US journal *October* (1985) is as important a part of Benjamin's work as his more scholarly writing, so also is 'A Berlin chronicle' (1979), a series of memories of growing up in Berlin. The 'chronicle' shows the influence on his writing of the new technology of film, photography and even the telephone which so fascinated him as a child. Memory for Benjamin was a struggle to recall, not a process of remembering or a linear development, but a set of flickering images. The work of remembering, and the form that memory takes, shows Benjamin to be engaging with Proust, whom he translated, and less directly with Freud. The non-linearity of memory and the availability, as a prompt to memory, of the reproduced image were to prove vital in Benjamin's understanding of history and in the method of writing he tried to develop in the *Passagenwerk* (Benjamin, 1982).

The question to be asked is what more sustained value this body of work has, or might now have, for those working in the field of cultural analysis, particularly in Britain where cultural studies has defined itself as more separate from other related fields (such as social history, literary studies, sociology, European studies, and even film and television studies)? Why was Benjamin important but marginal? Why did he suddenly drop from the reading lists of cultural studies? One of the most straightforward reasons for this is that the mode of writing employed by Benjamin, including the autobiographical fragments, was not considered as somehow appropriate to the methods of cultural studies as they developed through the 1970s and into the 1980s. While Benjamin continued to possess a kind of subterranean image as a figure of historical interest, he belonged somewhere else. This somewhere else lay in the history, not of the cultural left in Britain but of the European cultural left. (It might be suggested that even regarding Europe, British cultural studies has displayed the kind of narrow Anglocentrism many black critics now accuse it of [Gilroy, 1991].)

I want to suggest that a more detailed reconsideration of Benjamin's work is long overdue. What we find is a model for the practice of being a cultural intellectual. This comprises an inability to conform to the traditional requirements of the scholarly mode. Whatever personal pain his failure to get a tenured post might have caused Benjamin, it positioned him on the edge of intellectual life. (It would have been unlikely, for example, that any university appointments committee would have taken seriously his interest in the photographic image, the shopping arcades of Paris, or the fashions displayed in the windows of the new department stores.) There is nothing comfortable about anything Benjamin ever wrote. Instead it is shot through with difficulty and urgency. He was, of course, writing in a time more overshadowed by fear than our own. But what he was doing was new and inventive in every way. He was not a writer of fiction, or, like his friend Brecht, a playwright. Within the realms of what might be called non-fiction or the essay form, he was, however, an experimentalist. (I will say more on this later.) Equally important was the passion Benjamin displayed politically. As his 'A Berlin chronicle' records, he was, as a student, as much an activist as a young intellectual, organizing debates and making speeches in the meeting house which he and his friends in the youth movement rented. Later on he never got the permanent job he so much needed in a university and this consigned him to great financial insecurity. It also pushed him into the world of freelance writing which in turn meant that he had to be responding quite immediately to changes in the world around him. He was writing, from a critical perspective, about culture, and, in an underdeveloped field of study, he was grappling for the kinds of concepts and vocabulary which would best serve this purpose. What we find in this work is by no means restricted to journalistic comment, or indeed to what today might be called cultural journalism. There is instead a sustained critique of culture as a great unfolding history of ideas, and we also find a critique of culture as something cut off and separate from everyday life, which can be parcelled off for study in the traditional mode of, say, art history. In 'The artist as producer' Benjamin is using and extending an explicitly Marxist vocabulary in an attempt to understand not just how art relates to the world of production but how it *is* a form of production. He wants to demystify art by demonstrating those skills and practices which constitute the work of the artist. New technology also provides the means of overcoming the traditional boundaries which have separated the artist from the audience. It is here, in this space, that art can change itself. These ideas were immensely influential to critics and writers of the new left like John Berger (1972), Hans Magnus Enzensberger (1970) and, in the USA, Susan Sontag (1979), and they also prefigured much of Barthes's early writing (1977), particularly his concern with the photographic image, with aspects of popular culture and of course with 'the death of the author'.

There are other small but important ways in which Benjamin opened up for study areas which had been ignored as having little if any cultural value. In this way too his work can be seen as an important precursor of cultural studies. In the essay on Edward Fuchs, the historian and collector (Benjamin, 1979), Benjamin argues that Fuchs's interest in caricature, erotic art and 'manners' (what we would now call popular taste) pushed him into developing a language which was at odds with the official language of art criticism. The objects which Fuchs was interested in were not reconcilable with the vocabulary of high art. Fuchs's hobby (he had 'a Rabelaisian joy in quantity' [1979: 373]) as a collector, allowed him insight into the world of the trivial, the popular, the subordinate world of mass culture. 'It was the collector who found his way into grey areas . . . caricature, photography'(1979: 361). And, because he was also a powerful editor of an influential journal, Fuchs was able to undertake the 'popularization of knowledge' by using the mass media to address the masses. The way in which Fuchs's work reflected on culture as a living historical process encouraged Benjamin to develop a clearer conception of historical materialism as a critical force which 'conceives historical understanding as an after-life of that which is understood, whose pulse can still be felt in the present' (Benjamin, 1970a: 62).

'A small history of photography' (Benjamin, 1979) is equally packed with the kind of insight and analysis which have been so influential on cultural studies. In less than eighteen pages and with astonishing density Benjamin introduces what were to become the major thematics in the analysis of photography in the 1970s, including the destruction of 'aura' as a result of reproducibility of the image, the challenge of art which photography mounts and the extent to which it poses the question, not whether it counts as an art but if art can itself still exist after photography. Benjamin also considers the relation between the photograph and the caption anticipating Barthes's seminal work on text and image (Barthes, 1977) and even the title of John Berger's *Ways of Seeing* (1972) is taken from this essay, when Benjamin suggests that photography brings about a revolution in how we see. The close attention to the technology of photography and its effect on the image also foreshadows much of Barthes's later work in *Camera Lucida* (Barthes, 1981) and the whole curious, fascinated and even enchanted tone of the essay proved inspirational to Susan Sontag's *On Photography* (1979).

Most important perhaps is Benjamin's refusal to be constrained by the kind of academic mode which insists on conventional scholarship, on precise periodization, on the accumulation of facts, on naming, dating and conferring value. Instead Benjamin ruminates on photography. He explores the world of the photograph, not only suggesting the way in which the image could now be mass produced and could thus be everywhere in culture, but also evoking his own pleasure in the photographic image, the sense in which, as he was later to explain in the *Passagenwerk*, it epitomizes his notion of the 'dialectical image'. 'It is in the illumination of these sparks that the first photographs emerge, beautiful and unapproachable, from the darkness of our grandfathers' day' (Benjamin, 1979: 257). The photograph connects the past with the present by supplying the 'pulse', the rhythm and the motion of historical process, not as an unbroken chain but as a jumble of fragments and 'snapshots'. History is therefore connective but not linear, contingent but not without a pattern, a momentum, a force which could be challenged or transformed.

Many of these ideas are further developed in 'The work of art in the age of mechanical reproduction'. The cult of genius and of creativity is exposed and the emergence of a mass market for art, as a result of technological reproducibility, allows Benjamin to celebrate the final sundering of the ties which have linked ideas of art with those of ritual, originality, aura and eternal value. From now on, argues Benjamin, the work of art can be designed for, rather than against, reproducibility. Benjamin in effect created here the possibility of a non-canonic language of cultural criticism which, set against the rapid rise of fascism, also recognized the urgency of attempting to understand the politics of mass art and mass communication. In such circumstances there is no looking back with nostalgia for a moment when art could afford to be socially or politically unconnected, and when value could be debated in a more leisurely academic mode.

Finally there is in Benjamin's work a thread which is perhaps more evident now, in retrospect, than it was in the 1970s. As 'A Berlin chronicle' shows with great clarity, Benjamin was himself politicized not just by the broad social events which were happening around him, by the growth of anti-Semitism, for example, but by the constraints and hypocrisies of bourgeois society as they imposed themselves on the life of the young adult. The youth movement which Benjamin belonged to was greatly concerned with the 'brutalities' of middle-class family life, with the absurdities of sexual decorum which made it impossible for young people of both sexes to mix freely together and with the rigid authoritarianism of the education system. In this context the city itself (and the public sphere of freedom which it opens up in the form of entertainment and display), the prostitute, and the proletariat, play the role of the 'other' to whom and to which Benjamin inclines himself. He describes the pleasures of crossing the 'threshold of one's class' by procuring the services of a prostitute on the street for the first time. Later, in the *Passagenwerk* (Benjamin, 1982), this is an image and an experience which is at the heart of Benjamin's understanding of modernity. But in 'A Berlin chronicle' it is a fleeting, symbolic escape from his class of origin. It acquires heroic stature in his writing just as the prostitute and the brothel are key landmarks in his mapping of the modern metropolis.

Both of these identifications and inclinations, for the proletariat and the prostitute, had meaning and significance for the new left of the late 1960s. That is to say, they registered in the dominant political vocabulary of the moment. But on both counts, it is a good deal more complicated now. Benjamin's relationship to the world of prostitution might be seen, after twenty years of feminist debate and scholarship, as no different from that of any of his middle-class counterparts of the period. The prostitute remains a shadowy, anonymous figure in his writing. As in the writing of Baudelaire (on whom Benjamin wrote at least one volume and copious articles and notes) she is, at most, a fellow deviant, another outsider. Benjamin notes that she is a commodity, a 'mass article', but he takes this no further, preferring to remember the more pleasurable function of the prostitute and the even greater excitement of seeking her out. In 'The image of Proust' he writes, 'Anyone who has tried to get the address of a brothel in a strange city and has received the most long-winded directions ... will understand what is meant here ... and last but not least Proust's intransigent French spirit' (1970b: 209).

The critique of bourgeois society (and Benjamin shows no influence of feminism in his writing); the turning to the proletariat and to the politics of class as a means of overthrowing the old order; the links with the Communist Party particularly through the influence of his lover Asja Lacis but the rejection of the party in preference for a concern with culture and with political independence; the refusal to side with those on the left who underestimated the power of fascism, and the recognition

Figure 2 Walter Benjamin, uncharacteristically fashionable, on holiday with Gert Wissing and Maria Speyer, Saint-Paul de Vence, May 1931; photographer unknown. Reproduced by permission of Marbacher Magazin and the Theodor W. Adorno Archives, Frankfurt am Main

on his part of the 'powers of enchantment' which Nazism offered; the refusal perhaps to believe in Marxism as a redemptive force which could at the last moment change the tide of history as it was slowly closing in upon him; the small pleasures which could rally his spirits and rescue him, if temporarily, from despair and helplessness; the forms of these pleasures (small objects, fleeting sexual encounters), the place of these pleasures (in the city, on long walks, surrounded by the signs, landmarks and technologies of modernity) and the sheer excitement and sociability of these excursions (with friends including Franz Hessel, Gershom Scholem and Brecht, with Asja Lacis, and also alone): all of these describe not just a man, but the makings of a left culture, very different from the one we now inhabit, but one which we none the less have inherited and which we have looked to for a sense of our own place in history. It is, then, as a cultural intellectual that Benjamin plays so important a role, a figure who in every way experienced, sought to understand, and suffered at the hands of modernity. As Zygmunt Baumann has recently argued, the Holocaust and the rise of Stalin were as much part of modernity as the palaces of consumption (Baumann, 1989). Walter Benjamin occupies the space of modernity. White, male, middle-class and European, he is both a representative of and a critic of that moment which was so forma-tive for the new left generation of the late 1960s who turned away from the anti-intellectualism of the 1950s and 1960s, and away from the conservative world of establishment high culture, and went back instead to the time of Brecht and Benjamin where the politics of art was fiercely debated, and where low culture was already recognized as a powerful force offering many opportunities for political intervention.

Precisely because none of the 'advantages' of being white, middle-class and male saved Benjamin from the forces of history and from fascism, he might be seen as a symbol of European modernity in all its complexity. While some might now argue that the entire edifice of cultural studies was erected around the Eurocentric values of a small number of writers and intellectuals who had no interest in or understanding of their sexual or ethnic subordinates, this should not mean that we expunge their work from our own intellectual history and formation. To do so would be to refuse the challenge and the contradictions of history and to participate in the same kind of wilful forgetfulness which Benjamin frequently warns us against.

THE *PASSAGENWERK* AND *THE DIALECTICS OF SEEING*

Benjamin offered a more constructive way forward for the study of mass culture and popular culture than many of his counterparts, particularly Adorno (Adorno, 1967). Despite the difficult circumstances of his life, he displayed, in his writing, a distinct enjoyment of the pleasures of urbanism, a particular enjoyment of place, and of getting lost or straying in the city, a love of café culture as well as a fascination with shop windows and with the commodities they so proudly displayed. This capacity for enjoyment intensified rather than blunted his critical faculties and led him to examine the historical processes which gave the items, the objects and the urban areas or districts, their cultural meaning. Benjamin was also pioneering a new way of writing about culture characterized by a sense of uncertainty, a welcome rejoinder to the more emphatic Marxist orthodoxy on art and culture which held sway at that moment. Looking back, this sense of uncertainty, this force of prevarication, could be seen, not as pessimism or faint-heartedness, but rather as an unwillingness to profess a *faith* in Marxism, to embrace it as something which would somehow come to his rescue. A major part of Benjamin's critique of commoditization lay in the way in which it naturalized the process of its own production and presented itself as synonymous with progress. Benjamin disputed the idea of progress, historically and philosophically. He could not therefore participate in that account of Marxism which saw history as moving, progressively, towards socialism. As a result, his writing bears the mark, almost always, of the present or of the recent past. As many critics have since pointed out, it is the discarded ruins, the recent remains, the small trinkets and souvenirs of consumer capitalism and modernity which interested Benjamin and which were his raw materials. Benjamin sought out the older shops and café corners and the crumbling arcades of the cities in which he lived, rather than the magnificent boulevards or great buildings which so clearly expressed the bold modernist confidence of their architects. From watching and walking 'botanizing on the asphalt' (Benjamin quoted in Buck-Morss, 1989) he developed a cultural vision of the city as layered and labyrinthine rather than as being simply the highest expression of bourgeois civilization. It is this circumspect, convoluted and sometimes seemingly perverse mode of analysis which makes Benjamin a figure towards whom writers on postmodernity have recently turned.

Susan Buck-Morss's *The Dialectics of Seeing: Walter Benjamin and the Arcades Project* (1989) is, as she points out, a work of reconstruction. For over thirteen years, between 1927 and 1941, Walter Benjamin had thought about, talked about and prepared in note form what was to be one of his major pieces of work. The arcades project was to be a theory of modernity, a philosophy of history, a verbal montage of urban imagery, and a reflection on the meaning of consumer culture from the viewpoint of memory and experience. But this ambitious project which also came to represent a kind of unifying umbrella for Benjamin's entire *oeuvre* was destined not to come to fruition but to remain as fragments, notes, ideas and a series of longer pieces. What remains of the arcades project has been known about and discussed among Benjamin scholars in the UK, in the USA and in Germany for some time, but the work of translation and publication has been hindered by precisely the difficulty in assembling the material in book form. In Germany, it is available, but US and British publishers have been less certain of a market for this kind of work. The *Passagenwerk* notes and fragments were first brought together and edited by Rolf Tiedemann in 1982 (Benjamin, 1982). Susan Buck-Morss set herself the task of assembling these fragments for publication in English while retaining a commitment to the original fragmented 'montage' method of argument.

It is in the arcades project that Benjamin's more ambitious theoretical aims are pursued. As various critics have pointed out, a good many of the ideas in this work owe more to his earlier work on German baroque tragedy (Benjamin, 1977) than to the Marxist ideas found in the two seminal essays mentioned earlier, 'The work of art in the age of mechanical reproduction' and 'The artist as producer'. The arcades project has to be seen as a work which not only remained incomplete but which shifted and changed over the years in which it was being formulated. In some ways it is more like a diary, or a record of Benjamin's responses to history, philosophy, modernism and surrealism, as well as an attempt to theorize aspects of mass culture in the context of Europe on the brink of fascism.

What we find in Buck-Morss's book is an exposition not just of the *Passagenwerk*, but also of the other fragments and shorter pieces which have been referred to by critics but not as yet put into the context of Benjamin's larger project. Buck-Morss achieves an admirable balance between coherence and looseness in her reworking of the *Passagenwerk* material. She has managed to remain faithful to the method pioneered by Benjamin while also extending it into a commentary on contemporary urban life in the late 1980s, by drawing on images, photographs and other source material including advertisements which reflect now what Benjamin described then as 'dialectical images'.

There is a point, however, beyond which Buck-Morss goes no further. While Benjamin exists as a writer in *The Dialectics of Seeing*, his work is not seen as it might be, that is, as a kind of performance art. Precisely because his work resists the search for meaning and understanding which might be expected in more conventional cultural writing or literary criticism, it is, I would suggest, more productive to see Benjamin as fulfilling the role of the writer in the Barthesian sense (Barthes, 1977), as one who moves beyond and between genres, and who quite consciously breaks with the distinction between art and criticism, rather as Barthes himself does, who ushers in a new way of writing and a new way of seeing writing.

Without this *The Dialectics of Seeing* is forced into seeking some kind of intellectual resolution in the concepts and ideas found in the *Passagenwerk* which the work itself is incapable of providing. This is particularly true of the 'dialectical image' which Benjamin developed as a means of condensing, into a verbal flash, a few brief sentences or phrases which are simultaneously a representation of and a critique of a cultural event or item. This ambition grew out of Benjamin's admiration for montage techniques in the arts and in photography, and especially in the work of John Heartfield. As his notes suggest, he was as much interested in exhibiting as in writing: 'Method of this work: literary montage. I have nothing to say, only to show' (Benjamin quoted in Buck-Morss, 1989: 73). This illustrates Benjamin's aim to create a visual image out of words. The transcendent quality of these verbal images, the possibility of creating in a few words the kind of complex analysis and statement which John Heartfield produced in his photomontage work, requires on the part of the critic a conceptual leap. It means seeing Benjamin not only as a cultural theorist and as a historian but as a cultural practitioner. Benjamin is creating and practising a new and more active mode of cultural analysis and criticism. The analysis takes place inside his verbal images and aphorisms.

The problem is that even if we demystify art from notions of talent or genius, doing 'art work' still requires its own techniques and skills, learned and practised over the years. In the case of Benjamin, sometimes his method works with quite startling results – for example, in the image of the angel of history (Benjamin in Buck-Morss, 1989); but just as often it results in infuriatingly pretentious and self-important sets of statements. Despite this, a case can none the less be made for Benjamin as an experimentalist, a writer endlessly trying to adjust in language to the irreversible advances which have taken place in the visual mass media. It seems as though Benjamin wants to work with words as though they were images. This has repercussions for how we respond to the work. If the *Passagenwerk* is in part a compilation of prose images, then the conventional work of exposition and critique is no longer appropriate. The *Passagenwerk* instead asks of us that we sit back and read it as a series of often disconnected fragments, an exhibition or a performance, not as a conventional academic text.

That Benjamin became a practitioner in words of the kind of art work whose methods and strategies he most enjoyed and discussed at great length, should be no real surprise. He disliked the academy even though he sought, unsuccessfully, to earn a living there. His closest friends and the figures who influenced him most were creative artists. He occupied exactly that space of the writer which Barthes was later to espouse and himself represent where, as a point of principle, criticism and creative writing merge into each other and dissolve as separate categories, where fiction and non-fiction also overlap, and where the death of the author coincides with the birth of a different kind of writing and writer. The *Passagenwerk* should be read then like a modernist novel whose major influences were the growth of the cinema and photography, a series of speculations and reveries on urban culture, a surrealist documentary, a creative commentary.

This still leaves the critic with the difficult job of trying to evaluate the work. Buck-Morss reminds us of Adorno's disappointment with the project and his hostility to its unconventional methods. Earlier Adorno had rejected for publication another of Benjamin's articles (Buck-Morss, 1989). It is certainly difficult, if not impossible, to categorize it neatly as philosophical history, or as a sociology of consumer culture, or even as a lengthy piece of journalistic reportage. At many points in Buck-Morss's text there are repetitions and passages that simply do not make sense. The value that the work might have for cultural studies depends therefore on how we view it. While it certainly yields no unified account of modernity, it does exist, in my opinion, as a text of modernity, a lengthy, rambling, unedited piece of footage with a repetitious, irritating but compelling voice-over.

The form which Buck-Morss's compilation document of the *Passagenwerk* takes is as follows. Parts One and Two trace through the appearance in the work of four main threads. These are the fossil, the fetish, the wish-image and the ruin. Part Three examines the broader context of the work including its political and philosophical achievement, and Part Four takes the form of a visual homage to Benjamin's work comprising images and art work drawing on the contemporary world of mass culture. In Part One, Buck Morss considers the temporal and the spatial origins of the *Passagenwerk* project. First there is the context within which Benjamin embarked on the arcades work. *One Way Street*, first published in German in 1928, is seen as a key influence on what he was going to do. *The Origin of German Tragic Drama* (Benjamin, 1977) also reflects what was to be for Benjamin a lifelong interest in the idea of allegory. In the second chapter Buck-Morss describes the cities in which he lived during the late 1920s and the way in which he wrote about them. She shows him to be strongly influenced by Proust, by the work and ideas of his friend Franz Hessel, by the work of the surrealist movement, and by the politics of his Russian lover Asja Lacis who at the time was working for an experimental children's theatre in Moscow and was also a colleague of Brecht. Part Two of the book brings the reader more directly into the heart of the arcades project with Buck-Morss acting as a guide and interpreter. In 'Natural history: fossil', the fossil is where, according to Benjamin, nature and history merge together so that they cannot be prised apart. The symbiotic way in which historical change is subsumed under the guise of natural change, also leads Benjamin to reflect on the real rather than the mythic relation between the two. This interest in natural history was to run through the arcades work, in part a reflection of Benjamin's concern with the recent past, and in particular with the late nineteenth century when a more widespread fascination with natural history created a profusion of 'natural' images whose reproduction was made possible by advances in technology. Two additional concerns arise here: the notion of how Germany's 'natural history' might be alternatively constructed and the way in which John Heartfield's photomontage work represented an example of such a non-linear historical method, i.e. the creation of a modern-day emblematics, a visual rendering of the 'natural history' of Germany by allegorical means. Benjamin then takes up and adapts the photomontage form for his own purposes in the arcades project by pointing to the presence of the 'montage effect' already in existence in the cities through the 'piling up' and layering of neon and advertising which in turn become part of the architecture, and part of the visual experience of urbanism. As in so much of his work, Benjamin sees, in what has recently come into existence through new technology (what Buck-Morss calls the 'new nature'), a kind of dialectics at work. The effect is both fettering and emancipatory. Technology secures old relations while unleashing new ones which are as yet unimagined and hence unincorporated into the existing social arrangements. Drawing also perhaps on Brechtian ideas, Benjamin claims montage (itself the product of technological innovation) to be progressive because it 'interrupts the context into which it is inserted'.

In the section on the 'fetish', Buck-Morss introduces the complexity of Benjamin's thought in relation to consumerism. It is the vision of urban brilliance which pushes Benjamin to compare the city with the 'enchanted forest' of children's fairy-tales. The new consumer goods displayed in abundance, as well as the new urban experiences dreamt up to celebrate these forms, including the world expositions, the arcades, the panoramas and the lavish window displays, transform the city beyond the realms of the imagination and at the same time create a new public sphere produced not by artists and writers but by designers, commercial artists, copywriters, photographers, engineers and technicians. The sheer scale of their work (the toothpaste advertising billboard 'toothpaste for giants') contributes to the grandeur of this new dream world, a monumentalism which for the first time incorporates at a 'dream level' not just the aspirations of the ruling classes but also, in the form of the mass-produced commodity, a kind of popular utopia.

The contents of the wish-images of consumer capitalism, (outlined in chapter 5 of *The Dialectics of Seeing*) are similar to the utopias of pre-industrial folklore or fairy-tales. Their dialectical character exists in the way they are, on the one hand, products of a class-divided society, but on the other they also look forward to a more equal society free from scarcity and conflict. Benjamin's aim is to find a way of making conscious this 'desire for utopia' by somehow unleashing the potential of technology to make it work for social transformation rather than working as it does at present merely for the maintenance of the soporific 'dream state' brought about by the fairy-tale luxury of this new image world. The dialectic exists in that space between what Buck-Morss labels the sign and the referent. Fashion, for example, is a ritual of commodity worship, yet it is also progressive in its irreverent attitude towards tradition and in its vivid dramatization of change. Similarly, as Buck-Morss describes later in the book, the dream state cuts the individual off from others while at the same time creating a shared or collective experience by virtue of the mass availability of the dream material.

The ruin, the fourth of Benjamin's thematics, reminds us of the other side of consumer splendour, that which is deadly, repetitious and even hellish in its endless evocation of novelty. The image of the 'ruin' is also a symbol of the fragility of capitalist consumer culture; the transitoriness of fashion, for example, precisely because of its increasingly desperate attempts to preserve youthfulness and thus also halt the flow of time, ends up evoking death and decay. There is then a ruinous quality lurking just beneath the surface smiles of the fashionably dressed mannequins, the show girls and of course the prostitutes. Capital festers and decays from within and, as it does so, so also does it continually attempt to 'tart itself up'. Much of this section draws on a combination of Baudelaire's poetry and Benjamin's work on the baroque. If, as Buck-Morss says, 'Dialectical images are a modern form of emblematics' then 'in the *Passagenwerk* the devaluation of the new nature and its status as ruin becomes instructive politically. The crumbling of the monuments that were built to signify the immortality of civilisation become proof rather of its transiency' (Buck-Morss, 1989: 170).

Of the remaining chapters of Buck-Morss's volume it is the 'Dream world of mass culture' which draws together the fragments of the argument. She suggests that the *Passagenwerk* does indeed manage to convey the quality of historical experience through the dialectical image and the theory of montage even though the work itself frequently takes a literary or poetic rather than a critical or analytical mode. This 'mode of enchantment' which comes through in Benjamin's writing is also central to his argument which is that underneath the rationalization which creates the possibility of urban modernity, underneath the planning and the bureaucracy, lies a much more mythical landscape, a kind of undergrowth of chaos and abundance, of new consumer goods which quickly take on the character of ancient, pre-industrial symbols to the extent that the whole landscape can be viewed as a series of heavily iconographic signs and symbols. It was both the mundane objects and the extraordinarily endowed 'stars' of mass culture which the surrealists brought together in their own unique dream landscapes. Benjamin seeks to do something else with these same evanescent objects and images. He wants to use them as a means of waking up the masses from the slumber which, in their conventional representation, these wish-images invoke. With some difficulty Benjamin embarks on the work of explaining how, with the help of these objects (already overloaded with historical and mythical meaning), 'the collective' can empower itself by 'reconstructing the capacity for experience'. It is never quite clear in Benjamin's work how this can happen. But there are, however, the potentialities for change, including first that 'technical reproduction gives back ... what technical production takes away', second that the availability of technically produced images allows a 'new capacity to study modern existence reflectively', third that the unconscious wish-images hidden deep in the structure of the objects of consumer culture can be somehow brought to the surface, and fourth that it is also possible to read into and from the other discarded images, those which have only recently gone out of fashion, something useful and important about the conditions of their historical production. The potential for unlocking a kind of 'popular memory' lies in the substance and materiality of the childhood toy, or the now old-fashioned item of clothing.

There is, of course, a huge amount of other material included in *The Dialectics of Seeing* which cannot be summarized here. What remains to be done is to assess the significance for cultural studies of the highly condensed, heavily imagistic, highly imaginative but frequently cryptic ideas put forward by Benjamin in the *Passagenwerk* and translated and introduced in *The Dialectics of Seeing*. Buck-Morss is the first to agree that the meaning of the *Passagenwerk* project is often obscure. Part of Benjamin's plan was to challenge the immediacy of the present and the 'dream state' which mass culture induced, by recovering a sense of history. But what history and how? Benjamin was well aware of the power of what we would now call the ideologies of history, transmitted through culture and through generations, and of the role these play in creating a mystified understanding of contemporary reality. Without the aid of the concept of ideology but with a clear sense of the need for constructing an alternative history and an alternative historiography, Benjamin proposed that the everyday objects of industrial culture, particularly those entering a kind of twilight age in terms of their usefulness or attractiveness, could be rediscovered and rendered useful again in what he envisaged as a project of remembering and understanding the dynamics of the moment of their creation. This was indeed a radical proposal reflecting an outright rejection of conventional history in favour of a non-linear history, one which corresponded to the definition of history offered by his friend and colleague Bloch: 'A polyrhythmic and multi-spatial entity, with enough unmastered and as yet by no means revealed corners' (Bloch quoted in Chalmers, 1991). For Benjamin the task was to unravel the meanings of the discarded items lying in these dusty corners.

The Paris arcades, already in Benjamin's time well past their 'sell-by date' and replaced in grandeur by the new and luxurious department stores, could be looked to as a 'precursor of modernity', a set of buildings which the everyday life of the present rendered almost invisible in their unfashionable status but which precisely because of this eclipsing by progress could be returned to and dwelt upon afresh. In this sense the arcades become emblems, icons of an 'unmastered' past moment not yet defined as historical. The arcades become Benjamin's symbol for not one but a variety of social processes. The grandiosity and scale of their architecture tell us something about the confident way in which pre-modernity anticipated the rise of consumerism, at the same time their cathedral-like ceilings, the dim light from the windows, and the long passageways like church aisles, flanked on either side not by small chapels to pray in but by chapels of consumption, demonstrated exactly what Benjamin recognized as a recurring theme in the conception of new cultural forms; that is, the tendency to incorporate at some unconscious level familiar and comforting reminders of those things which new technology and social progress and indeed which the new object itself make redundant. This looking back to the non-contemporary signifies not simply nostalgia but rather a stirring of discontent or dissatisfaction with the present, a deeper anxiety which cannot be extinguished even by the brilliance, the luxury and the apparent mass availability of the new.

This dimension does indeed draw us into a deeper level of thought, one which is continually present in Benjamin's work but which remains difficult to extrapolate. Benjamin is concerned with the way in which the present bears traces of the recent past within it and with how popular sentiments are embedded into the materiality of the objects which themselves are evidence of and embody the process of historical change. His interest is not then in how great architects, urban planners and designers combine their imaginative skills with the technology and political and ideological power at their disposal, but rather with a more dispersed, more general 'structure of feeling' (Williams, 1961) which brings to bear on these forms and environments a more popular strain, a vernacular. But this is not a question of bricolage, it is not just how 'they' (the collective) add their imprint to an environment, an economy, and a mode of production not of their own choosing. Instead it is about how utopian hopes for emancipation come to be embedded right inside the cultural objects and artefacts, from the point of their inception and design, and how these 'wishes' have to be heeded in the act of refashioning the future.

Benjamin is here providing us with a kind of pre-history of urban modernity through the currency of the commodity. There is, in the commodity form and underneath the glossy packaging and all the promises of the new, a pre-history which includes a 'backward' anti-capitalistic impulse (Chalmers, 1991). It is only very recently that theorists like

John Fiske (Fiske, 1989) and Michel de Certeau (de Certeau, 1984) have attempted to unravel a similar dynamic in contemporary consumer culture. As Fiske writes, 'The commodities produced and distributed by the culture industries that are made into popular culture are those that get out of control, that become undisciplined. . . . The economic needs of the industries can be met only if the people choose their commodities as adequate resources for popular culture . . . and they will choose only those texts that offer opportunities to resist, evade, or scandalise' hegemony (1989: 104–5).

Modernity desperately seeks to deny the presence of volatile and unstable elements. One way of doing this is by attempting to stifle their memory by simply producing more and more objects for more and more people. It is this aspect, along with the simultaneous rapid change and deadly repetition brought about by modernity, which leads Benjamin to describe it as 'hell'. Fashion, according to Benjamin, is hellish because, despite its irreverent attitude towards tradition (mentioned above), it intensifies and accelerates the act of social forgetting, indeed is predicated on it. Benjamin returns repeatedly to fashion, though it is significant that he links fashion with prostitution and that he also takes it as emblematic of the trivial and of course of the feminine. Fashion, he claims, is both the invention and the archetypal symbol of modernity. Its denunciation of the recent past (i.e. of last season's styles) must be challenged if we are to understand the way in which utopian or emancipatory ideals manage to find some latent expression in mass culture.

There are problems and inconsistencies in Benjamin's ideas on fashion, as there are in his whole understanding of the cultural meaning of the commodity form. There is no point in pretending these can be easily explicated and then found a place in cultural studies alongside existing work on this area. In Benjamin's favour, however, it could be said that in his own way he recognized, long before popular culture existed as a topic of any academic or political debate in this country, what since has been called the 'multi-accentuality' of the sign, the instability of meaning, its capacity for change and the extent to which historical change itself was condensed and encapsulated in the forms and the meanings of the consumer goods which filled the display shelves of the shops and arcades. He also recognized that the commodity worked, for the mass of the people, primarily as an image. They could look but not buy, or at least the rate of buying lagged far behind the opportunities for looking. What they were looking at, whether 'window-dressed' or photographed and put on the pages of the magazines, were texts replete with meanings which were activated, however, only at the point of reception. In fashion Benjamin also, and not surprisingly, brings to bear the baffled, fascinated but also patronizing gaze of the male writer. He looks in bewilderment, finds some cause to retrieve positive elements, but remains more firmly on the side of disapproval as bourgeois culture celebrates itself by so lavishly renewing itself in fashion each season. Benjamin's uneasy relation to women, the absence of any sense of sexual politics in his writing and the constant references to the charms of the prostitute, make it unlikely that in discussing fashion he might consider the fact that here 'disruptive' elements exist all the more forcefully. Benjamin does not consider, for example, that for women, fantasies of emancipation might well take shape in and through the language of fashion.

Benjamin's aim in the *Passagenwerk* remained incomplete. It is, in effect, to develop a theory of culture, which is also a form of cultural practice. But the people or the masses possess only a metaphorical presence here. Even as a *flâneur* (the emblem of the emptiness of modernity) Benjamin exists in a strangely depopulated urban landscape where only the prostitutes, pathetic in their state of physical decay, and as such entirely appropriate to their chosen business environment, the upper floors of the deserted arcades, hang out. They too are discarded 'mass articles'. Benjamin's turning away from the people or from the interactive dimension of consumer culture was no doubt a philosophical as well as a methodological decision. His cultural theory is one of objects rather than of social relations. As a consequence it makes it even more difficult to unravel or extend the meaning of this shadowy presence of living people and their utopian impulses in everyday goods and artefacts. Where exactly do these come from, what do they mean? Is it the idea of an abundance where there is enough for everybody, which provides the anti-élitist, democratic spark? If so, is this a kind of nascent or transcendent class consciousness? Or is it a historical residue, a reminder of an earlier folk culture where the fruits of the land were not entirely controlled by the laws of bourgeois property? Or, is Benjamin relying on the Marxist idea that capitalism contains within it the seeds of its own destruction and that signs of this transcendence can indeed be caught sight of in everyday life? The problem of clarity here is compounded not just by the note form in which so many of the *Passagenwerk* ideas are jotted down, but by the fact that, having gone so far, Benjamin leaves off and continues his analysis by casting his gaze back to childhood.

Buck-Morss does a remarkable job of exegesis here. She puts into a clearer framework what in the *Passagenwerk* remained a series of theoretical flashes, ideas, or prose images. There is the way in which consumer culture enters into our unconsciousness by providing the raw material for our dreams. We do not just dream of any old tie or any old pair of shoes, but of those shoes or ties which are themselves emblematic of a particular social moment. In this sense fashion enters into and gives shape to our internal and unconscious thought processes. Likewise in memory, the fondly remembered moment where the child is clutching at the mother's skirt, contains not just some archetypal skirt but a skirt of that moment,

114

a commodity of consumer capitalism for which the passage of time is as merciless as it is for its wearer. It is like saying that commodities chart part of our lives, they constitute our reality, they are the fabric of the culture in which we live, they are not just commodities.

But it is to childhood which Benjamin repeatedly returns, and to many of the ideas and experiences recorded in his 'Berlin chronicle' which are given a more theoretical treatment. These include remembering the shopping expeditions with his mother, the huge variety of luxury goods delivered to their Berlin apartment as a result of his father's business contacts, and also the way in which his family was socially positioned at the forefront of modernity, a position which was later to prove so tragic for them. Before the rise of Nazism, Benjamin's father had a financial stake in the first artificial ice rink in Berlin which Benjamin also remembered as being both an 'ice palace' and a night-club where he caught sight of a prostitute dressed in a sailor suit, a figure who subsequently became a source of fantasy and desire.

Benjamin was fascinated by the often unnoticed but daily signs of contemporary urban life, the sandwich men, the gas stations, the neon signs, the women's fashions, the brightly lit shop windows. He was most drawn by those recently discarded objects existing still in what Buck-Morss describes as a 'half-life'. Such commodities seemed to be emblematic of the passing of time which was peculiar to modern capitalism. To Benjamin their place in the history of modernity was particularly important in that they represented an earlier moment, where modernity was just in sight, and where it was more possible, as a result, to recognize some of those utopian elements which existed alongside, but were not as yet wholly taken over by, consumer capitalism. It was these impulses which gave Benjamin some hope that through the object and the commodity form there could be expressed wishes and ideals other than those merely of acquisition, wealth and private property.

In approaching consumer culture from this angle Benjamin was also trying to pull back from the grip of 'bourgeois capitalism' its hegemony over all that it produced and the historical conditions of that production. If the objects possessed the ability to enchant and be forgotten, then Benjamin would describe another mode of enchantment which occurred in and through these same objects and which in the process of being revealed and remembered could play an active role in the re-enchantment of society (i.e. through the revolutionary process). Benjamin therefore offers another history of place, space and culture through reading its objects backwards. Hence the arcades project itself. By the 1920s and 1930s the arcades existed as exemplary symbols of the ever-changing experience of modernity. Their crumbling façades, their ornate glass ceilings, the lavish iron-work, the atmosphere of the luxury of the recent past, the forlorn items left standing in the windows, once the epitome of fashion but now hopelessly old-fashioned, all of these provide Benjamin with a rich source of raw material from which he was to produce his verbal slide show of 'cognitive images'.

There are a number of points which remain to be made in relation to Benjamin as looked at from the perspective of cultural studies. Some of these have been mentioned already, in passing, and require a few further words, others are more open-ended, questions which Benjamin, in his own indirect way, might ask of cultural studies now. Benjamin's distinctive and imaginative mode of argument coheres around the idea of 'looking back'. While he too is entranced by many of the signs and sights of urban modernity, he obstinately insists that we hold the tide of rapid change at bay by looking at the recent past. However, he is not proposing a full or a linear historical account of the late moment of pre-modernity. Instead, his method is to work in and through the 'dialectical image'. Thus he chooses the painting by Paul Klee titled *Angelus Novus* as an opportunity to reflect on the process of historical change. Where capitalism celebrates itself and its achievements and victories with 'great monuments to mythic progress' (Buck-Morss, 1989: 93) Benjamin looks to this painting as a representation of a different way of seeing. Here the 'angel of history' who 'looks as if he were about to move away from something at which he is staring' (Benjamin quoted in Buck-Morss, 1989: 93) sees not a 'chain of events' but a series of catastrophes which appear like a pile of wreckages in a scrapyard. Progress is that 'storm' which is carrying the angel forward through space and time, against his will. With his back towards the future he fixes resolutely on the scale of the damage below him. It is characteristic of Benjamin to look to a small, delicate and modernist work, like Klee's painting, to demonstrate the power of the image itself and to use it as a means of illustrating his historiographical approach.

Not only does Benjamin continually remind us of the need for history but his method proves particularly appropriate to cultural studies. A more radical use of history like that developed by Benjamin would complement existing work on popular images and textuality. If the precise way in which this might be done is clouded by his use of poetic language, where his own 'text' is condensed almost to the point of obscurity, then this should not, as perhaps it has in the past, lead us to dismiss the value of Benjamin's 'other work'. Of course he was influenced by Baudelaire, of course he was sitting in the street cafés of Paris and Berlin composing prose images which he then set to work in the name of cultural history, theory, or philosophy. What he was doing was a kind of archaeology on the commodities and images of consumer culture. But this is not so far removed from our own contemporary practice of semiology. It is a cultural history in the most literal of senses, a style of writing and a mode of work which could perhaps be compared with Dick Hebdige's many 'readings' of images drawn from the world of contemporary pop culture, in particular the skinheads photograph which is the focus of attention in the essay entitled 'Hiding in the light' (Hebdige, 1988). It is also strongly reminiscent of Hebdige's use of the image of the car in his run-down inner-city street, transformed by its owner into a kind of temple, 'a cathedral among hovels'. Significantly perhaps, Hebdige opens this piece with the 'angel of history' quote from Benjamin (Hebdige, 1988).

The second way in which Benjamin's interest in history is of value to cultural studies in the 1990s is in the challenge he poses to the way in which history is actually done. He is arguing for a sense of recent history to be continually with us in our inhabiting of the present. This requires some effort for the reason that we live in a consumer culture predicated on forgetting or else on highly selective remembering, e.g. through nostalgia or the 'heritage industry'. But it also raises a number of additional questions. Which recent history? How is that history to be chosen? According to what criteria? The *Passagenwerk* is a history and documentation of selected items drawn from the 'window' of urban life as seen by Benjamin. What characterizes his chosen images is that they have become less visible as a result of their age. However, they are by no means old. It is rather that the pace of historical change has accelerated as a result of the technological and social changes brought about by this later stage of industrialization. These 'emblematic' goods have been outmoded by the abundance of the new. History is then doubly a fiction. It is not the passing of time but the pacing of capitalist production manifest in the language of consumer culture.

Most important to Benjamin's work is the immediate history of the time in which he himself was writing. Fascism too had an unnatural, almost magical ability to naturalize itself. It had quickly understood the power of the mass media and the power of myth and ritual. Benjamin's historical method was also a riposte to the grandiosity of fascism, to its claims of universalism, to its monumental vision. Declining the redemptive, grand narrative of communism, Benjamin persevered against the odds, with his modest, *imagistic* practice of cultural history.

Benjamin tightly grips on to the past, like a child clinging on to his mother's hand. He carefully records and analyses the small pleasures and enjoyments of the present in which he feels the 'pulse' of the past. Benjamin's best work is fuelled by a love of culture, a love of collecting cultural items, including books and picture postcards, and by a love of those urban experiences which are not conventionally the subject of academic study (e.g. walking, café culture). These strands of thinking put him at odds with the left in Germany at the time (with a few exceptions including Bloch to whom he owed a great deal in his conception and writing of the *Passagenwerk*).

It often seems as though he was writing against the inexorable forces of history and fascism rather than in favour of socialist revolution.

117

Uncertain of Marxism as a political practice or as a theory of history, Benjamin pursues his own singular path, drawing on Marxist ideas, and influenced by Brecht and Lacis on questions of art and culture, but concerning himself in the *Passagenwerk* with modernity as a multiply layered social reality, one which could only be grasped in the form of the philosophical fragment, the 'dialectical image', or in the note form itself. This kind of writing was also a literary experiment, an attempt to create a new practice of theory, history and philosophy which could be compressed into a series of tightly worked prose images. These fragments become the hallmarks of Benjamin's style. For the *Passagenwerk* to be of use to cultural studies it would be necessary for those working in cultural studies to remember the value of experimentation, the importance of interdisciplinarity, the breaking down of the distinctions not just between philosophy, history, literary criticism and cultural analysis, but also between art and criticism, not for the sake of the new, but for social change and transformation.

* * * *

During the time I was living in Birmingham, one of my closest friends and neighbours was the feminist Soviet historian Lizzie Waters. Because she was married to a Soviet citizen Lizzie was able to travel to and from Moscow regularly, although she had to publish her work under an assumed name. After a long winter in Moscow Lizzie returned to Birmingham with stories of queues and no fruit or vegetables for months. One day she had waited several hours because she had heard that there were frozen chickens available. When she got home with the chicken, a treat for academic friends visiting from Australia, she discovered from the small print on the wrapping that it had come from Germany and that its sell-by date had expired two years earlier.

A few weeks later (and still many years before *perestroika*, never mind the coup of August 1991), I dreamed that I did eventually make it to Moscow to visit Lizzie. But when I arrived the city centre was thronged with smiling, well-dressed men and women. There was a festive feel in the air. The architecture was dark and magnificent, like the great gloomy tenements and municipal buildings of my childhood in Glasgow. The shops were full of clothes and domestic gadgetry, but most of all it was the cafés whose light flooded out through the frosty windows on to the street, which seemed like the heart of the city. I eventually caught sight of Lizzie who waved me over to join the group of friends she was with. The place was awash with colour and warmth. Steaming coffee, hot chocolate and cakes were ordered. (In *Moscow Diary* Benjamin writes: 'The hotel has no kitchen so one can't even get a cup of tea' [1985: 41].)

I remember this as a profoundly political dream. The so-called socialist society which I was visiting, contrary to my expectations, provided me with many of the consumer goods and items around which I organize my own everyday life; coffee, for instance, city lights and clothes. (In *Moscow Diary* Benjamin also writes: 'The scarcity of living quarters here creates a strange effect: unlike in other cities, here the streets in the evening are lined with large and small houses with almost every window lit up . . . you might imagine you were looking at an illumination' [104].) Sociability and friendship also flourished in this loud, crowded dream environment. There was no fear, no silence, no guarded words.

Perhaps, in the end, it is not insignificant that one of the ways Benjamin exists for left intellectuals today is, as Susan Sontag (1979) has shown, as an image. We look back to the many photographs of him, and see what looks like a stubborn scholar, a reluctant refugee, a critical intellectual. Benjamin understood the pressing need for change and, more immediately, for the struggle against fascism, but he was not politically didactic. He was non-dogmatic and non-authoritarian in his thinking and in his practice. One of the values of his work to cultural studies today is that while Benjamin, like the contemporary postmodernists, rejects the notion of progress and rejects history as a straight line, he argues all the more forcibly for the place of history in the study of culture. For this reason, the sadness and the suicide are not simply biographical notes. They are part of a recent history which cultural studies must continue to remember.

REFERENCES

Adorno, Theodor (1967) *Prisms*, trans. Samuel and Shierry Weber, London: Neville Spearman.

Barthes, Roland (1977) 'The death of the author' and 'The rhetoric of the image', *Image, Music, Text*, London: Fontana, pp. 142–9 and 32–52.

Barthes, Roland (1981) *Camera Lucida*, London: Fontana.

Baumann, Zygmunt (1989) *Modernity and the Holocaust*, Ithaca, NY: Cornell University Press.

Benjamin, Walter (1970a) *Understanding Brecht*, London: NLB.

Benjamin, Walter (1970b) *Illuminations*, London: Jonathan Cape.

Benjamin, Walter (1973) *Gesammelte Schriften*, Vol. 1, ed. T. W. Adorno, Frankfurt am Main: Suhrkamp.

Benjamin, Walter (1977) *The Origins of German Tragic Drama*, trans. J. Osborne, London: NLB.

Benjamin, Walter (1979) *One Way Street*, London: NLB.

Benjamin, Walter (1982) *Gesammelte Schriften* (including Vol. 5, *Das Passagenwerk*), ed. R. Tiedemann, Frankfurt am Main: Suhrkamp.

Benjamin, Walter (1985) *Moscow Diary*, Special Issue, *October* 35, ed. G. Smith, trans. R. Sieburth, Cambridge, MA: MIT Press.

Bennett, T. *et al.* (eds) (1981) *Culture, Ideology and Social Process*, London: Batsford.

Berger, John (1972) *Ways of Seeing*, Harmondsworth, Mx: Penguin/BBC.

Bloch, Ernst (1991) *Heritage of Our Times*, Oxford: Polity.

Buck-Morss, Susan (1989) *The Dialectics of Seeing: Walter Benjamin and the Arcades Project*, Cambridge, MA: MIT Press.

Chalmers, Martin (1991) 'Carnival time in Weimar', *Times Literary Supplement*, 6 September.
Chambers, Iain (1985a) *Metropolitan Culture*, London: Macmillan.
Chambers, Iain (1985b) *Urban Rhythms: Pop Music and Popular Culture*, London: Macmillan.
de Certeau, Michel (1984) *The Practice of Everyday Life*, Berkeley, CA: University of California Press.
Eagleton, Terry (1981) *Walter Benjamin: Or Towards a Revolutionary Criticism*, London: Verso.
Enzensberger, Hans Magnus (1970) 'Constituents of a theory of the media', *New Left Review* 64.
Featherstone, Mike (ed.) (1980–) *Theory, Culture and Society: Explorations in Critical Social Science*; journal published in London by Sage.
Fiske, John (1989) *Understanding Popular Culture*, London: Unwin Hyman.
Gilroy, Paul (1991) 'Against ethnic absolutism', in L. Grossberg, C. Nelson and P. Treichler (eds) *Cultural Studies*, New York: Routledge, pp. 189–99.
Grossberg, Lawrence, Nelson, Cary and Treichler, Paula (eds) (1991) *Cultural Studies*, New York: Routledge.
Hall, Stuart (1981) 'Two paradigms in cultural studies', in T. Bennett *et al.* (eds) *Culture, Ideology and Social Process*, London: Batsford, pp. 19–39.
Hebdige, Dick (1979) *Subculture: The Meaning of Style*, London: Routledge.
Hebdige, Dick (1988) *Hiding in the Light*, London: Routledge/Comedia.
McRobbie, Angela (1991) 'New Times in cultural studies', *New Formations* 13, Spring: 1–17 (reprinted in this book as chapter 2).
McRobbie, Angela (1992) 'Post-Marxism and cultural studies', in L. Grossberg, C. Nelson and P. Treichler (eds) *Cultural Studies*, New York: Routledge, pp. 719–30 (reprinted in this book as chapter 3).
Puttnies, Hans and Smith, Gary (1991) *Benjaminmania: Ein Biografische Recherche*, Ananbas: Verlag Giessen.
Rabinbach, Anson (1985) 'Benjamin, Bloch and modern Jewish messianism', *New German Critique* 17, Spring, 78–125.
Sontag, Susan (1979) *On Photography*, Harmondsworth, Mx: Penguin.
Sontag, Susan (1983) 'Under the sign of Saturn', in *Under the Sign of Saturn*, London: Writers and Readers, pp. 109–37.
Williams, Raymond (1961) *The Long Revolution*, New York: Columbia University Press.

7

STRATEGIES OF VIGILANCE: AN INTERVIEW WITH GAYATRI CHAKRAVORTY SPIVAK

Gayatri Chakravorty Spivak's three seminal essays published in *Yale French Studies* (hereafter *YFS*) and *Social Text* (hereafter *ST*) are still a great deal better known among feminists and others working in the field of literary studies in America, than they are on the British side of the Atlantic.[1] *YFS* is primarily a literary journal and has been responsible for introducing to the USA much of the work of Lacan, Derrida and their followers. It has also provided a forum for an emergent American structuralist and poststructuralist criticism. *Social Text* spans a wide political and theoretical spectrum, and it has done much to familiarize American readers with Foucault and his critics. Alongside this there has been, in *ST*, a continual engagement with debates around popular culture, cinema, imperialism, racism and of course Marxism, with contributions from writers like Fredric Jameson and Edward Said.

My own knowledge of many of the theoretical excavations found in the pages of these journals is not too extensive. But I have returned to Gayatri Chakravorty Spivak's articles because of their intellectual scope and their ability to absorb and reformulate many of those ideas and concepts which often seem to float around in the poststructuralist universe unanchored. Gayatri's starting point in her article 'French feminism in an international frame',[2] is the feminist inflection of much of this French critical work. What she manages to do is to put this work not so much in context, as in relation to a set of 'other' signifiers; for example, the representation of 'Third World women'.

Having marked out the parameters of this forceful critique, Gayatri then locates those points within 'high French feminism' which *could* conceivably suggest a space where women's interests, on an international basis, do indeed coincide.

There are other reasons why I have wanted to make Gayatri's work more available to the British reader. Here is a feminist working within that terrain labelled poststructuralism, using extremely difficult concepts and, undaunted, juggling with them to suit her own ends. And while she refuses to console the reader with a series of neat conclusions, neither is she tempted into the elegant play of much poststructuralist writing. I can only enthusiastically refer the reader to her extended preface to *Of Grammatology*[3] and the text itself, as well as her translation. It is a stunning work of elucidation and critique. In this preface she describes the connections between Derrida's work and that of Nietzsche, Freud and Heidegger. She also clarifies Derrida's critique of Barthes and Lévi-Strauss, before going on to outline the method of deconstruction itself. As a final note, Gayatri discusses the work of translation, which she sees as not so much a flawless or accurate reproduction, but rather an extension, or rewriting, of something which was never an 'original'.

Two other points are worth commenting on. As a black woman working in an overwhelmingly white environment, Gayatri adamantly refuses to claim marginality. None the less the experience of being black does lend an urgency to her desire to see the practical consequences of a particular mode of intellectual work. And then as a teacher Gayatri insists, also, that in the seminar room new meanings outside those of the textbook, or, indeed, her own discourse as teacher, come into play. Both of these make it difficult to sustain a purely text-bound adherence to deconstruction.

In relation to the contents of the interview, Gayatri declined, in the discussion we had before the tape recorder was switched on, to comment on her impressions of Britain in 1984. She explained this in terms of a preference not to be drawn on the question of 'local colour'. But her avoidance of any form of intellectual tourism wasn't altogether unconnected with her quiet insistence on dislocating the centrality which many British intellectuals still assume they have in the international field. Her plea was for more modesty, as well as a greater degree of attentiveness and interest in those others who have had a minimal audience. Perhaps she was referring here to the continual lack of interest in translations, other than those coming from France, and the too easy complacency about knowing the politics of other European, as well as Third World countries which still characterizes much of British intellectual life. As Gayatri pointed out, left internationalism, with its cycle of enthusiasms, is often not so far removed from colonialist benevolence. We are still tempted when we look at the so-called Third World, to drop the complexity with which we view our immediate environment. We regard this 'other' as a unity, a transparent realism (in grainy black and white). Homi Bhabha has developed this argument in his excellent piece in *Screen* magazine,[4] one that also deserves a wider audience. Bhabha poses this realist gaze as the complement of the desire for exoticism sought out and therefore found in the Third World. Bhabha's essay could be extended. The left and the women's movement have also participated in the search for the pleasurable exoticism which *partially* makes it possible to begin to deal with the terrible enormity of the legacies of colonialism and imperialism. And these popular fantasies often fulfil deeper social needs. The left in West Germany has embraced Third World struggles as an alternative to a political situation in their own country which has seemed so rigidly stabilized, as a result of postwar reconstruction, consumerism, and everything else we associate with the German economic miracle. There was also the desire to expunge the legacy of their fathers and, alongside all of this, the allure of the 'dark' races. It is these themes which Gayatri, towards the end of the interview, seeks to question.

Angela McRobbie I came across your article 'French feminism in an international frame' almost three years ago and since then I've read it several times. Partly this was because of its broad intellectual sweep, and partly because of its strongly political focus. I was both surprised and excited by its conclusion (although of course it is not really a conclusion). Especially where you pull together all the strands you've been working with around the notions of pleasure and the female body.

Gayatri Chakravorty Spivak That article was very important to me because it helped bring together a lot of things that had in fact already come together in my intellectual and practical life, although I hadn't realized it. I can tell it in a kind of story. Two prestigious American journals, *Critical Inquiry* and *Yale French Studies*, simultaneously asked me to write about French feminism. And I thought, 'Isn't it strange that I should have become spokeswoman for French high feminism, what's going on here?' So, to *Critical Inquiry*, I said that what I really wanted to do was to translate a piece of revolutionary Bengali feminist fiction (my native language is Bengali), and that I would write an introduction for it. They said quite properly that they didn't take fiction but would give me a chance. To *YFS* I suggested talking about my predicament as a spokeswoman for French feminism in the United States. Perhaps it's a moving article because it articulates a real change in my life. Since then I've been trying to work out seriously (and not just emotionally, though one is never very far away from the affects in a project like this), how literary criticism (because that is my discipline) and more, feminist literary criticism, can be placed with a critique of imperialism. Not just imperialism in the nineteenth-century sense, but as it was displaced into neo-colonialism and the international division of labour. I've been concerned with how critics of colonialist discourse forget that it's at work now, but then also how, when one looks at, let's call it racism, in the contemporary context in the First World, one forgets that its history looked a little bit different in the nineteenth century. For me 'Feminism', the movement with a proper name, gets caught within a double bind between the two. That is the direction my work has taken.

123

AMcR It's still difficult for us here to get to grips with the American left. Despite the number of journals that are available, periodicals like *Monthly Review, Signs, Feminist Studies* as well as the more theoretical *Diacritics, October, Social Text, Camera Obscura* and *Yale French Studies*, we rarely get much of a sense about where it all comes from. We don't know about the institutions, the practices and the politics which are behind these publications. The same goes for the highly successful fiction of black American writers like Alice Walker, Toni Cade Bambara and Maya Angelou. Has, for example, poststructuralism had much impact on the intellectual left stage?

GCS I think the scene has changed in the last three years. There is now a good deal of effort to see the impact of both French structuralism and poststructuralism. The American left is a complex phenomenon and rather easy to trivialize. It is marked by the fact that it has no serious national political arena and that every attempt at carving out such a space reduces itself to social democracy. Given this, the most appropriate answer to your question has to be given in terms of isolated groups and single figures. Thus I draw attention to the influence of Foucault on the intellectual left, as shown by, say, the *GRIP*[5] project. Edward Said combines a critique of imperialism with a critical reworking of Gramsci and Foucault. The work of Fredric Jameson and his students (such as Tom Lewis) attempts to focus on questions raised by deconstruction and Lacanian psychoanalysis. Younger scholars such as Michael Ryan, Andrew Parker and Satya Mohanty reinscribe Marxism by way of deconstruction. Outside of literary Marxism, the only significant figure combining poststructuralism and Marxism is Stanley Aronowitz.

But within Marxist feminism the impact of French structuralism has not been very significant. There the force of the ideology of humanism (feminism as revolutionary humanism) is still hegemonic. The most emancipatory 'critical' intelligence here is still the Frankfurt School, and a brilliant single figure there is Nancy Hartsock.

AMcR As you know, much of the recent work of radical politics and social movements has been one of recovery. That is, bringing to the surface and into visibility those who have been hidden from history. For women, black people and others, this has frequently been articulated in terms of finding a voice, discovering an identity, seeking out an authentic sense of oneself, and helping others to do the same thing. Much of the structuralist and poststructuralist project, however, is opposed to all notions of the self, the whole person, or the constituted subject. How can one reconcile these two movements, and is it a problem when one is working around issues of how a people came to be absolutely subjected?

GCS Yes, I think it should be a problem, especially within the bastion of polycentric activism. Because there is a real danger in thinking that one can easily graduate into a critique of the sovereign subject. But that said, when I was concentrating more strongly on Marxist feminism I was trying to cope with this question through the strategic use of essentialism. I have found that it has been helpful for a lot of people to think in this way. It comes back to me from the collectivity over and over again, that anti-essentialism is equally as fetishized as essentialism itself. The idea that you can have clean anti-essentialist hands, is nonsense if you take essentialism or transcendentalism as only a moment in a whole spectrum of things... Derrida touches on this in the thought of *minimal* idealization... when idealization is of course, by definition maximal. So once you begin selectively to use idealization, empiricism, transcendental-ism, essentialism, as positions promised within an awareness of the limits of (self-) positioning – individual – collective – then you can see them to be strategically effective. This offers a more practical take on poststructur-alism than the kind of negative metaphysics that is nervous about essen-tialism always crouching around the corner.

It is only such a negative metaphysics that would oppose 'all notions of the self, the whole person or the constituted subject'. I am more interested in that aspect of poststructuralism that would situate the subject (on another level of ideological abstraction, the self or the real person) as the *effect* of an orchestrated cut within a much broader text. This would allow us to see that those 'collectivities' or 'individuals' who were made to cathect the space of an 'other' that would consolidate the hegem-onic self, relate to the critique of the sovereign subject obliquely.

To take up the second part of your question – the critique of imperial-ism is not identical, and cannot be identical, with the critique of racism. Nor is our own effort to see the identification of the constitution of race within First World countries, identical with the problem of capitalist territorial imperialism in the context of the eighteenth and nineteenth centuries. Just as race is not chromatism... that is determined only by skin colour... imperialism is not just race. Within the specific imperialist theatres I am concentrating on, these places were already inscribed in a kind of proto-racism, and they were then reinscribed. They were never 'virgin territory', and I use that term advisedly, with reference to racist discourse. This needs to be disclosed carefully if the critique of imperial-ism is to have anything other than euphonic value. Just as it must be disclosed that the operations of racism in the First World today are by no means homogenous.

AMcR There has been some discussion here about the consequence which the kinds of critique offered by, say, Foucault or Derrida, have for Marxism. Foucault frequently seems to be eliding what might be described

125

as left positions, as though this allows him to work at once more strategically and to move densely around those issues which interest him. And Derrida apparently commented that his own work is not inconsistent with Marxism. How would you place yourself amidst the debates as to what of Marxism might be rescued, or indeed what it means today to be a Marxist?

GCS I'm not in the same place as Derrida or Foucault. I'm not coming from the French context, though of course I'm deeply influenced by both these figures. The problems with Marxism in France stem from, among other things, the existence of two left parties, an uneasy relationship with the Soviet Union, and then what Mike Davis has described as late American imperialism: the period from '53–'73. As for me, I don't have to think about holding on to Marxism in that situation in that specific way. The project of the left in West Bengal – it has a United Front government – already reflects an uneasy balance between something near to the Eurocommunist model, but within the context of the critique of western Marxism from the peasant and guerrilla phenomena, and, at the same time, the great example of the rewriting of revolution in China, on the other side. Within that context I'm committed to saving Marxism from its European provenance, where it remains useful and where almost nothing else is practically useful. I am suspicious of the great narrative of Marx anyway, the mode of production narrative. It's so closely tied to all kinds of imperialist notions because Marx was himself writing in the nineteenth century. My problems are not, therefore, with saving Marxism over post-structuralism. I am a bricoleur, I use what comes to hand.

In relation to West Bengal I have no role. But if as a student or reader (in the broadest possible sense) of the politico-sexual text, the other side makes of me a token, I won't throw that away. Being a token in the superpower of the twentieth century, in the US university system, gives me a kind of clowning 'leadership' role. Otherwise, to focus on small things, to look around and intervene at random, as you put it earlier, is I think the best way for the academic intellectual to stay honourable and alive in the social world. I am deeply suspicious of colleagues who periodically produce formulas for saving the world. Nor do I want to *distance* myself from Marxism or feminism. At a recent conference on nuclear criticism run by *Diacritics*, one woman said that I was talking in a way that was inimical to US feminism. 'Look,' I said, 'I am a white liberal feminist, my skin colour may not be white, my avowed politics may not be liberal, but what has produced me? It would be an incredible luxury to say that I have not been enabled by white liberal feminism, white socialist feminism.'

What I would say to socialist feminist sisters (we were also talking about this earlier), is simply to put a situation-specific adjective, 'British' or 'American', or whatever, in front of Marxism, when they are describing what they are doing or writing. The real critic is not so much interested in distancing him- or herself, as in being vigilant. To universalize the local is a very dangerous thing and no good practice comes out of it. That's why identifying race issues within the First World, with imperialism or neo-colonialism, is a version of the same thing; it should develop this process of criticism from the inside.

AMcR Does the emphasis on working from within, on considering the local in its historical context, allow one to get away from the search for unity (theoretical, political . . .) and does it also offer, do you think, greater grounds for a kind of optimism?

GCS Working simply on this basis can lead to seeing the local as the text, and history as the context. That too is deeply problematic. Within the cultural politics that operate just now, there is always the desire to conflate the local and the individual. This too calls for vigilance. Sometimes it can be elided by insisting that there is nothing like a 'big solution'. I'm optimistic, but because I take this stance that there are no big solutions, I make people suspicious who want to see me as some kind of nihilist. But from the point of view of the so-called Third World, I'm suspicious of the production of elegant solutions because: (a) it is through these that we have been betrayed, and (b) we have been paying the price of that elegance. We have been defined as the deviation in the equation, that which the solution has to compensate for. I'm not offering any solutions. What I do offer is vigilance.

AMcR Derrida, and after him Lyotard, Deleuze and Guattari, make much of the notion of 'play' as though, ironically, the vigilance you describe can be achieved through some kind of dissembling. I think they also stress plurality as better to think with than the old and much over-used duality. Can fluidity and the element of play find a place within your present interests?

GCS It's not really possible to think of the other side of the world with that kind of gaiety. Gaiety is situational. Alliance politics, this 'rhizome' politics,[6] is only possible within socialized capital because there the lines of communication, even within the unemployed, the oppressed, the Euro-worker, have already been established, and they are working even when they are not working. However, when we are talking about the other side, we are conscious of the international division of labour, of international subcontracting, and in this situation those lines do not exist. The politics of play, or of rhizomes, may be valid enough within the First World but not when it's called planetary or global. If play is not identified with

127

game-playing or playfulness in the narrow sense, one might suggest that that other side, questioning the history of nationality, is the place to play, but the play does not resemble the vagaries of western versions of what used to be called decadence, on the same chain of displacement that today produces postmodernism.

AMcR I'm not sure about how to push this strand of thought. But if we go back for a moment to bricolage and to dissembling, or playing from within with the signs which give order and meaning to the society around us, then I have to say that some of this 'writing on the body' which we talked briefly about in connection with Dick Hebdige's[7] work, gives me a great deal of pleasure. The way, for example, that young girls today in Britain refuse the orthodox signs of femininity not by seeking after a kind of state of naturalness or purity, which feminism for a long time was linked with, but rather by jumbling up the neat equations and making them almost indecipherable to patriarchy.

GCS But aren't these phenomena also localized? When I think of the women in the so-called Third World countries for whom *I* am foreign, these counter-culture movements became another part of the processes of hegemony. And when you talk of this writing on the body, and I'm not being pathetic, this is not a tear-jerking remark, but I can tell it in terms of my home town where more than 300,000 people live on the streets. The little kids have to shit in the gutter because there is no other place. And when you look at the colour of the shit you know whether they are going to last or not. That is a political bodily inscription which makes the inside-outside indeterminate. This kind of stuff is a lot different.

AMcR I have two final questions. The first is rather an obvious one to ask you. It's what to do with the category of experience and how, by all the structuralist and poststructuralist accounts, it is merely an effect of discourse, or the text within whose discourse it is inscribed.

GCS There are a number of points to be made here and so if you don't mind I will give you a rather long-winded reply. What comes up here is the positionality of the subject. And there is no doubt that post-structuralism can really radicalize the old Marxist fetishization of consciousness. But then all of this has also been recuperated by disciplinary formations. Discourse analysis has become the privileging of language, and the ones who are talking about the critique of the subject are the ones who have had the luxury of a subject.

And then there is also the question as to what is our identity? In everyday life our identity, that is our ID, at the important level, has already been undermined and deconstructed. Our ID cards, without which we can do nothing, carry a complicated set of numbers. So that the deconstruction of the subject to mathemes, that has already happened.

Then there are those who have been obliged to cathect the state of the other. Historically they have always occupied the position of the subject in the lower case, they have been subjected so that the other subject can be sovereign. In these cases the question of the strategic use of the category of experience is very different and that is situational. And so I can quite see that in a certain situation I would go along with a white woman speaking against white phallocentrism as long as it is not universalized. I have many enthusiastic and thoughtful white students for whom, always, the final arbitrator is concrete experience. And I have to tell them that the whole hierarchical taxonomy of concrete experience which has been regarded as completely valid for so long is exactly what has to be got under. At the same time one cannot use that as a terrorism on the people who were obliged to cathect the place of the other, those whose experiences were not quite 'experience'.

AMcR Again this question is tentative. I'm throwing it out as a kind of prompt. It's also one which has fuelled my own interest recently. If we are in the business of talking, inevitably, about images or representations, then one could say that the touchstone for horror and suffering in Europe and America, in modern times, has been the profusion of images, diaries, and documentation of the Holocaust ... the gas chambers, and the forced extermination of the Jews. How does this strike the Third World person? Are these images and experiences which serve as a symbolic dividing line between the First and Third Worlds?

GCS In answering that, can I quote from an article that I recently wrote for a US journal? It goes:

> I would like it to be understood that I do of course think that the eventuality of a nuclear holocaust must be resisted in every possible way. Having said that with complete conviction, I would like to consider for a moment a certain problem that the nuclear issue, the representation of the nuclear issue, serves. It has seemed to me, as it has seemed to other critics of imperialism, that the liberal West has a tendency to bestow great proper names to events of human suffering and thus dole out a quota system, a ranked quota system of moral outrage which allows it to repress the anonymous and myriad chronicles of suffering daily perpetrated by imperialism and neo-colonialism.
>
> In our own time the two most powerful proper names are the Holocaust of the Second World War and Stalin. The nuclear

129

holocaust has now been added to the list. One of the strongest appeals of the anti-nuclear movement is that in the face of the nuclear threat we are all equal. This would no doubt be true in the event of a nuclear war. But *while the resistance mobilizes*, this appeal allows the liberal humanists often politically committed to the social (if not psycho-sexual) relations of society, to forget that some of us are perpetrators and others victims. By generating a spurious feeling of equality for this section of the West, by far the largest majority of 'concerned adults' this name for the worst possible human suffering *can* once again *permit* a repression of the anonymous quotidian and continual holocaust of international exploitation.

As for sections of the First World left, or anti-humanist post-Marxist radicals in the First World, who are involved in the anti-nuclear movement, I think John Keane's suggestion that they should recognize themselves as calling for a 'democratic civil society against the State', would be a powerful move. As an Asian, with long experience of the co-optation of religion for political purposes, and with the scandal of Israel on our western shore, I am not enthusiastic about the privileging of the Holocaust as Chosen Suffering.

I have a comparable resistance to focusing on imperialism as Chosen Suffering. My paper at the Sociology of Literature Conference at Essex, with the somewhat unwieldy title 'Overdeterminations of Imperialism: David Ochterlony and the Ranee of Sirmoor' takes this up. There I am critical of the binary opposition colonizer/colonized. I try to examine the heterogeneity of 'colonial power', and to disclose the complicity of the two poles of that opposition as it constitutes the disciplinary enclave of the critique of imperialism.

This last quote ended our interview. Not really an end because it set other processes of transcribing, editing and corresponding, in motion. Some months later I'm struck by the incisiveness of Gayatri's comments, and I am reminded of the curious role of the interviewer. In the drafts which followed the first transcription, both Gayatri and myself slowly edited out the spaces in between... the little comments, the domestic details, the paragraphs which at the time seemed rightly to give priority to the *I* as the perpetrator of experience, but which later were equally disposable. None of these is such a mysterious process. The interview is no more a pure example of unconditional 'speaking out' than any other form of social exchange. It is certainly not the quick easy mode of publication commonly assumed. How well it has worked here is for the reader to assess. Perhaps its real value will depend on the extent to which it encourages further re-excavations on the critique of imperialism.

This interview first appeared in *Block* 10 (1985): 5–9.

NOTES

1 Gayatri Chakravorty Spivak, 'French feminism in an international frame', in Gayatri Chakravorty Spivak, *In Other Worlds: Essays in Cultural Politics*, London, Routledge, 1988, pp. 134–54; Gayatri Chakravorty Spivak, 'The letter as cutting edge', ibid.: pp. 3–15; Gayatri Chakravorty Spivak, 'Finding feminist readings – Dante, Yeats', ibid.: pp. 15–30.
2 Spivak, 'French feminism', op. cit.
3 Jacques Derrida, *Of Grammatology*, trans. Gayatri Chakravorty Spivak, Baltimore, MD and London, Johns Hopkins University Press, 1976.
4 Homi Bhabha, 'The other question – the stereotype and colonial discourse, *Screen*, November-December 1983, vol. 24, pp. 19–35.
5 GRIP: Group for Research on the Institutionalization and Professionalization of Literary Study (Professor J. Sosnosky, Department of English, University of Miami, Oxford, OH).
6 Gilles Deleuze and Félix Guattari, 'Rhizome', *Ideology and Consciousness*, 'Power and Desire', Spring 1981, no. 8, pp. 42–53.
7 Dick Hebdige, *Subculture: The Meaning of Style*, London, Routledge, 1979.

Part III

YOUTH, MEDIA, POSTMODERNITY

8

SECOND-HAND DRESSES AND THE ROLE OF THE RAGMARKET

Miss Brooke had that kind of beauty which seems to be thrown into relief by poor dress. Her hand and wrist were so finely formed that she could wear sleeves not less bare of style than those in which the Blessed Virgin appeared to Italian painters.

(George Eliot, *Middlemarch*)

She's dressed in old European clothes, scraps of brocade, out-of-date old suits, old curtains, odd oddments, old models, moth-eaten old fox furs, old otterskins, that's her kind of beauty, tattered, chill, plaintive and in exile, everything too big, and yet it looks marvellous. Her clothes are loose, she's too thin, nothing fits yet it looks marvellous. She's made in such a way, face and body, that anything that touches her shares immediately and infallibly in her beauty.

(Marguerite Duras, *The Lover*)

INTRODUCTION

Several attempts have been made recently to understand 'retro-style'. These have all taken as their starting-point that accelerating tendency in the 1980s to ransack history for key items of dress, in a seemingly eclectic and haphazard manner. Some have seen this as part of the current vogue for nostalgia while others have interpreted it as a way of bringing history into an otherwise ahistorical present. This chapter will suggest that second-hand style or 'vintage dress' must be seen within the broader context of postwar subcultural history. It will pay particular attention to the existence of an entrepreneurial infrastructure within these youth cultures and to the opportunities which second-hand style has offered young people, at a time of recession, for participating in fashion.

Most of the youth subcultures of the postwar period have relied on second-hand clothes found in jumble sales and ragmarkets as the raw material for the creation of style. In the early 1980s the magazine *iD* developed a kind of *vox pop* of street style which involved stopping

135

young people and asking them to itemize what they were wearing, where they had got it and for how much. Since then many of the weekly and monthly fashion publications have followed suit, with the result that this has now become a familiar feature of the magazine format. However, the act of buying and the processes of looking and choosing still remain relatively unexamined in the more academic field of cultural analysis.

One reason for this is that shopping has been considered a feminine activity. Youth sociologists have looked mainly at the activities of adolescent boys and young men and their attention has been directed to those areas of experience which have a strongly masculine image. Leisure spheres which involve the wearing and displaying of clothes have been thoroughly documented, yet the hours spent seeking them out on Saturday afternoons continue to be overlooked. Given the emphasis on street culture or on public peer-group activities, this is perhaps not surprising, but although shopping is usually regarded as a private activity, it is also simultaneously a public one and in the case of the markets and second-hand stalls it takes place in the street. This is particularly important for girls and young women because in other contexts their street activities are still curtailed in contrast to those of their male peers. This fact has been commented upon by many feminist writers but the various pleasures of shopping have not been similarly engaged with.[1] Indeed, shopping has tended to be subsumed under the category of domestic labour with the attendant connotations of drudgery and exhaustion. Otherwise it has been absorbed into consumerism where women and girls are seen as having a particular role to play. Contemporary feminism has been slow to challenge the early 1970s orthodoxy which saw women as slaves to consumerism. Only Erica Carter's work has gone some way towards dislodging the view that to enjoy shopping is to be passively feminine and incorporated into a system of false needs.[2]

Looking back at the literature of the late 1970s on punk, it seems strange that so little attention was paid to the selling of punk, and the extent to which shops like the 'Sex' shop run by Malcolm McLaren and Vivienne Westwood functioned also as meeting places where the customers and those behind the counter got to know each other and met up later in the pubs and clubs. In fact, ragmarkets and second-hand shops have played the same role up and down the country, indicating that there is more to buying and selling subcultural style than the simple exchange of cash for goods. Sociologists of the time perhaps ignored this social dimension because to them the very idea that style could be purchased over the counter went against the grain of those analyses which saw the adoption, for example, of punk style as an act of creative defiance far removed from the mundane act of buying. The role of McLaren and Westwood was also downgraded for the similar reason that punk was seen as a kind of collective creative impulse. To focus on a designer and

136

an art-school entrepreneur would have been to undermine the 'purity' or 'authenticity' of the subculture. The same point can be made in relation to the absence of emphasis on buying subcultural products. What is found instead is an interest in those moments where the bought goods and items are transformed to subvert their original or intended meanings. In these accounts the act of buying disappears into that process of transformation. Ranked below these magnificent gestures, the more modest practices of buying and selling have remained women's work and have been of little interest to those concerned with youth cultural resistance.[3]

The literature on youth culture provides by no means the only point of entry to the question of second-hand fashion. It retains a usefulness, however, in its emphasis on the wider social and historical factors which frame youth cultural expressions and in the emphasis on the meaning and significance of the smallest and apparently most trivial of gestures and movements. Second-hand style has, in fact, a long history in British culture, but it was Peter Blake's sleeve for the Beatles' *Sgt Pepper* album which marked the entrance of anachronistic dressing into the mainstream of the pop and fashion business. In their luridly coloured military uniforms, the Beatles were at this point poised midway between the pop establishment and hippy psychedelia. The outfits, along with John Lennon's 'granny' spectacles and the other symbols of 'flower power' depicted on the cover, comprised a challenge to the grey conformity of male dress and an impertinent appropriation of official regalia for civilian anti-authoritarian, hedonistic wear.

Military uniforms were first found alongside the overalls and great-coats in army surplus stores and on second-hand rails of shops such as 'Granny Takes a Trip', in the King's Road. Metal-rimmed glasses added a further element to that theme in the counter-culture suggesting an interest in the old, the used, the overtly cheap and apparently unstylish. Standard male glasses had been until then black and horn-rimmed. National Health Service gold-coloured rims retained the stigma of poverty and the mark of parental will imposed on unwilling children. Lennon's cheap, shoddy specs became one of his trade marks. At the same time they came to represent one of the most familiar anti-materialist strands in hippy culture. They suggested a casual disregard for obvious signs of wealth, and a disdain for 'the colour of money'.

Stuart Hall saw in this 'hippy movement' an 'identification with the poor', as well as a disavowal of conventional middle-class smartness.[4] His comment touches on issues which are still at the heart of any analysis of second-hand style because the relationship to real poverty, or instead to particular stylized images of poverty, remains central. At an early point in its evolution the hippy subculture denounced material wealth and sought some higher reality, expressing this choice externally through a whole variety of old and second-hand clothes. None the less, these clothes

137

were chosen and worn as a distinctive style and this style was designed to mark out a distance both from 'straight' and conventional dress, and from the shabby greyness of genuine poverty. A similar thread runs right through the history of postwar second-hand style. This has raised questions engaged with at a journalistic level by Tom Wolfe and then more recently by Angela Carter.[5] She asks whether rummaging through jumble sales makes light of those who search in need and not through choice? Does the image of the middle-class girl 'slumming it' in rags and ribbons merely highlight social class differences? Tom Wolfe poked fun at the *arriviste* young middle classes of America in the 1960s who were so well off that they could afford to look back and play around with the *idea* of looking poor. Almost twenty years later Angela Carter made the same point in relation to the 'ragamuffin look' favoured by post-punk girls, an image which held no attraction, she claimed, for working-class girls whose role-model was Princess Diana. Each of these writers sees in second-hand style a kind of unconsciously patronizing response to those who 'dress down' because they have to. It is an act of unintended class condescension.

While it is still the case that those who possess 'cultural capital' can risk looking poor and unkempt while their black and working-class counterparts dress up to counter the assumption of low status, there have been crucial social shifts which confuse this simple divide. Not all students in the 1980s are white, affluent and middle-class. Nor is it any longer possible to pose the world of street style or second-hand style against that of either high fashion or high street fashion. A whole range of factors have intervened to blur these divisions. For example, the street markets have themselves come into prominence and have been subjected to greater commercial pressure, while high street retailing has been forced to borrow from the tactics of the street trader. The sharpest illustration of these overlaps and cross-fertilizations lies, at present, in the wardrobes of the so-called young professionals, male and female. The new items which now make up his or her wardrobe were almost, to the last sock or stocking, discovered, restored and worn by the young men and women who worked in, or hung around, Camden Market and a whole series of provincial ragmarkets, in the late 1970s and early 1980s.

The ladies' suit announced as the high fashion item of summer 1988, is a reworking of the early 1960s Chanel suit worn by Jackie Kennedy and other celebrities. A bouclé wool version in pink and orange can be found on the rails of Next this season, but it is not simply a 1980s revamp of the Chanel original, because it was in the late 1970s, as part of her challenge to conventional femininity, that Poly Styrene first wore this most 'unflattering' of outfits, the ladies' two-piece found in the jumble sale or ragmarket in abundance for 50p. Exactly the same process can be seen at work in the recent 'respectabilization' of the classic gents' lightweight poplin raincoat. Designed by Jasper Conran and retailing at £350 in expensive department stores, with the cuffs turned up to reveal a quality striped lining, these were first found by great numbers of second-hand shoppers on the rails at Camden or even cheaper in the charity shops. Finally, there is the so-called 'tea dress', heavily advertised in the summers of both 1987 and 1988 by Laura Ashley, Next, Miss Selfridge and Warehouse. These are new versions of the high-quality 1930s and 1940s printed crêpes sought out by girls and young women for many years, for the fall of their skirts and for their particularly feminine cut.

The parasitism of the major fashion labels on the post-punk subcultures is a theme which will be returned to later in this chapter. While fashion currently trades on the nostalgia boom, it also, more specifically, re-works the already recycled goods found in the street markets. It produces new and much more expensive versions of these originals in often poor-quality fabrics and attempts to sell these styles, on an unprecedented scale, to a wider section of the population than those who wander round the ragmarkets. To understand more precisely the mechanisms through which this predatory relation reproduces itself, it would be necessary to examine questions which are beyond the scope of this chapter. In the concluding section they will be referred to briefly. They include the dependence of the fashion industry on media 'hype' and the consequent prominence of the 'designer' fresh out of college and surviving, in fact, on the Enterprise Allowance Scheme but none the less featured regularly in *Elle*; the huge explosion of the media industries in the 1980s and their dependence on an endless flow of fashion images again on an unprecedented scale; and finally, with this, a broader process sometimes described as 'the aestheticization of culture'. This refers to the media expansion mentioned above, and with it the renunciation by some young people of the grey repertoire of jobs offered in the traditional fields of youth opportunities, and their preference for more self-expressive 'artistic' choices... part-time or self-employed work which offers the possibility of creativity, control, job satisfaction and perhaps even the promise of fame and fortune in the multi-media world of the image or the written word.

THE ROLE OF THE RAGMARKET

Second-hand style owes its existence to those features of consumerism which are characteristic of contemporary society. It depends, for example, on the creation of a surplus of goods whose use-value is not expended when their first owners no longer want them. They are then revived, even in their senility, and enter into another cycle of consumption. House clearances also contribute to the mountain of bric-à-brac, jewellery, clothing and furniture which are the staple of junk and second-hand shops and stalls. But not all junk is used a second time around. Patterns of taste and discrimination shape the desires of second-hand shoppers as much as they do those who prefer the high street or the fashion show-room. And those who work behind the stalls and counters are skilled in choosing their stock with a fine eye for what will sell. Thus although there seems to be an evasion of the mainstream, with its mass-produced goods and marked-up prices, the 'subversive consumerism' of the ragmar-ket is in practice highly selective in what is offered and what, in turn, is purchased. There is in this milieu an even more refined economy of taste at work. For every single piece rescued and restored, a thousand are consigned to oblivion. The sources which are raided for 'new' second-hand ideas are frequently old films, old art photographs, 'great' novels, documentary footage and textual material. The apparent democracy of the market, from which nobody is excluded on the grounds of cost, is tempered by the very precise tastes and desires of the second-hand search-ers. Second-hand style continually emphasizes its distance from second-hand clothing.

The London markets and those in other towns and cities up and down the country cater now for a much wider cross-section of the population. It is no longer a question of just the art students rubbing shoulders with the poor and the down-and-outs.[6] Unemployment has played a role in diversifying this clientele; so also have a number of other less immediately visible shifts and changes. Young single mothers, for example, who fall between the teen dreams of punk fashion and the reality of pushing a buggy through town on a wet afternoon, fit exactly with this new constitu-ency.[7] Markets have indeed become more socially diverse sites in the urban landscape. The Brick Lane area in London, for example, home to part of the Bangladeshi population settled in this country, attracts on a Sunday morning, young and old, black and white, middle-class and working-class shoppers as well as tourists and the curious browsers. It's not surprising that tourists include a market such as Brick Lane in their itinerary. In popular currency, street markets are taken to be reflective of the old and unspoilt, they are 'steeped in history' and are thus particularly expressive of the town or region.

The popularity of these urban markets also resides in their celebration of what seem to be pre-modern modes of exchange. They offer an oasis of cheapness, where every market day is a 'sale'. They point back in time to an economy unaffected by cheque cards, credit cards and even set prices. Despite the lingering connotations of wartime austerity, the market today promotes itself in the language of natural freshness (for food and dairy produce) or else in the language of curiosity, discovery and heritage (for clothes, trinkets and household goods). There is, of course, a great deal of variety in the types of market found in different parts of the country. In London there is a distinction between those markets modelled on the genuine fleamarkets, which tend to attract the kind of young people who flock each weekend to Camden Lock, and those which are more integrated into a neighbourhood, providing it with fruit, vegetables and household items. The history of these more traditional street markets is already well documented. They grew up within the confines of a rapidly expanding urban economy and played a vital role in dressing (in mostly second-hand clothes), and feeding the urban working classes, who did not have access to the department stores, grocers, or other retail outlets which catered for the upper and middle classes. As Phil Cohen has shown, such markets came under the continual surveillance of the urban administrators and authorities who were concerned with 'policing the working-class city'.[8] The street markets were perceived by them not only as interrupting the flow of traffic and therefore the speed of urban development, but also as hindering the growth of those sorts of shops which would bring in valuable revenue from rates. These were seen as dangerous places, bringing together unruly elements who were already predisposed towards crime and delinquency; a predominantly youthful population of costermongers had to be brought into line with the labour discipline which already existed on the factory floor.

The street market functioned, therefore, as a daytime social meeting place as much as a place for transactions of money and goods. It lacked the impersonality of the department stores and thrived instead on the values of familiarity, community and personal exchange. This remains the case today. Wherever immigrant groups have arrived and set about trying to earn a living in a largely hostile environment a local service economy in the form of a market has grown up. These offer some opportunities for those excluded from employment, and they also offer some escape from the monotony of the factory floor. A drift, in the 1970s and 1980s, into the micro-economy of the street market is one sign of the dwindling opportunities in the world of real work. There are now more of these stalls carrying a wider range of goods than before in most of the market places in the urban centres. There has also been a diversification into the world of new technology, with stalls offering cut-price digital alarms, watches, personal hi-fis, videotapes, cassettes, 'ghetto-blasters' and cameras. The hidden economy of work is also supplemented here by the provision of goods obtained illegally and sold rapidly at rock-bottom prices.

This general expansion coincides, however, with changing patterns in urban consumerism and with attempts on the part of mainstream retailers to participate in an unexpected boom. In the inner cities the bustling markets frequently breathe life and colour into otherwise desolate blighted areas. This, in turn, produces an incentive for the chain stores to reinvest, and in places such as Dalston Junction in Hackney, and Chapel Market in Islington, the redevelopment of shopping has taken place along these lines, with Sainsbury's, Boots the Chemist and others, updating and expanding their services. The stores flank the markets, which in turn line the pavements, and the consumer is drawn into both kinds of shopping simultaneously. In the last few years many major department stores have redesigned the way in which their stock is displayed in order to create the feel of a market place. In the 'Top Shop' basement in Oxford Street, for example, there is a year-round sale. The clothes are set out in chaotic abundance. The rails are crushed up against each other and packed with stock, which causes the customers to push and shove their way through. This intentionally hectic atmosphere is heightened by the disc jockey who cajoles the shoppers between records to buy at an even more frenzied pace.

Otherwise, in those regions where the mainstream department stores are still safely located on the other side of town, the traditional street market continues to seduce its customers with its own unique atmosphere. Many of these nowadays carry only a small stock of second-hand clothes. Instead, there are rails of 'seconds' or cheap copies of high street fashions made from starched fabric which, after a couple of washes, are ready for the dustbin. Bales of sari material lie stretched out on counters next to those displaying makeup and shampoo for black women. Reggae and funk music blare across the heads of shoppers from the record stands, and hot food smells drift far up the road. In the Ridley Road market in Hackney the hot bagel shop remains as much a sign of the originally Jewish population as the eel pie stall reflects traditional working-class taste. Unfamiliar fruits create an image of colour and profusion on stalls sagging under their weight. By midday on Fridays and at weekends the atmosphere is festive. Markets like these retain something of the pre-industrial gathering. For the crowd of shoppers and strollers the tempo symbolizes time rescued from that set aside for labour, and the market seems to celebrate its own pleasures. Differences of age, sex, class and ethnic background take on a positive quality of social diversity. The mode of buying is leisurely and unharassed, in sharp contrast to the Friday afternoon tensions around the checkout till in the supermarket.

Similar features can be seen at play in markets such as Camden Lock on Saturday and Sunday afternoons. Thousands of young people block Camden's streets so that only a trickle of traffic can get through. The same groups and the streams of punk tourists can be seen each week, joined by older shoppers and those who feel like a stroll in the sun. Young people go there to see and be seen if for no other reason than that fashion and style invariably look better worn than they do on the rails or in the shop windows. Here it is possible to see how items are combined with each other to create a total look. Hairstyles, shoes, skirts and 'hold-up' stockings; all of these can be taken in at a glance. In this context shopping is like being on holiday. The whole point is to amble

142

and look, to pick up goods and examine them before putting them back. Public-school girls mingle with doped-out punks, ex-hippies hang about behind their Persian rug stalls as though they have been there since 1967, while more youthful entrepreneurs trip over themselves to make a quick sale.

SUBCULTURAL ENTREPRENEURS

The entrepreneurial element, crucial to an understanding of street markets and second-hand shops, has been quite missing from most subcultural analysis. The vitality of street markets today owes much to the hippy counter-culture of the late 1960s. It was this which put fleamarkets firmly back on the map. Many of those which had remained dormant for years in London, Amsterdam, or Berlin, were suddenly given a new lease of life. In the years following the end of the Second World War the thriving black markets gradually gave way to the fleamarkets which soon signalled only the bleakness of goods discarded. For the generation whose memories had not been blunted altogether by the dizzy rise of postwar consumerism, markets for old clothes and jumble sales in the 1960s remained a terrifying reminder of the stigma of poverty, the shame of ill-fitting clothing, and the fear of disease through infestation, rather like buying a second-hand bed.

Hippy preferences for old fur coats, crêpe dresses and army great-coats, shocked the older generation for precisely this reason. But they were not acquired merely for their shock value. Those items favoured by the hippies reflected an interest in pure, natural and authentic fabrics and a repudiation of the man-made synthetic materials found in high street fashion. The pieces of clothing sought out by hippy girls tended to be antique lace petticoats, pure silk blouses, crêpe dresses, velvet skirts and pure wool 1940s-styled coats. In each case these conjured up a time when the old craft values still prevailed and when one person saw through his or her production from start to finish. In fact, the same items had also won the attention of the hippies' predecessors, in the 'beat culture' of the early 1950s. They too looked for ways of by-passing the world of ready-made clothing. In the rummage sales of New York, for example, girls and women bought up the fur coats, satin dresses and silk blouses of the 1930s and 1940s middle classes. Worn in the mid-1950s, these issued a strong sexual challenge to the spick and span gingham-clad domesticity of the moment.

By the late 1960s, the hippy culture was a lot larger and much better off than the beats who had gone before them. It was also politically informed in the sense of being determined to create an alternative society. This subculture was therefore able to develop an extensive semi-entrepreneurial network which came to be known as the counter-culture.

This was by no means a monolithic enterprise. It stretched in Britain from hippy businesses such as Richard Branson's Virgin Records and Harvey Goldsmith's Promotions to all the ventures which sprang up in most cities and towns, selling books, vegetarian food, incense, Indian smocks, sandals and so on. It even included the small art galleries, independent cinemas and the London listings magazine *Time Out*.

From the late 1960s onwards, accompanying this explosion of 'alternative' shops and restaurants were the small second-hand shops whose history is less familiar. These had names like 'Serendipity', 'Cobwebs', or 'Past Caring' and they brought together, under one roof, all those items which had to be discovered separately in the jumble sales or fleamarkets. These included flying jackets, safari jackets, velvet curtains (from which were made the first 'loon' pants) and 1920s flapper dresses. These second-hand goods provided students and others drawn to the subculture, with a cheaper and much more expansive wardrobe. (The two looks for girls which came to characterize this moment were the peasant 'ethnic' look and the 'crêpey' bohemian Bloomsbury look. The former later became inextricably linked with Laura Ashley and the latter with Biba, both mainstream fashion newcomers.) Gradually hippie couples moved into this second-hand market, just as they also moved into antiques. They rapidly picked up the skills of mending and restoring items and soon learned where the best sources for their stock were to be found. This meant scouring the country for out-of-town markets, making trips to Amsterdam to pick up the long leather coats and making weekly trips to the dry cleaners. The result was loyal customers, and if the young entrepreneurs were able to anticipate new demands from an even younger clientele, there were subsequent generations of punks, art students and others.

The presence of this entrepreneurial dynamic has rarely been acknowledged in most subcultural analysis. Those points at which subcultures offered the prospect of a career have warranted as little attention as the network of small-scale entrepreneurial activities which financed the counter-culture. This was an element, of course, vociferously disavowed within the hippy culture itself. Great efforts were made to disguise the role which money played in a whole number of exchanges, including those involving drugs. Selling goods and commodities came too close to 'selling out' for those at the heart of the subculture to feel comfortable about it. This was a stance reinforced by the sociologists who also saw consumerism within the counter-culture as a fall from grace, a lack of purity. They either ignored it, or else, employing the Marcusian notion of recuperation, attributed it to the intervention of external market forces.[9] It was the unwelcome presence of media and other commercial interests which, they claimed, laundered out the politics and reduced the alternative society to an endless rail of cheesecloth shirts.

There was some dissatisfaction, however, with this dualistic model of creative action followed by commercial reaction. Dick Hebdige and others have drawn attention to the problems of positing a raw and undiluted (and usually working-class) energy, in opposition to the predatory youth industries.[10] Such an argument discounted the local, promotional activities needed to produce a subculture in the first place. Clothes have to be purchased, bands have to find places to play, posters publicizing these concerts have to be put up . . . and so on. This all entails business and managerial skills. The fact that a spontaneous sexual division of labour seems to spring into being is only a reflection of those gender inequalities which are prevalent at a more general level in society. It is still much easier for girls to develop skills in those fields which are less contested by men than it is in those already occupied by them. Selling clothes, stage-managing at concerts, handing out publicity leaflets, or simply looking the part, are spheres in which a female presence somehow seems natural.[11]

While hippy style had run out of steam by the mid-1970s the alternative society merely jolted itself and rose to the challenge of punk. Many of those involved in selling records, clothes and even books, cropped their hair, had their ears pierced and took to wearing tight black trousers and Doc Marten boots. However, the conditions into which punk erupted and of which it was symptomatic for its younger participants were quite different from those which had cushioned the hippy explosion of the 1960s. Girls were certainly more visible and more vocal than they had been in the earlier subculture, although it is difficult to assess exactly how active they were in the do-it-yourself entrepreneurial practices which accompanied, and were part of, the punk phenomenon. Certainly the small independent record companies remained largely male, as did the journalists and even the musicians (though much was made of the angry femininity of Poly Styrene, the Slits, the Raincoats and others).

Punk was, first and foremost, cultural. Its self-expressions existed at the level of music, graphic design, visual images, style and the written word. It was therefore engaging with and making itself heard within the terrain of the arts and the mass media. Its point of entry into this field existed within the range of small-scale youth industries which were able to put the whole thing in motion. Fan magazines (fanzines) provided a training for new wave journalists, just as designing record sleeves for unknown punk bands offered an opportunity for keen young graphic designers. In the realm of style the same do-it-yourself ethic prevailed and the obvious place to start was the jumble sale or the local fleamarket. Although punk also marked a point at which boys and young men began to participate in fashion together, girls played a central role, not just in looking for the right clothes but also in providing their peers with a cheap and easily available supply of second-hand items. These included 1960s' cotton print 'shifts' like those worn by the girls in the Human League in the early

1980s (and in the summer of 1988 'high fashion' as defined by MaxMara and others), suedette sheepskin-styled jackets like that worn by Bob Dylan on his debut album sleeve (marking a moment in the early 1960s when he too aspired to a kind of 'lonesome traveller' hobo look), and many other similarly significant pieces.

This provision of services in the form of making available dress and clothing for would-be punks, art students and others on the fringe, was mostly participated in by lower middle-class art and fashion graduates who rejected the job opportunities available to them designing for British Home Stores or Marks & Spencer. It was a myth then, and it is still a myth now, that fashion houses are waiting to snap up the talent which emerges from the end-of-term shows each year. Apart from going abroad, most fashion students are, and were in the mid-1970s, faced with either going it alone with the help of the Enterprise Allowance Schemes (EAS), or else joining some major manufacturing company specializing in down-market mass-produced fashion. It is no surprise, then, that many, particularly those who wanted to retain some artistic autonomy, should choose the former. Setting up a stall and getting a licence to sell second-hand clothes, finding them and restoring them, and then using a stall as a base for displaying and selling newly designed work, is by no means unusual.

BABY DRESSES AND GIRLS IN MEN'S SUITS

The 'implosionary' effect of the mass media means that in the 1980s youth styles and fashions are born into the media. There is now an 'instantaneity' which replaces the old period of subcultural incubation. The relentless forces of consumerism operate at the style-face with teams of stylists being sent out by the magazines each month to scour the market places and end-of-term fashion shows for commercial ideas. Students who start off working on the stalls move, often to their own labels, within a year of leaving college, with the help of the EAS and a bank loan. They provide magazines and journalists with strong images and lively copy and the whole system reproduces itself at an increasingly frenzied speed. Thanks to the vitality of the style glossies, the fashion business becomes more confident about and more conversant with fashion language. As more column inches are given over to fashion in the daily and weekly quality newspapers (adding a dash of colour to the black and white format and catering for the 'new' women readers at the same time) fashion learns to talk about itself with a new fluency, it can even mock itself.[12]

Mainstream fashion has a lot to thank youth subcultures for. It can gesture back in time knowing that its readers have been well educated, through the media, in postwar pop culture history. Often it is enough just to signal Brian Jones's hairstyle, or Jimi Hendrix's hat and scarf, or Cathy McGowan's floppy fringe, as though they have already been immortalized. They remain recognizable as traces, signs, or fragments. This instant recall on history, fuelled by the superfluity of images thrown up by the media, has produced in style a non-stop fashion parade in which 'different decades are placed together with no historical continuity'.[13] Punk do-it-yourself fashion has transformed fashion into pop art, and collecting period fashion pieces into a serious hobby.

From the mid-1970s punk girls salvaged shockingly lurid lurex minis of the sort worn in Italian 'jet-set' films of the mid-1960s. They reinstated the skinny-rib jumper and plastic earrings (worn by Pauline of Penetration and Fay Fife of the Rezillos) as well as any number of 'shift' dresses into the fashion mainstream. They also reclaimed tarty fishnet stockings, black plastic mini-skirts and, of course, ski pants. When Debbie Harry first appeared in this country she was dressed in classic New York hooker style with white, knee-length, 'these boots are made for walkin'' boots, micro mini-skirt and tight black jumper. Television shows, even puppet TV shows, as well as 1960s movies such as *Blow Up* and, of course, all the old James Bond films, were continually raided by the 'new' stylists in search of ideas. Paul Weller, for example, joined this rush in the early 1980s and uncovered old pieces of 1960s 'mod' clothing which were then installed as part of the 1980s 'soulboy' wardrobe ... Jon Savage has described this plundering of recent style history displayed each week at Camden Lock as follows: 'Fashion, cars, buildings from the last hundred years piled up in an extraordinary display ... a jungle where anything could be worn, driven, even eaten as long as it was old.'[14] Savage reinforces Fredric Jameson's gloomy prognosis of the postmodern condition in this 'mass flight into nostalgia'.[15] Loss of faith in the future has produced a culture which can only look backwards and re-examine key moments of its own recent history with a sentimental gloss and a soft focus lens. Society is now incapable of producing serious images, or texts which give people meaning and direction. The gap opened up by this absence is filled instead with cultural bric-à-brac and with old images recycled and reintroduced into circulation as pastiche.

It is easy to see how this argument can be extended to include second-hand style, which in the early and mid-1980s did indeed appear to the observer like a bizarre pantomime parade where themes and strands from recognizable historical moments seemed to be combined at random. Against Savage and Jameson, however, it might be argued that these styles are neither nostalgic in essence nor without depth. Nostalgia indicates a desire to re-create the past faithfully, and to wallow in such mythical representations. Nostalgia also suggests an attempt at period accuracy, as in a costume drama. While both of these are true, for example, of Laura

Ashley fashions, they are certainly not apparent in contemporary second-hand style. This style is marked out rather by a knowingness, a wilful anarchy and an irrepressible optimism, as indicated by colour, exaggeration, humour and disavowal of the conventions of adult dress.

The best known examples of this are the two girl groups, Bananarama and Amazulu, and the pop presenter Paula Yates. The wardrobes of Yates and the others are still drawn in spirit, if not in practice, from the jumble sale or the second-hand market. Paula Yates's 'silly' dresses and gigantic hair bows are like outfits salvaged from a late 1950s children's birthday party. The huge baggy trousers worn by Bananarama, tied round the waist 'like a sack of potatoes', their black plimsolls and haystack hairstyles caught up with straggly cotton headscarves are equally evocative of an urchin childhood or a *Grapes of Wrath* adolescence. It is as though the Bananarama girls tumbled out of bed and put on whatever came to hand without their mothers knowing. Amazulu's gypsy dresses worn with cascades of hair ribbons and Doc Marten boots creates a similar effect. Again and again they gesture back to a childhood rummage through a theatrical wardrobe and the sublime pleasure of 'dressing up'. There is a refusal of adult seriousness and an insistence on hedonism and hyperbole. The 1950s ball-gown glamour sought out by Paula Yates is undercut by the sheer excessiveness of it. Paula Yates's wardrobe exists within the realms of high camp. Her style of presentation and style of dress create an image of pure pastiche.

However this pastiche is celebratory rather than reflective of a sterile and depthless mainstream culture. It plays with the norms, conventions and expectations of femininity, post-feminism. Each item is worn self-consciously with an emphasis on the unnatural and the artificial. Madonna remains the other best-known exemplar of this rags, ribbons and lace style. She wore her mid-1980s image like a mask and with what Kaja Silverman has described as a sense of 'ironic distance'.[16]

The other most influential image in the fashion horizons of the 1980s which also drew on second-hand style flirted with the idea of androgyny. Punk androgyny was never unambiguously butch or aggressive, it was slim, slight and invariably 'arty'. The Robert Mapplethorpe cover of Patti Smith's first album made a strong impression on those who were less keen on studs, chains and bondage trousers. Smith appeared casual, unmade-up with a jacket slung over her shoulders and a tie loosened at her neck. The cuffs of her shirt were visibly frayed and she faced the camera direct with a cool, scrutinizing gaze. This cautious but somehow threatening androgyny had a much greater resonance than, for example, Diane Keaton's very feminine take-up of the male wardrobe in the Woody Allen film *Annie Hall*. She too ransacked the traditional gents' wardrobe but her image was New York 'kooky' and eccentric (ex-hippy), and not even vaguely menacing. Smith was unmistakably from the New York underground. She was pale-faced, dark, undernourished, intense and 'committed'.

Patti Smith sent girls and young women off in search of these wide, baggy and unflattering clothes, while *Annie Hall* alerted others to the feminine potential of the male wardrobe. The film made the do-it-yourself look attractive to those less familiar with the ragmarket, and balanced shirts and ties with soft, floppy, feminine hats. Suddenly all those male items which had lain untouched for years in second-hand shops, charity shops and street markets came to life. Nothing was left untried including cotton pyjama tops, shirts, jackets, evening suits and tuxedos, overcoats, raincoats, trousers and even the occasional pair of shiny black patent evening shoes, small enough to fit female feet. Men's jackets replaced early 1970s figure-hugging jackets with an inverted pyramidic line. The exaggerated shoulders narrowed slowly down to below the hips creating a strong but none the less slimming effect. This was immediately taken up by fashion writers as 'liberating'. It covered all 'irregularities' in size, imposing instead a homogeneously baggy look. It was a style open to all, not just the size 10s and 12s. As a result these jackets began to appear 'new', in chain stores and exclusive boutiques up and down the country. They were soon being worn by high-flying businesswomen as well as by secretaries, professionals and others. These 'new' jackets imitated what had been a necessary alteration on those bought second-hand. Instead of shortening male-length sleeves, these had simply been turned up revealing the high-quality, soft, striped silk lining. Again, the effect of this was to lighten an otherwise dark and fairly heavy image. The same feature appeared in the second-hand winter coats found in 'Flip' and in markets like that at Camden Lock. The huge surplus of tweed overcoats kept prices low and the range of choice extensive. These too were adapted for female use by turning up the sleeves, as were their summer equivalents, the lightweight cotton raincoats of which there was, and still is, a vast discarded 'mountain'. This effect was soon copied in new overcoats for both men and women. It can be seen in outlets as exclusive as Joseph's and Paul Smith's and also in Warehouse and Miss Selfridge. However, the cost of such garments in fabric comparable to that found in their second-hand equivalents makes them prohibitively expensive. This in itself forces a much wider range of shoppers, including the so-called young professionals, back towards Flip and Camden Lock.

These items of male clothing never conferred on girls and women a true androgyny. There was instead a more subtle aesthetic at work. The huge, sweeping greatcoats imposed a masculine frame on what was still an unmistakably feminine form. All sorts of softening devices were added to achieve this effect – diamante brooches, lop-sided berets, provocatively red lipstick, and so on. A similar process took place round the appropriation of the male shirt. It too seemed baggy and egalitarian and thus in

149

keeping with 1970s feminist critiques of fashion. But these shirts were tightly tucked into a thick waistband which emphasized the traditional hour-glass figure. Men's shirts ushered in the new shape for female clothing. Their sleeve line fell far below the shoulder on women, often connecting with the body of the garment half-way down the arm. This produced a 'batwing' effect which in turn was taken up by manufacturers and marketed as such. The inverted pyramid shape here took the form of an elongated arm and shoulder line narrowing down at each side to a small and feminine waist.

Alongside these, other 'stolen' items began to appear in the high street. Tuxedos (favoured by Princess Diana), bow ties, silk evening shirts, and for everyday wear, flat, black patent, lace-up shoes. For two consecutive winters these were as ubiquitous as leggings were in the summer. And in both cases the point of origin was the man's wardrobe. Indeed, leggings offer a good example. These first appeared alongside the gents' vests, in a cream-coloured knitted cotton fabric, as winter underpants, again in places like Camden Market. They had an elasticated waistband and a button opening at the front. Punk girls began to buy them as summer alternatives to their winter ski pants. Dyed black, they created a similar effect. Then, the stall-holders dyed them and sold them in a dark, murky, grey-black shade. But they still suffered from the design faults which arise from adapting male lower garments for women. They were cut too low at the waist and frequently slid down. The fly front cluttered the smooth line across the stomach and they were often too short at the crotch. It was not long, therefore, before the same stall-holders were making up their own models in the professionally dyed brushed cotton fabric popularized through consumer demand for track suits and sweatshirts. By the summers of 1985 and 1986 these were being worn by what seemed to be the entire female population aged under 30. They were combined with wide, baggy male-shaped shirts, headscarves knotted on top 1940s munitions-worker style, children's black plimsolls (or else smart walking shoes) and lightweight cotton jackets.

The popularity of the male wardrobe therefore reflects a confusion of meanings similar to that thrown up by second-hand 'baby' dressing. In this apparently androgynous context these meanings highlight an appreciation of high-quality fabrics of the sort rarely found in mass-produced goods, a desire also to reinstate them to their former glory, and even a desire to wear something 'socially useful'. By recycling discarded pieces of clothing new wearers are not only beating the system by finding and defining high fashion cheaply, they are also making good use of the social surplus. An ecological ideal thus resides alongside the desire for artifice, decoration and ambiguous, double-edged femininity.

THE DEATH OF THE DESIGNER

Writing in the early 1970s Tom Wolfe offered one of the few fragments on the subject of second-hand dress when he labelled this style, along with that ethnic look made fashionable for whites by the Black Panthers, 'radical chic'. This meant dressing down, looking righteous and wearing 'jeans of the people . . . hod carrier jeans . . . and woolly green socks, that kind you get at the Army surplus at two pair for twenty nine cents'.[17]

Wolfe went on to suggest that on a grander scale *'nostalgie de la boue'* marked the arrival of a thrusting new middle class sufficiently confident culturally and socially to outrage their stuffier class equals by asserting in an upfront way where they have come from, through dressing in the 'styles of the lower orders'. These 'Peter, Paul and Mary' hippy types and with their apparently unwashed appearance and preference for old, discarded clothes brought out, on the part of the urbane Wolfe, a tone of disdain: 'She didn't wear nylons, she didn't wear makeup, she had bangs and long straight hair down below her shoulders . . .'[18] The point which Wolfe made is one commonly enough asserted, that this 'poverty dressing' is both insulting to 'the people' and ill judged: 'today the oppressed, the hard core youth of the ghetto, they aren't into . . . Army surplus socks. If you tried to put one of those lumpy lumberjack shirts on them, they'd vomit.'[19]

In a more recent piece in *New Society*, Angela Carter made the same point.[20] The focus here is on an image widely displayed on the city centre hoardings and in the London Underground in 1983 to advertise the magazine *19*. The model is dressed in an assortment of wide, baggy clothes, in this case new but drawn in spirit from the ragmarket: 'But if you didn't know she was a fashion model, the girl in the poster . . . would in fact look like nothing so much as a paper bag lady (or rather person), in her asexually shaped jacket, loose trousers, sagging socks, with a scarf of dubious soiled colour wrapped round her head like a bandage, beneath a hat jammed firm down. . . .'[21] Carter sees this as a style favoured, once again, by the rich who can afford to play at looking poor: '. . . it is ironic that rich girls (such as students) swan about in rancid long johns with ribbons in their hair, when the greatest influence on working class girls would appear to be Princess Di. . . .'[22] Both Angela Carter and Tom Wolfe recognise that for working-class people the structure of the working day, the tyranny of the clock, and the monotony of work, with its uniforms, overalls and aprons, conspire to produce in leisure an overwhelming desire to mark out distance from the factory floor. In contrast, the middle classes, who can achieve individuality in dress on a day-to-day basis, have no need for a 'Sunday best'. Likewise, because they have to dress up during the working day for their professional roles, they are able to dress down in leisure and to 'slop about' as students.

The problem is that this is now being changed by forces beyond the control of either of the two groups. In the 1980s, for old and young alike, the discipline of the factory clock no longer prevails. The unemployed and semi-employed have been cast adrift, and for many young men and women their attention has turned inwards towards the body. Wild peacock punk dressing of the type seen on the streets in the early 1980s signified this body politics, this making strange through an excessive masquerade, a 'quotidien marvellous'.[23]

There have been changes on both sides of the class divide. Students are not, as Angela Carter suggests, 'rich girls'. Many are barely scraping along on their grants with no parental back-up. This is even more true for the ranks of the student body who would once have proceeded into training or an apprenticeship but are now finding their way into further and higher education. This too marks the increasing fluidity across the old class lines which previously distinguished working-class from middle-class youth. Of course, it does not mean that all young people now dress in what Carter labelled 'recession style'. There are as many girls who still aspire to the Princess Di look as there are boys who model themselves on the 'casual' elegance of Italian style. It does mean, however, that there is a much wider constituency for ragmarket shopping than was once the case.

This fluidity is reflected across all the other social sites and fashion spheres engaged with here. The high street emulates the style of the market place and takes up the ideas of those who produce for the markets. At the same time, for the do-it-yourself 'designers' and stall-holders the lure of the mainstream is not altogether unattractive. Many sell simultaneously to the department stores and to the passing crowds at Camden or Kensington Market. Self-employment in these fields is both an attempt to participate in an economy unwilling to open itself up to school-leavers and graduates alike and an act of evasion, an evasion of those sorts of dull jobs which are promised at the end of a work experience programme.

All of the styles described above have been seen as part of the contemporary interest in 'retro'. They have therefore been linked with other visual images which draw on and 'quote' from past sources or earlier genres. These are now most prominent in the world of advertising and in pop videos where some vague notion of popular memory is evoked in the swirl of a petticoat or the sweep of a duster coat. It is unwise, however, to place second-hand style unproblematically within that cultural terrain marked out by Fredric Jameson as the sphere of postmodernity. This would be to conflate retro-dressing as merely yet another cultural re-run, no different from the nostalgic remakes of 1940s 'B' movies, or the endless re-releases and revivals of old hit records.

These trends, including that of second-hand dress, require much more specific analysis. While pastiche and some kind of fleeting nostalgia might indeed play a role in second-hand style, these have to be seen more precisely within the evolution of postwar youth cultures. Second-hand style in this context reveals a more complex structure offering, among other things a kind of internal, unofficial job market within these 'enterprise subcultures'. Girls and young women have played a major role, not just in providing youth subcultures with their items of style and dress, but also in rediscovering these items and imaginatively re-creating them. Despite being at the vanguard of style in this respect, these young women have been passed over and eclipsed in the fashion pages by the young 'geniuses' of fashion in the 1980s like John Galliano or John Flett. In fact fashion designers play a much less central role in setting fashion trends than is commonly imagined. There is even a case to be made for the 'death of the designer', since the main impetus for changes in fashion and in contemporary consumer culture, as this chapter has argued, comes from below, from those who keep an eye open for redeemable pieces which are then reinscribed into the fashion system.

This article first appeared in Angela McRobbie (ed.) *Zoot Suits and Second-Hand Dresses: An Anthology of Fashion and Music*, London, Macmillan, 1989, pp. 23–49.

NOTES

1 P. Cohen, 'Policing the working-class city', in B. Fine *et al.*, *Capitalism and the Rule of Law*, London, Hutchinson, 1979, pp. 118–37.
2 E. Carter, 'Alice in consumer wonderland', in A. McRobbie and M. Nava (eds) *Gender and Generation*, London, Macmillan, 1979, pp. 185–214.
3 S. Hall and T. Jefferson (eds) *Resistance through Rituals*, London, Hutchinson, 1977; and D. Hebdige, *Subculture: The Meaning of Style*, London, Routledge, 1979.
4 S. Hall, 'The hippies: an American moment', CCCS Stencilled Papers, University of Birmingham, 1977.
5 T. Wolfe, *Radical Chic and Mau-Mauing the Flak Catchers*, New York, Bantam Books, 1974; and A. Carter, 'The recession style', *New Society*, January 1983, vol. 63, no. 1052, pp. 25–6.
6 Paddy's Market in Glasgow, in the early 1970s, offered one of the best examples of absolute social polarity in second-hand shopping.
7 The Birmingham Ragmarket in the late 1970s provided many similar examples of social diversity in second-hand shopping.
8 Cohen, op. cit.
9 J. Clarke, 'Style', in S. Hall and T. Jefferson. (eds) *Resistance through Rituals*, London, Hutchinson, 1977, pp. 175–92.
10 Hebdige, op. cit. and A. McRobbie, 'Settling the accounts with subcultures: a feminist critique', in A. McRobbie (ed.) *Feminism and Youth Culture: From Jackie to Just Seventeen*, London, Macmillan, 1991, pp. 16–35.
11 A. McRobbie and J. Garber, 'Girls and subcultures: an exploration', in ibid., pp. 1–16.
12 Sally Ann Lasson reviewed Nicholas Coleridge's *The Fashion Conspiracy* by

poking fun at her own profession which specializes in lines like 'Paris was awash with frothy femininity', *Observer*, 20 March 1988, p. 25.

13 J. Savage, 'Living in the past', *Time Out*, February 1983, p. 32.
14 ibid.
15 F. Jameson, 'Postmodernism, the cultural logic of capital', in H. Foster (ed.) *Postmodern Culture*, London, Pluto Press, 1985, pp. 111–25.
16 K. Silverman, 'Fragments of a fashionable discourse', in T. Modleski, *Studies in Entertainment: Critical Approaches to Mass Culture*, Bloomington and Indianapolis, IN, Indiana University Press, 1986, pp. 108–29.
17 Wolfe, op. cit.
18 ibid.: 48.
19 ibid.
20 Carter, op. cit.
21 ibid.: 25.
22 ibid.: 26.
23 A. Breton, *What is Surrealism?*, London, Pluto Press, 1981.

9

SHUT UP AND DANCE: YOUTH CULTURE AND CHANGING MODES OF FEMININITY

Like Helmut Hartwig (1993), I too feel a sense of acute anxiety at the thought of writing about youth. It is at once too close and too far away. I am too old. I have a daughter of 15 who lives these experiences and in talking or writing about them I feel I am encroaching on her private space. Frequently the difference between being a sociologist interested in youth and being the parent of a teenage girl reaches a crisis point. Sometimes this entails the simple recognition of the huge gap between the loose and tentative sociological observations of my own early work carried out in Birmingham in the late 1970s, and the psychological complexity of growing up, a process which now, as I see it happening on a day-to-day basis, causes me to question almost everything I ever wrote about teenage girls (McRobbie, 1991). At other moments the crisis is of a different nature, more like that described by Dick Hebdige (1987) when he too is given cause to ponder his earlier writing on youth and his present position as somebody who, when kept awake for nights at a time by the loud music played by his young neighbours, eventually gets dressed and goes out in the middle of the night and angrily complains. Getting dressed and going out in the middle of the night and sometimes in the early hours of the morning to pick up my daughter from 'raves' held in empty warehouses on trading estates on the outskirts of North London precipitates the same kind of reaction in myself, though this time it is extreme anxiety rather than anger and frustration which I feel, driving out into the early light looking for the appointed spot where I wait, as the sweat-drenched, pale-faced youths come out in straggly bunches.

In the final part of this chapter I will return to the question of rave, bringing to bear on my analysis some of these new contradictions which emerge from this uncomfortable overlap of roles. Despite the acute feelings of anxiety verging on terror which I experience in my capacity as mother, it still seems important to stand back and ask what is going on and why. How young people, male and female, experience the society around them and how they in turn express this experience, continue to be immensely important questions. Youth remains a major point of symbolic investment for society as a whole. What I will be doing in this chapter is selecting from an immensely rich and complicated landscape of social change in Britain, through the Thatcher years and beyond, a few critical examples in the field of youth culture and youth mass media. These examples indicate a direct engagement with change – change also indicative of new emergent modes of femininity, which in turn tell us something of real significance about the society in which we now live. I will also argue that these changes must prompt a revision of some of the ways in which cultural studies has defined itself in recent years. It is not that social change alone forces such a revision but that by returning, for instance, to the category of youth as I am doing here, one is also in a sense returning to those frameworks for analysis which came to characterize the field from the mid-1970s onwards, with the result that it is possible to see more clearly how these frameworks now need to be amended.

I shall be arguing that in recent youth culture, what may be responses to some of the more oppressive aspects of life in Britain for young people in the 1980s and into the 1990s, for example, the frightening reality of AIDS, may also be where new and unanticipated social meanings are actively produced. This symbolic and aesthetic material is developed in what often seems like a frenzy of cultural production. It marks, in my view, an absolute engagement with the social. Youth cultures, in whatever shape they take, stake out an investment in society. It is in this sense that they are political. One rather clichéd way of putting this is to say that they make 'statements'; but these statements take different shape under different historical conditions and they keep on being made. It is this activity which has of course provided the raw material for the study of subcultures, but it seems to me worth both repeating the exercise of looking at subcultures and taking this analysis further and in a slightly different direction. Of course it is also the case that the intensity of the subcultural activity means that it almost immediately spills out of its youth cultural 'home', becoming part of a wider popular culture which is continually looking to the innovative elements in youth culture in order to claim a dynamism for itself. While in the early days of subcultural theory from the Centre for Contemporary Cultural Studies (CCCS) it was important to draw a line between youth culture and pop culture, crediting the former with a form of symbolic class authenticity and the latter with all the marks of the consumer culture, in reality the two were always merged, involved in an ongoing relationship (Hall and Jefferson, 1977). But now that the search for the fundamental class meaning underpinning these formations no longer constitutes the rationale for their cultural analysis, we can also afford to be more speculative, more open to reflecting on meanings other than those of class. It is not so much that these meanings can now openly include questions of gender, sexuality, race and identity, but rather how in different youth cultural 'venues' different permutations of class, gender and racial meanings are being explored. In each of the examples I look at in this chapter one or another of these will be recognized as occupying a position of prominence.

For example, in relation to changing modes of femininity, I do not claim that we can simply see evidence of progress, i.e. girls being more independent than they were in the late 1970s when I first started working in this field. But neither do I endorse the argument put forward recently by the American feminist Susan Faludi (1991), namely that after a short period of gains, women (and by implication young women) are now experiencing the full force of a backlash led by the emergent 'new right' and moral majority movements. I would offer here neither a narrative of progress nor one of backlash, but instead suggest a dramatic 'unfixing' of young women in British society over the last fifteen years which has been effected in the social institutions and can be seen in the field of commercial mass culture and in the various youth subcultures. There is now a greater degree of fluidity about what femininity means and how exactly it is anchored in social reality. I know of no major study which has assessed with any precision how things have actually changed for girls and young women in and across the main social institutions of the family, education and employment. As is often the case for cultural studies, where there is a complete absence of sociological material which would in effect do the work of illustrating or acting as evidence in support of an argument, we have to rely more loosely on less hard evidence and look to some of the most widely available 'texts' of youth culture for the clearest expression of these changes.

My use of the phrase 'changing modes of femininity' is used here as a reminder of just how fluid gender practices and meaning structures are. Even in adverse political circumstances (i.e. throughout the Thatcher years) it can by no means be assumed that, for example, the position of women, and young women, simply worsened. Despite the hostility of the tabloid press, feminism has had a dramatic impact on almost every level of social life in Britain. It has made issues around sexual inequality part of the political agenda in both the private sphere of the home and in domestic relations, and in the more public world of work. Likewise institutions themselves (particularly in education) have been alerted to the question of women and young women as economic agents, participating in the economy for the greater part of their lives. Altogether this kind of heightened activity around questions of gender has radically undermined what might be described as the old domestic settlement which tied women (and young women's futures) primarily to the family and to low-paid or part-time work. There is, as a result, a greater degree of uncertainty in society as a whole about what it is to be a woman, and this filters down to how young women exist within this new *habitus* of gender relations (Bourdieu, 1984). It might even be suggested that in Britain, girls – both black and white – have been 'unhinged' from their traditional gender position while the gender and class destiny of their male counterparts has remained more stable.[1]

This state of flux in relation to what now constitutes feminine identity can certainly be detected in the new girls' magazines as well as in the whole expansive field of the mass media. It is in culture, above all, that there has been a discursive explosion around what constitutes femininity and its ambiguous relationship with feminism. Feminist issues are now firmly implanted not only in those traditional spheres of femininity – e.g. women's magazines, radio programmes like *Woman's Hour* – but also in other less gender-specific areas of radio and broadcasting, in arts programmes and drama in particular. Nor is such a shift restricted to culture for a middle-class female audience or readership. In mainstream television thanks to writers like Carla Lane and others, feminist topics are now a standard part of the staple of 'sitcom' material, soap opera, plays and series. But this does not mean that younger women now identify themselves as feminist. They are more likely to resist such a label and assert, at least as an image, an excessively conventional femininity. At the same time they frequently expressly strongly feminist views in their day-to-day discussions. What they are rejecting is a particular image of the feminist which they associate either with an older generation or with a stereotypically unfeminine image. In other words the old binary opposition which put femininity at one end of the political spectrum and feminism at the other is no longer an accurate way of conceptualizing young female experience (maybe it never was). It is no longer a question of those who know (the feminists, the academics) against those who do not, or who are the 'victims' of ideology. As Charlotte Brunsdon (1991/2) has recently argued, a quite dramatic realignment between feminism and the lived experience of femininity (and its textual representations) has taken place. As feminist ideas have slowly worked their way into the material and ideological structures of society and become part of the general culture of femininity, so also has the fragile unity of feminism (or feminist theory) itself been challenged and disputed from within as black women, for instance, ask the question of what the women's movement or the feminist theory of the 1970s meant for them. While it is as yet impossible to predict whether a new 'sexual settlement' will emerge from this fragmentation and realignment, what is clear is that there is a good deal more noise; there are many more voices eager to participate in this postfeminist cultural field and anxious to be listened to. Charlotte Brunsdon has pointed out how these shifts have real consequences for what we as feminist academics teach, how we engage with our students, male and female, and how we define and pursue our chosen objects of study.

How should youth culture in Britain in the 1990s be approached, bearing in mind not only the late 1970s feminist critique of subcultural theory, but also those shifts in gender relations outlined above which have traversed the whole society? One way of proceeding is to look at a number of particular examples and to draw from them those elements and developments which seem to be most significant. Since class no longer underwrites the critical project of cultural analysis, and ideology seems too monolithic a category, too focused on social passivity and conformity to be usefully alert to the more micrological level of dispute and contestation, we can scale down the field of study and abandon claims on unity or totality in favour of pursuing what Laclau has called the 'dignity of the specific' (quoted in McRobbie, 1992).

GIRLS, CULTURAL PRODUCTION AND YOUTH CULTURE

Let us start by saying that there have been some key changes in youth culture in the last decade. In fact things were never the same after punk. The turning-point it marked meant that youth subcultures, whatever the guise they had taken, could no longer be seen as occupying only a 'folk devil' position in society. There were too many of them, and they were increasingly able to counter whatever charges were made against them by the mass media since they had at their disposal – partly as a result of the availability of cheaper technology – the means to defend themselves and to discuss the issue with a wider audience than themselves. These means of communication were not restricted solely to fanzines and to the self-generated style magazines, since spaces were opened up for 'youth TV', first on Channel Four and more recently in BBC2's *Def II* programmes. With their clear commitment to employing young people, these programmes continue to reflect an image of youth different from that found, for example, in the *Daily Mail*.[2]

The increasing interest among a wider section of the population in style, and then in 'design' in the 1980s, reflected a situation in which youthfulness became virtually synonymous with subculture. Earlier subcultures were revived for the umpteenth time; some, like heavy metal, remained unchanged in appearance but continued to recruit new followers from boys aged 13 upwards. Hippie culture, with the new interest in vegetarianism, the environment and peace, proved ready not just for revival but for a permanent place in this 'endless' youth culture. There was a black inflection too with musicians like De La Soul in the USA, and Soul to Soul in Britain, celebrating the connection between mid-1960s black liberation and civil rights, and the language of radical politics it spawned for white students and hippies soon after.

Out of punk, goth, hippie and reggae, 'crusties' (white, pallid Crass fans, their own unkempt hair literally encrusted with 'dreadlocks') emerged marking the place of the underdog, the right to the streets or the common land, the desire for disenfranchisement from the legacy of

159

Thatcherist values, the rejection of clean consumer culture in favour of 'ecological' dirt. Accompanied by decrepit but much-loved mongrel dogs, these 'convoys' continue to occupy key spaces (with a can of beer in hand and dog on tow) in the urban environment, like outside the Sainsbury's store at Camden in North London for example, a building celebrated as an example of the best of postmodern architecture. Crusties often merge with squatters, young anarchists and homeless young people, and with such a dramatically 'dirty' visual style, they stage 'homelessness' or 'the end of welfare'. These groups continue to make an extraordinarily strong impression on the urban landscape. They contribute directly to our experience of social reality. They play back a particular version of that reality, and they function as strong social texts, signs of response that indicate an active registering of broad social changes over which such groupings otherwise have no control.

Despite the longevity of subcultures like these in the British urban landscape, there were certain quite straightforward questions which for some reason were never asked even during the heyday of subcultural theory in the late 1970s. For instance, who was doing what? Where did the style come from? Where was it purchased, who was selling it to whom? More abstractly, what were the social relations which informed the production of the subculture? What pre-existing skills were called upon to produce the graphics and the posters and even the music itself? In my own earlier work so much effort was put into attempting to problematize the marginalized experience of girls in youth culture that it never occurred to me to explore this further and find out what exactly they were doing on a day-to-day basis. Likewise, in Dick Hebdige's work, so much attention was put on the final signifying products of the subculture and the permutations of meaning produced by these images, that the cultural work involved in their making did not figure in the analysis (Hebdige, 1979).

In my article 'Second-hand dresses and the role of the ragmarket' (McRobbie, 1990) I argued that subcultural theory was resistant to investigating some of these processes because they brought an analysis, itself dependent on notions of class and resistance, directly up against a set of practices which seemed far removed from the politics of class and resistance. Buying and selling and participating in subcultures as consumers represented to subcultural theorists only the moment of diffusion, the point at which the oppositional force is incorporated or 'recuperated' back into society through the processes of commodification. As the subculture is commodified for a mass market so also is it de-politicized and made palatable for popular consumption. The problems with this model have now become a familiar strand in cultural studies with contributions from Erica Carter (1984), Frank Mort (1994), Mica Nava (1992) and myself, each having confronted in different ways the complex pleasures and the politics of consumption. But introducing the practices of selling clothes and records and other items to those involved in the subculture was also to bring to the analysis the reality of an infrastructure in the subculture which involved both production and marketing. The assumption implicit in subcultural theory was that those who did this sort of thing were simply 'hustlers' who pushed their way into the subculture from outside, making a profit from something which in reality had no interest in or connection to commerce. As a result music and style and other related activities sprang on to the subcultural theory stage as though from nowhere.

It soon became clear, particularly after punk, that this romanticism of authenticity was a false and idealized view. Not only Malcolm McLaren and Vivienne Westwood, but the whole punk phenomenon used the predatory, easily exploited and above all open-ended mass media for publicity, and actually set up, right from the start, a string of shops selling clothes directly to young people.[3]

Since then the old model which divided the pure subculture from the contaminated outside world, eager to transform anything it could get its hands on into a sellable item, has collapsed, even though there still remains an ideology of authenticity which provides young people in youth cultures with a way of achieving social subjectivity and therefore identity through the subcultural experience.

However, my concern here is with the way in which the magazines produced by fans, the music produced by DJs, the clothes bought, sold and worn by subcultural 'stylists', do more than just publicize the subculture. They also provide the opportunity for learning and sharing skills, for practising them, for making a small amount of money; more importantly, they provide pathways for future 'life-skills' in the form of work or self-employment. To ignore the intense activity of cultural production as well as its strongly aesthetic dimension (in graphics, fashion design, retail and music production) is to miss a key part of subcultural life – the creation of a whole way of life, an alternative to higher education (though often a 'foundation' for art school), a job creation scheme for the culture industries. The point is then that far from being merely the commercial, low ebb of the subculture, as far removed from resistance as it is possible to imagine, these activities can be seen as central to it. They are also expressions of change and of social transformation. De-industrialization, class de-alignment, the changing place of women, and the consolidation of black people at the bottom end of the labour hierarchy, have all affected young people during the 1980s. The turn to fashion and music as career rather than consumer choices (no matter how shaky these careers might be) represents a strong preference for the cultural sphere. I would suggest that this involvement can be an empowering experience, particularly for young people with no access to the skills and qualifications acquired as a matter of course by those other young people destined for university and for the professions. Subcultures are often ways of creating job opportunities as more traditional careers disappear. In this undocumented, unrecorded and largely 'hidden economy' sector, sub-cultures stand at one end of the culture industry spectrum and the glamorous world of the star system and the entertainment business at the other.

If, for the moment, we deconstruct the notion of resistance by removing its metapolitical status (even when this exists in some disguised, magical, or imaginary form, as it did in CCCS theory), and if we reinsert resistance at the more mundane, micrological level of everyday practices and choices about how to live, then it becomes possible to see the sustaining, publicizing and extending of the subcultural enterprise as a way of attempting to earn a living within what has been described as the aestheticization of culture (against a backdrop of industrial decline).

The buying, selling and producing do not take place in a vacuum. They are integrally connected to much longer chains of meaning and value-systems. Second-hand clothes and the recycling ethic which goes with them, for example, do not just produce 'retro' images on the streets: they also provide a counterpoint to overpriced high street fashion. Selling such clothes requires organizational skills as well as imagination. Selling usually exists alongside designing and making up new clothes as well as restoring and selling old ones. The shop assistant is also therefore a fashion designer. Involvement often develops into a proper career choice. At the same time the interconnection in the subculture between fashion, image and music can be seen as reflecting more generally what Helmet Hartwig (1993) has described as a 'longing for art'.

This can also be understood as a preference over against the 'training' pathways provided for young people in Britain today. While self- or semi-employment in the world of subcultures could be interpreted as examples of the enterprise culture of the Thatcher era at work, they are, in my view, better considered as angry ripostes to the rhetoric of Thatcher. If *she* said be enterprising then *their* enterprise would be pursued in precisely those 'soft' art areas, relatively unprofitable but personally rewarding, which have always found little favour with the conservatives. If *she* abandoned substantial sectors of the youth population to the forces of the free market and thus to unemployment, *they* refused such subordination and carved out spaces for themselves in the interstices of the *hidden* cultural economy, by setting up a stall selling retro clothes, for example, at Camden Lock in London. Or by setting up at home with a turntable and learning the DJ skills.

Alternatively, they stayed on at school or at college on BTec fashion and design courses. In education and in the art colleges far from finding an outright rejection of these subcultural ideas, young people experienced reinforcement, since, as Frith and Horne (1987) have argued, the British art schools, despite the lingering influence of the great traditions, have shown themselves in the postwar period to be at least open to pop and to the blurring of the distinction between high art and low culture. Art student culture itself, often as a result of working-class, particularly male, students' access to the art colleges in the postwar years (in contrast to other institutions of higher education), forged a direct line between adolescent youth cultures pursued in leisure and what these students brought with them to their art education. Where this overlapped with the interests of the younger teachers and lecturers (perhaps from the same background and experience themselves) a rich output often emerged, incorporating music, graphics, magazines and fashion as well as 'fine art' pop art.

It is in buying and selling clothes that girls and young women have been more active. The male bias of subcultural analysis has relegated these activities to the margins, just as it has elevated style to a special place while locating fashion at a lower level. But when we look at these activities we can see not just their key importance to youth culture, but also their lasting contribution to the particular integration of fashion and subcultural style which exists in Britain. Fashion in Britain, because of its roots in youth subcultures (rather than in *haute couture*) is a more popular form. It is in the 'designs' and in the 'fancy dress' often inspired by what once again Helmut Hartwig (1993) calls the 'crazy fantasies' of youth culture, that we see those ideas which find their way into the vocabulary of high street fashion. That these images have no clear-cut point of origin, that they belong to no one person, that they emerge from the space of the subculture, tells us something important about the creative process itself and about the rich aesthetic opportunities afforded by subcultural involvement. For black people whose expressive cultures have been so consistently marginalized and disregarded by the art establishment, this is a particularly intense struggle, which once again is carried out all the more insistently in popular black youth culture.

CODING THE FEMININE IN THE 1990s

Where subcultural theory concentrated on the final signifying product (the punk, the mod, the hippie, the bike boy, the new romantic, etc.) rather than on the material processes of cultural production involved in the creation of subculture, feminist readings of girls' magazines, including my own, have concentrated on the seamless text of oppressive meanings held together by ideology, rather than on the disruptions and inconsistencies and spaces for negotiation within the magazines. Where an emphasis on cultural production (and on ethnography) can reveal a much greater level of involvement on the part of young women in subcultures – i.e. in fashion and style and other creative processes – so also can a more open-ended reading, particularly of the new girls' magazines like *Just Seventeen*, reveal a whole world of changes in the construction of femininity. Let me summarize both new ways of conceptualizing these popular texts and the new ways they themselves have found of coding the feminine.

As I describe at greater length in 'From Jackie to Just Seventeen: girls' magazines in the 1980s' (McRobbie, 1991), *Just Seventeen* has replaced *Jackie* as the top-selling magazine among a female readership aged approximately between 12 and 16. If we look closely at the magazine, it is immediately clear how different it is from its predecessor. Most strikingly, the girl is no longer the victim of romance. She is no longer a slave to love. She no longer waits miserably outside the cinema knowing that she has been 'stood up'. She no longer distrusts all girls including her best friend because they represent a threat and might steal her 'fella'. She no longer lives in absolute terror of being dumped. She is no longer terrified of being without a 'steady'. In fact she no longer exists because the narrative mode in which she appeared three or four times over every week, i.e. the picture love-story, no longer exists. Romance is an absent category in *Just Seventeen*. There is love and there is sex and there are boys, but the conventionally coded meta-narratives of romance which, as I argued in my earlier work on *Jackie*, could only create a neurotically dependent female subject, have gone for good.

Launched in the early 1980s *Just Seventeen* took a risk in doing away with the stories. But its editors did it because they detected a new climate of confidence and self-esteem among their potential readers. They commissioned a detailed market research study which confirmed that the readers of popular girls' magazines no longer wanted to be 'talked down to'. They did not want 'silly' love stories and they did not want to be portrayed as 'boy mad'. The editors and staff, mostly young graduates, many of them familiar with debates around feminism and representation and the politics of pop, attempted therefore to create a publication which was highly commercial, exciting to look at, easy to read, but which also confronted 'real issues' and which abandoned the patronizing and condescending tone which had characterized girls' magazines in the past.

We can stop here for a moment and make a couple of points. Judging from the evidence of the market research conducted by the new magazines it seems that girls have changed. They do not want to be represented in a humiliating way. They are not dependent on boys for their own sense of identity. Magazines (like *Jackie*) which continue to offer this passive stereotype of femininity will simply lose their readers. As young consumers girls are therefore able to exert some power in the market place. They will buy a magazine as long as it presents an image of themselves which is compatible with those selves that exist outside the text. These other changing modes of femininity – in the school, in the family and in other leisure spaces – would therefore have to be considered in relation to the changing textual representations in the magazines and in pop culture, if we are to build up a more coherent account of changes in femininity. While a single piece of market research can hardly be relied upon as a guide to social change and transformation, what are important are the new editorial practices inside the magazine which see such a survey as a necessary part of the process of creating a popular product.

The second point is that this dimension of cultural analysis lies outside the sphere of textuality. Looking at a magazine only as an interrelated series of texts can produce a 'reading' which does indeed pick up and respond to new and emergent modes of femininity, in the image or in the written text, but what it cannot do is to understand the complex and contested social processes which accompany the construction of new images. Looking not only at the finished products, the visual and verbal texts, but also at the professional ideologies alerts us to wider social changes, to social connections across otherwise conceptually separate spheres like the media and higher education, and to the magazine form itself as a non-homogeneous entity, a system with 'openings'. Helen Pleasance has recently described this non-monolithic approach to popular magazines in the following terms (Pleasance, 1992: 79–80):

> There are all sorts of people involved in making meaning out of *Smash Hits* and *Just Seventeen*. Even within the company of EMAP Metro there are different kinds of producers, different kinds of power, which might not sit easily together, and are, at best, in contingent alliance.... Theirs is only one of the many relationships which are played out across the magazines pages. Journalists, photographers, advertisers, the music industry (with all its own groupings and differences), and for *Just Seventeen* the fashion and beauty industries all contribute to the final product.

In *Just Seventeen*, femininity does indeed emerge as an altogether less rigid category. It is still predicated round the pursuit of identity (in beauty), the achievement of success (through fashion consumption) and search for some harmony or stability (through happiness). There is more of the self in this new vocabulary of femininity, much more self-esteem, more autonomy, but still the pressure to adhere to the perfect body image as a prerequisite for the success in love which is equated with happiness. However, even here prettiness has given way to strikingness. Models are chosen from the world of real readers; they are no longer all excessively tall and exceptionally thin. There are black, mixed race and Asian models appearing on the front covers as well as on the fashion and beauty pages. There is also a redefinition of the feminine self. It can be endlessly constructed, reconstructed and customized. No longer lavishing attention on the male partner, the girl is free to lavish attention on herself and she is helped in this task by the world of consumer goods at her disposal. In love, the new female subject can expect to be treated like an equal or

165

else feel quite entitled to 'dump him'. Pictures of boys, from real life and from the world of entertainment, are found on many pages of the magazine, but the self-mocking tone of the accompanying copy indicates a playful attitude.

How complicated and ironic all this is. The enslavement of romance is escaped partly, though not exclusively, through the freedom of the commodity. Images of bold, assertive and ambitious girls leap out in their Doc Marten boots, from the pages of the magazine. Far from having to relinquish their femininity to achieve 'equality' these girls have demanded their right to hold on to it intact, even excessively (note the new love of cleavage evidenced in Kylie Minogue's pop video for her hit single 'Give Me Just a Little More Time' and in the sudden rising sales of the Gossard Wonder Bra). The chains of meaning which emerge from these bold, confident and strongly sexualized images interact with all the other new modes of femininity found beyond the world of the text or of popular culture. The more general meaning of these hypersexual modes of femininity will be looked at in more depth in the concluding section of this chapter.

But remaining for the moment with the magazines, it would be impossible to ignore the presence of various strands of postmodern culture on the pages of *Just Seventeen*. This too is relevant to the construction of femininity in the 1990s. If the meta-narratives of romance have gone, they have been replaced by an avalanche of information. Fragments of 'info' about favourite pop stars, film stars and TV celebrities are now the raw material of fantasy. They too can now be customized to fit the reader's own unique desires. She no longer needs the story format when she can simply be given the information. There is an absolute excess of information and 'gossip' about the stars in *Just Seventeen*. But even here, in this 'ecstasy of communication', there is a detached ironic tone. The reader is expected not to take it all too seriously. 'We know it's silly', is what the editors seem to be saying, when they announce this week's celebrity pin-up, 'but it's fun and it's harmless.' In this sense superficiality and pastiche allow readers to position themselves at a distance from the subordination of being 'just' a fan or just a silly girl. Trivia presented in a knowing guise seems to mark an advance on the awful cloying claustrophobia of conventional romance. *Just Seventeen* is not anti-love or anti-sex but it does express a new horizon of possibilities in the field of sexual and social relationships for its readers. Girls are encouraged to think clearly about whether or not they want to have sex with their partners. They are given all the available information about contraception, about protection from AIDS, and about how to make sense of love. Having friends of both sexes is given a prominent place too, and it is this new, more equal climate of sexual relations that girls are encouraged to enjoy.

This begs a question which I will return to in the final section because it has clear repercussions for feminists and academics working in the field of cultural studies. If feminist academics (see, for instance, Radway, 1984; Modleski, 1982) have done a great deal to restore the status of romance by reclaiming it as a hidden pleasure of femininity, how historically specific is this pleasure? Do girls now simply have to look elsewhere for romantic narratives? Or do they no longer need them? Do these narratives no longer serve a useful as well as a pleasurable function? My feeling is that romance has indeed been dislodged from its place of cultural pre-eminence. The pleasures of popular narrative are now found in TV soap operas like *Brookside, Neighbours*, or *Home and Away*. But these are hardly romances. There seems to be a shift away from the fixity of gender relations inscribed in the romance. It may well be that young women today prefer the quirky postmodern subjectivities offered in films like *Heathers* and in *Twin Peaks*. While the TV series deployed an intensely heightened sexuality in its cast of exceptionally beautiful female characters and good-looking men, it was sex, danger, terror and 'strangeness' rather than love or romance which held the fragmented structure of the episodes together. Yet for all its weirdness and violence, the postmodern style of *Twin Peaks* seemed to address its audience adventurously, as knowing, intelligent consumers of postmodern culture rather than as hostages to the realist text. Perhaps one of the problems with romance in the 1990s is that its subject positions of masculinity and femininity no longer tally either with the more fluid subjectivities of the postmodern mass media, or with the ways of making sense of sexuality now required by young people in the post-AIDS era.

RAVE, GENDER AND CULTURAL STUDIES

In the first part of this chapter I advocated an approach to youth culture which emphasized the role of cultural production. Not only would such a perspective offer a more active picture of the involvement of girls and young women, particularly in relation to fashion and style, it also would encourage a more longitudinal dimension which would connect being in a subculture with what happens next, especially in the world of education, training, or employment. It was also my intention to emphasize the aesthetic element in youth cultures, particularly the creative interplay between music, dance, fashion, graphic design and other forms of visual image-making. While it would be unwise to suggest that involvement in these spheres alone facilitates a shift from being a consumer to a producer of culture on the part of the young person, that transition into culture-related areas has been and continues to be (perhaps at an accelerated rate) part of a broader social trend which has gone relatively unrecorded in the sociological literature on young people.

In the second section I argued for an analysis of those cultural forms

167

associated in this instance with young girls' magazines which was open to extra-textual factors including both the views and ideas which young editorial staff brought to the magazines and the tensions inside the magazines between the various different departments and sections. This was a way, I argued, of allowing for the changing views and experiences which do find expression in culture (in this case in the magazines) to be recognized and understood. It was therefore a way of gauging the parameters of change in the popular representations of femininity.

When it comes to my third example, rave culture, both of these arguments, first about the aesthetics of subculture and second about changing modes of femininity, are less easily maintained. Indeed rave seems to overturn many of the expectations and assumptions we might now have about youth subcultures and for this reason it reminds us of the dangers of looking for linear development or 'progression' in, let us say, the sexual politics of youth. Girls appear, for example, to be less involved in the cultural production of rave, from the flyers, to the events, to the DJing, than their male counterparts. We cannot be certain therefore that the broader changing climate of sexual politics is automatically reflected in rave. It is precisely the unexpected social relations and cultural practices which give the subculture its distinctive character. For example, just at the point at which class has receded as the conceptual key for understanding what subcultures are really about, and as questions of race, gender and cultural and aesthetic practice have come to the forefront, suddenly there appears from some unspecified site in the symbolic landscape of youth, a subculture which rescues working-class youth from the distant memories of the sociologists and provocatively places working-class masculinity shirtless, sweating, *en masse*, in the vast hangars of the rave party.

The scale is huge and ever increasing, the atmosphere is one of unity, of dissolving difference in the peace and harmony haze of the drug Ecstasy. The trope of masculinity is visually one of largely white unadorned, anti-stylish 'normality'. But laddishness has been replaced by friendliness. Indeed the second irony of this present social moment is that working-class boys lose their 'aggro' and become 'new men' not through the critique of masculinity which accompanies the changing modes of femininity I referred to above, but through the use of Ecstasy. They undergo a conversion to the soft, the malleable and the sociable rather than the anti-social, and through the almost addictive pleasure of dance they also enter into a different relationship with their own bodies, more tactile, more sensuous, less focused round sexual gratification. The orgiastic frenzy of dance culture also hints at the fear of AIDS among young people. Rave dance legitimates pure physical abandon in the company of others without requiring the narrative of sex or romance. The culture is one of childhood, of a pre-sexual, pre-oedipal stage. Dancing provides the rationale for rave. Where other youth subcultures have focused on street appearances, or have chosen live rock performances for providing the emblematic opportunity for the display of style, in rave everything happens within the space of the party.

There is always something arbitrary and almost absurd about the objects or favoured ritualistic practices of subcultural choice. The spray of spit which showered down on those standing near the stage at punk performances was as obviously 'meaningful' as it was shocking. Likewise the sight of rave girls in hot pants and bra tops dancing with a 'dummy' in their mouths, and a whistle round their necks, is as unexpected as it is unprecedented in the visual repertoire of stylish femininity (the rave equivalent perhaps to the laddered fishnet tights and suspenders of punk). This is a drug culture which masquerades its innocence in the language of childhood. Ice lollies help the 'revellers' to chill out or cool down. All three of these objects, the lolly, the dummy and the whistle, also mediate between the drug E and its absorption by the physical body. The symbols and imagery are self-consciously childlike and direct. Primary colours, psychedelic doodles, images taken from familiar advertisements, phrases and tunes lifted from children's TV programmes like *The Magic Roundabout*, *Sesame Street* and others, all of these along with electronically produced music with a dance-defying beats-per-minute ratio are crafted together creating a rapturous response on the part of the 'revellers'.

Some features of rave are of particular significance in relation to the questions I have posed above. What kind of image of femininity, for example, is being pursued as female ravers strip down and sweat out? Dance is where girls were always found in subcultures. It was their only entitlement. Now in rave it becomes the motivating force for the entire subculture. This gives girls a new-found confidence and a prominence. Bra tops, leggings and trainers provide a basic (aerobic) wardrobe. In rave (and in the club culture with which it often overlaps) girls are highly sexual in their dress and appearance, with 1960s TV stars like Emma Peel as their style models. The tension in rave for girls comes, it seems, from remaining in control, and at the same time losing themselves in dance and music. Abandon in dance must now, post-AIDS, be balanced by caution and the exercise of control in sex. One solution might lie in cultivating a hypersexual appearance which is, however, symbolically sealed or 'closed off' through the dummy, the whistle, or the ice lolly. This idea of insulating the body from 'invasion' is even more apparent in the heavy duty industrial protective clothing worn by both male and female fans of German techno music, a European variant of rave. In both cases the body signifies sociability and self-sufficiency. The communality of the massive rave crowd is balanced by the singularity of the person. Subcultural style is in this instance a metaphor for sexual protection.

The attraction of rave can partly be explained through the way in which in the 1980s club culture (which itself emerged out of black culture, the gay scene and punk, and was symbolized in Britain in the figure of Boy George) had become exclusive in terms of 'in' clubs, places, people and other 'insider' knowledge. Getting into clubs had become so difficult that many dance and music fans ended up staying away. At the same time the other club scenes had fragmented into so many specialist interests around music, race and sexual preference, that choosing where to go in this segmented dance market depended on an already stable cultural identity. You had to know exactly what you liked and who you wanted to be with and then you had to know where to look for it. But for 16-year-olds, growing up and going out is at least partly about exploring what sort of person you are, and who you want to become. In rave, even though it, too, as it grew out of Acid House had developed its own 'underground of authenticity' and, as Sarah Thornton described (1993), its own VIP culture, this cultural foreknowledge was never a precondition of entry. Likewise the selective door policies which had characterized the club culture of the late 1980s were also swept away in favour of the 'mass rave'. As the venues grew bigger, so did the crowd and so also the takings at the door and behind the bar. Rave promoters have become wealthy businessmen employing large numbers of people, including DJs, technicians, security staff, bar staff and professional dancers. This kind of level of organization put rave alongside the mainstream of club and concert promotion and removed it from the kind of small-scale entrepreneurialism associated with youth subcultures and with the level of cultural production which has allowed young people to play a more participative role in music. For raves to succeed they have to attract a large number of people. Rave organizers as a result tend to be older, male and with some experience in club promotion, often starting as DJs in smaller clubs and in illegal radio-stations. Girlfriends help on the till, work behind the bar, or else do 'PR' by going round pubs distributing flyers. The rave culture industry thereby reproduces the same sexual division of labour which exists not just in the pop music industry but in most other types of work and employment.

Who supplies this market with clothes? Is this where young women might be found? Once again the answer to this lies in the 'mass subcultural' market for rave. The kind of outrageous styles which have in the past been linked with subcultures and have therefore emphasized the line between subculture and mainstream, now reflect the disappearance of this divide. Rave style is the style of the moment, neither mainstream nor marginal, but both. Cat suits, leggings, bodies, 'playsuits' and trainers are available on the rails in Selfridge's or Pineapple. Rave style for girls is provided at every level of the fashion chain. It can be purchased in Camden Market and in other similar new and second-hand markets around the country, it can also be found in the high fashion stores as well as in the small designer outlets. (Pam Hogg, for example, designs largely for club and dance culture. Her clothes are worn by pop stars like Shakespeare's Sister. Helen Storey's best-selling beaded bra tops were also bought for wearing in the sweaty atmosphere of the club.) What this means is that as dance culture has expanded so also has the variety of activities involved in the production of fashion and style. There is still space for setting up a stall and selling new and second-hand clothes, but there is less of a gulf between the items found in the markets and what is available on the High Street.[4]

The scale of rave, however, applies not just to the hugeness of the events and parties but also to the scale of cultural plundering which makes it so expansive. From British and American black culture it takes over two fundamental forms and practices, the dance party and the pre-eminent role of the DJ. These supply, with the help of new music and sound technology and pirate radio, a huge world of possibilities. The DJ with all of this at his disposal ('his' disposal because nine out of ten are male) becomes a kind of magician, creating a 'total experience', a controlled exercise in crowd excitement. The music generates this effect through combining an accelerating but monotone beat with a much lighter, often highly melodic fragment (taken from TV soundtracks like *Twin Peaks*, or else from a Phil Collins record, or even from a James Bond soundtrack) and 'laced' on to the underlying beats-per-minute. Just as some strands of the drug culture of the late 1960s enjoyed bringing into their musical repertoire 'silly' children's theme tunes and strains of popular 'ditties', this drug culture eschews social or political comment in favour of a kind of simple, happy 'matey music' (happy hard core) articulated with the 'smiley' logo of the early phase of Acid House. This in turn raises the question of the politics of youth culture in a post-Thatcher but also seemingly post-socialist moment.

The other attraction of rave is that unlike the concert or 'gig' it goes on, it doesn't stop. This hyper-reality of pleasure, this extension of media (one which is found also in 24-hour TV and radio) produces a new social state, a new relationship between the body, the pleasures of music and dance, and the new technologies of the mass media. Rave takes pleasures which have sustained black and gay cultures and makes them available to a wide audience. It also transports this dance, drugs and music 'cocktail' into a distinctively British landscape, one which uses and celebrates a geography of small towns, new towns, motorways and rural 'beauty spots', not just all night or all day but for up to three days at a time. Not surprisingly these raves, especially during the summer, begin to look like the hippie gatherings or festivals of the late 1960s. The sight, in the summer of 1992, of working-class male football fans converging in secret rural locations to dance out of doors and sleep in their cars before returning, after this saturnalia of mind and body experiences, to Liverpool, Leeds, or wherever, is a strong statement about the appropriation of pleasure and the 'right to party' on the part of this particular (but expansive) group of young people.

There are social tensions in rave (including those around gender and sexuality) which are manifest in the particular aesthetics of dance, music and drugs which have come to characterize the phenomena. If there is as Maria Pini (1993) argues, a 'text of excitement', an intense and relentless desire for pleasure which finds gratification in the combination of the sociability of the event, the 'friendliness' of the drug and the individual physical pleasure of its effects, there is also not only a 'text of anxiety', one which, out of fear of AIDS, results in the downgrading of sexual pleasure in favour of a childlike body pleasure (polymorphous perversity) but also a 'text of avoidance'. Rave contains nothing like the aggressive political culture found in punk music. It is as though young ravers simply cannot bear the burden of the responsibility they are being expected to carry. There are so many dangers (drugs, cigarettes, alcohol, unprotected sex, sexual violence and rape, ecological disaster), so many social and political issues which have a direct bearing on their lives and so many demands made on them (to be fully responsible in their sexual activity, to become good citizens, to find a job and earn a living, to find a partner and have a family in a world where marriage has become a 'temporary contract') that rave turns away from this heavy load headlong into a culture of avoidance and almost pure abandonment. It does this as visibly and spectacularly as many of its subcultural predecessors and thereby provokes a strong social reaction. As a result a dialogue is established, one which, as in the past, includes the intensification of policing and social control. The question then is the extent to which a subcultural aesthetic that asks its fans to 'shut up and dance' produces in the haze of pleasure and enjoyment a cultural politics of any sort.

But just how possible is it to talk about a cultural politics of youth in the 1990s? While I have insisted throughout this chapter on the importance of positioning young people as active negotiators and producers of culture rather than simply its consumers, the very notion of a cultural politics implies a unity of focus and a direction which it is difficult to find in youth culture and which perhaps is not what we should be looking for in any case. Youth is not a stable undifferentiated category; it is cut across by ethnic, gender, class and other differences. What are more realistic to look for are cultural forms and expressions that seem to suggest new or emergent 'structures of feeling' on the part of sections of the young population; for example, among young girls.[5] Such a confluence of change can be seen, I have argued, in a magazine like *Just Seventeen* where patterns of meaning which were once emblematic of the experience of teenage femininity (i.e. romance) have disappeared and have been replaced by a more diffuse femininity, one which has been cut loose from the firm underpinning provided by romance. What results from this process of detachment from the poles of identity provided by romance is that femininity is constructed as the product of a number of less stable, emergent subject positions. Femininity is no longer the 'other' of feminism; instead it incorporates many of those 'structures of feeling' which emerged from the political discourse of feminism in the 1970s. But it also, and perhaps most powerfully, exists as the product of a highly charged consumer culture which in turn provides subject positions for girls and personal identities for them through consumption. Finally the subject of the new femininity also enters into social and sexual relationships from a different position than the one she occupied ten or fifteen years ago. Here too there has been contestation and change. Friendship, equality and difference are all now part of the vocabulary of relationships, alongside love, sex and pleasure. What remains to be explored is the way in which being 'emancipated' from romance coexists with new anxieties and fears of AIDS. We also need to understand the dangers which young women confront in a world where they no longer look for or believe in the prince who will come riding by and protect them from such dangers. The absent prince could also be seen as precipitating a crisis of female subjectivity.

Perhaps the most appropriate way to conclude is to return to the 'micrological' level and to the subject position of parent which I hesitantly took up in the opening paragraphs of this article. What, for example, are the debates and dilemmas which go through my head as I wait anxiously for my daughter to return from all-night raves? I find that the pleasure and excitement which my daughter and her friends experience as they discover new clubs and locations for raves, as they get to know new people inside the raves and as they uncover places and spaces where raves carry on and wind down when the clubs shut, are all clouded by my own fears and even panic about a number of things including drugs ('Is it possible to enjoy the music without the drugs?'); the people (i.e. men or boys) they meet; the dangers of being in cars driven by boys who have taken E; the dangers of being in such large crowds of people ('Do they have fire and safety regulations?' I ask, nervously) – in fact almost every conceivable part of rave which contributes to its attraction, and to its thresholds of thrill and excitement.

And yet, of course I am both interested in and pleased by my daughter's absorption in culture. I had forgotten the wide range of knowledge about music which such involvement in a subculture produces. Television fades in interest as Kiss FM and many of the other illegal radio stations take over, broadcasting direct to this audience. Subcultural novels and video films, usually mythologizing some earlier subcultural or underground moment, begin to circulate among the group of friends. The cultural politics which emerges for these girls and their friends from the experience of rave fixes them in a space of identity which knows first and

173

foremost what it is not. It is not conventionally middle-class. It is not too tightly bound to the 'parent culture'. Instead this is a cultural space dominated by the experience of mostly working-class young people, black and white, and it is their culture and language as well as their creativity and work which establish the subculture in the first place. It is also a place of spectacle and display, as one club or rave tries to outdo the other in special effects or theme park attractions or videos. This interplay of dance, music and image produces a powerful popular aesthetic. Immersion in rave also influences patterns of love and friendship. Despite being ostensibly open to all, the codes of 'rave authenticity' which include 'white label' tracks, fanzines, flyers as collectors' items, well-known DJs, famous clubs, legendary raves, double meanings in music lyrics, argot, ritual and special items of clothes, are continuously drawn upon as resources for constructing who the raver is.

Perhaps the emphasis on authenticity is a precondition for acquiring subjectivity and identity in adolescence, one of the attractions of subculture being precisely that it offers strong subjectivity through the collective meanings that emerge from the distinctive combination of signs, symbols, objects, styles and other 'signifying texts'. These are not experienced in isolation from other more commercial teenage texts such as those of TV soap opera, or series like *Twin Peaks*, or films like *Flatliners*, or other 'brat pack' movies. But the subculture far outstrips other forms of youth entertainment because of where it takes place. Outside the regulatory space of the home or school, the more autonomous space of the subculture contributes directly to the weakening of these other institutional ties. For this reason the attraction to subcultures lies partly in the modes of empowerment they offer. It is the extent to which such cultural forms and practices exist and take shape outside the controlling and defining gaze of otherwise more powerful others, including parents, which also accounts for the feelings of anxiety, fear and powerlessness experienced by conventional 'moral guardians' and also by parents. Sociologists have described and explained the power of youth subcultures as resistance, and the social reaction to these phenomena as 'moral panics'. These often nebulous terms find clarification and confirmation when the position of the parent, or mother, is taken into account.[6]

This article was first published in *Cultural Studies* 7, 3 (1993): 406–26; and simultaneously in *Young: the Nordic Journal of Youth Research* 1, 2 (1993): 13–32.

NOTES

My thanks to Sarah Thornton for discussing this article. See also S. Thornton, 'From record hops to raves: cultural studies of youth, music and media', PhD thesis, John Logie Baird Centre, University of Strathclyde, Glasgow, 1993, for a much fuller account of club culture.

1 Only a detailed research study would reveal the precise shifts and changes in the youth labour market along the lines of sex, class and race. What evidence there is shows that black working-class young women are more likely to return to further or higher education than their male counterparts. While middle-class girls continue to move into professional fields like law, dentistry and medicine, it is more difficult to find material on white working-class women's training and employment.

2 See, for example, TV programmes like BBC Def II's *Reportage* series, edited by Janet Street Porter, which addresses the question of drugs seriously while avoiding the sensationalist reporting of the tabloid press.

3 There has always been a direct link between small shops and boutiques selling specifically youth culture styles before they get into the high street and the club scene. For instance, flyers and publicity leaflets for clubs and raves list such shops as the places where tickets can be purchased. These clothes shops as well as record stores will also supply information about local clubs and raves.

4 For example, the Revive Clothing shop in Coventry sells rave-style clothes which include new designer club clothes in rubber, lycra and cotton, but also 'restored' second-hand items, as well as new, 'perfect' copies of old classics, e.g. American silk bomber jackets.

5 Raymond Williams (1961) used the term 'structure of feeling' in *The Long Revolution*.

6 Drawing on the work of Foucault, Erica Carter (1984) uses the term 'micrological' to describe exactly this interface of power and powerlessness between mother and adolescent daughter. Carter is referring to conflicts over particular items of clothing, and in so doing offers a more local and contextual definition of 'resistance'. Far from reducing the scope of the term Carter's analysis brings into play questions of gender and the family, both of which were conspicuously missing in the model of 'resistance through rituals' developed by the CCCS.

REFERENCES

Bourdieu, Pierre (1984) *Distinction*, London/New York: Routledge & Kegan Paul.

Brunsdon, Charlotte (1991/2) 'Pedagogies of the feminine: feminist teaching and women's genres' *Screen* 32, 4: 364–82.

Carter, Erica (1984) 'Alice in consumer wonderland', in Angela McRobbie and Mica Nava (eds) *Gender and Generation*, London: Macmillan, pp. 185–214.

Faludi, Susan (1991) *Backlash: The Undeclared War Against American Women*, New York: Doubleday.

Frith, Simon and Horne, Howard (1987) *Art into Pop*, London: Methuen.

Hall, Stuart and Jefferson, Tony (1977) *Resistance through Rituals*, London: Hutchinson.

Hartwig, Helmut (1993) 'Youth culture forever', *Young: The Nordic Journal of Youth Research* 1, 3: 2–16.

Hebdige, Dick (1979) *Subculture: The Meaning of Style*, London: Routledge.

Hebdige, Dick (1987) 'The impossible object: towards a sociology of the sublime', *New Formations* 1, 1: 47–76.

McRobbie, Angela (1990) 'Second-hand dresses and the role of the ragmarket', in Angela McRobbie (ed.) *Zoot Suits and Second-hand Dresses: An Anthology of Fashion and Music*, London: MacMillan, pp. 23–49 (reprinted in this book as chapter 8).

McRobbie, Angela (1991) 'From Jackie to Just Seventeen: girls' magazines in the 1980s', in Angela McRobbie, *Feminism and Youth Culture: From Jackie to Just Seventeen*, London: Macmillan, pp. 135–89.

McRobbie, Angela (1992) 'Post-Marxism and cultural studies', in Lawrence Grossberg, Cary Nelson and Paula Treichler (eds) *Cultural Studies*, New York: Routledge, pp. 719–30, (reprinted in this book as chapter 3).

Modleski, Tania (1982) *Loving with a Vengeance*, New York/London: Methuen.

Mort, F. (1994) *For What It Is Worth*, London: Lawrence & Wishart.

Nava, Mica (1992) *Changing Cultures: Feminism, Youth and Consumerism*, London: Sage.

Pini, Maria (1993) 'Rave, dance and women', unpublished MA dissertation, Thames Valley University.

Pleasance, Helen (1992) 'Open or closed: popular magazines and dominant culture', in S. Franklin, C. Lury and J. Stacey (eds) *Off Centre: Feminism and Cultural Studies*, New York: HarperCollins, pp. 69–85.

Radway, Janice (1984) *Reading the Romance; Women, Patriarchy and Popular Literature*, Chapel Hill, NC/London: University of North Carolina Press.

Thornton, Sarah (1993) 'From record hops to raves: cultural studies of youth, music and media', unpublished PhD thesis on club culture, John Logie Baird Centre, University of Strathclyde, Glasgow.

Wiliams, Raymond (1961) *The Long Revolution*, London: Chatto & Windus.

10

DIFFERENT, YOUTHFUL, SUBJECTIVITIES: TOWARDS A CULTURAL SOCIOLOGY OF YOUTH

The purpose of this chapter is first to review and update work on youth falling within the fields of both sociology and cultural studies; second to consider in more depth questions of ethnicity and questions of sexuality within this overlapping field; and third to argue for a new convergence of cultural studies and sociology where each might benefit from the strengths of the other and in so doing overcome the tendency to disciplinary boundary-marking and hostility which has become disappointingly commonplace over the last few years. Cultural studies has been characterized as excessively concerned with texts and meanings and has been seen by many sociologists as lacking in methodology and in rigour. Sociology in turn is often regarded in cultural studies as being uninterested in questions which cannot be contained within the existing language of 1970s Marxist/feminist theory. Cultural studies flaunts its wild style while sociology prides itself on its materialist steadfastness. This is not a conflict which has come out in the open. Instead it has bubbled underneath and has taken the form of barbed references and footnotes, with occasional outbursts of overt hostility. The debate has emerged more clearly in the contents of the academic curriculum, where sociology sees itself as concentrating on the real world while castigating cultural studies for daring to suggest that there is no 'real' world, an issue to which I will return in the course of this chapter.[1]

Both sides, it will be suggested, need to consider issues which have been marginalized in the course of their own development. Cultural studies, while continually on the cutting edge of theory, must be willing to substantiate this interest, not necessarily through recourse to empiricism, but through a mode of research and analysis which explores more fully the rich suggestiveness of theoretical work. Sociology in turn must be willing to consider two possibilities. The first is that culture, however it is defined, now exists in a position of dominance in a world where the television and the visual image have become the primary means through which the mass communications industry works, and where alongside this

177

the map of the world, its borders and boundaries have been redrawn by the international corporations, for whom the production of culture and information is the 'logic of late capital' (Jameson, 1984). The second is that the consequences of Jameson's view are that one of the marks of postmodernity is that it is no longer possible to conceptualize and analyse society as a whole, or even as a layered and uneven totality. There can no longer be one big picture, and that kind of theoretical imaging of 'society' which gave sociology its existence, is exactly what is now being disputed. With this, sociology must contend.

Calls for a convergence of these two disciplines have begun to appear, the most notable being Michèle Barrett's chapter 'Words and things: materialism and method in contemporary feminist analysis' in the collection she has coedited with Anne Phillips (Barrett, 1992). In this piece Barrett argues that sociology needs to engage more directly with those strands of poststructuralist thinking which it has in the past consigned to the field of literary studies. This is all the more important given the extent to which there seems to have been within academic feminism over the last ten years a 'turn to culture'. Barrett is referring here to a shift in interest away from sociological 'things' to 'processes of symbolization and representation ... and attempts to develop a better understanding of subjectivity, the psyche and the self ... and towards a more cultural sensibility of the salience of words' (1992: 2).

While it is also the intention of this chapter to propose that sociology might regard more favourably concepts like subjectivity and difference in relation to youth, it will equally be argued that sociology continues to offer not just the valuable sound of 'spoken voices' in much of the work on youth, something which is largely absent from cultural studies, but that it has also insisted on the importance of institutional practices as key forces for shaping continuity and change in the experience of young people in Britain today. This too is something that should not be ignored. In short the purpose of this chapter will be to set a new agenda for the sociology of youth, informed not only by recent developments in cultural theory but also by that emphasis on lived experience and on spoken voices which continues to be found in sociology.

To begin such a discussion it is assumed that, without presenting youth as an essentialist category, there are none the less a sufficient number of shared age-specific experiences among young people which still allow us to talk meaningfully about youth. And while it is recognized that differences of social class continue to play a considerable role in determining the landscape of opportunity for young people, the emphasis here will be on questions of ethnicity and questions of sexuality. Drawing on Stuart Hall's category of 'new ethnicities' (Hall, 1992a) and with what I have elsewhere referred to as 'changing modes of femininity' (McRobbie, 1993), and adding to this the admittedly clumsy notion of 'different, youthful, subjectivities', I will, in the pages that follow, indicate some areas for discussion and for research.

But first, why youth? For a variety of social, historical and psychological reasons which have already been explored in depth in that area of work which has come to be known as 'subcultural theory' (Hall and Jefferson, 1977), youth remains a site of cultural innovation. The social processes of construction which underpin this flow of creativity remain relatively undocumented as a number of sociologists have recently pointed out (Frith, 1992; McRobbie, 1993; Thornton, 1993). There is certainly no longer a case to be made for the traditional argument that youth culture is produced somehow in conditions of working-class purity, and that such expressions are authentic and in the first instance at least uncontaminated by an avaricious commercial culture. That argument has long since been replaced by a more complex understanding of the dynamics between subculture, the mass media, commercial culture and the state. These vibrant, noisy products which emerge from in between the spaces for expression, discovered by young people inside and outside of the large social institutions which regulate and control their movements and experiences, might still seem trivial and unimportant if judged from the perspective of traditional youth politics. But the proliferation of hairstyles and musics, of events and rituals, of fashions and magazines, of images and articles, of complex systems of cross-referencing and of reviving past youth cultures, and finally the sheer speed with which this all takes place, represent exactly what Michèle Barrett refers to as the 'turn to culture' and the 'processes of symbolization'.

In addition the volume of culture being created and the high turnover of ideas and images from week to week, appearing on the street, in the magazines and on TV, must logically collide at some point with Jameson's suggestion that culture is now dominant. If he is right then it seems that it is young people who are largely responsible for maintaining this high level of output. This puts young people, and the apparent ease with which they participate in this form of informal cultural production, in an even more pivotal position. All the more reason then to return to the field of youth studies. Many of these powerful symbolic formations can then be interpreted as the voice of young people and the new subjectivities which changing social conditions bring into being. We are thus starkly reminded of the extent to which young people tell us a good deal about the scale and the dynamics of social change itself. And because as academics we are teachers and many of us are also parents it is not surprising that we are curious about how their 'difference' and their 'subjectivities' are historical formations, the expressions of 'a generation'. Youth subcultures are symbolically so highly charged and so energetic in their output of cultural forms, that they come to represent or even stand in for a particular historical moment and its generation, e.g. the 'rave' generation of the late 1980s and early 1990s. This does not mean that there is a singular youth experience, but rather that there is a range of 'different, youthful, subjectivities', and what we have to be able to do as sociologists is to move beyond journalistic terms like 'Thatcher's children' or 'the rave generation' and understand those factors which appear to reach to the unconsciousness of young people and re-emerge in their socially perceptible subjectivities.

While sociology has been interested in the social characteristics of expressions of 'generational consciousness' (Murdock and McCron, 1977) it has implicitly relegated detailed questions about subjectivity to the field of psychology (see the work of Valerie Walkerdine, 1991, for example). It has also treated the voices of young people, as reported in ethnographic studies, as transparently meaningful and as evidence in themselves, rather than as complex social constructs which are the products of pre-given discourses, in effect 'written' in advance as scripts made available by dominant culture for their teenage speakers. This is how structuralists and many within the field of cultural studies would now approach the same material. By taking elicited responses as generally unproblematic at this level, while being alert to methodological issues, sociology has no vocabulary for asking the sort of questions which cultural studies has been asking. Among these questions is the way the discourses of popular culture, including those of music, magazines and youth TV, position their readers or viewers in a particular relationship to the text and its meaning and in doing so play a concerted role in constructing and organizing subjectivity as it comes into being in the 'inter-discursive space' where these cultural forms and their meanings meet and interact with each other.

The difficulty with this approach, as I will go on to argue later, is that it too easily slides into analysis of the specific discourses, most often forms of mass media, which then look as though they do virtually all of the positioning work. What get ignored are the interactions between the various discourses, and also between the young people and the wider social and institutional relations which they inhabit. It is this kind of exclusive concentration on specific texts which then gives cultural studies a reputation for being closer to film and media studies and which also encourages sociology to consider itself as more grounded in social reality and more concerned with observable social behaviour.

Meanwhile youth remains a key point for social and political anxiety. It has been one of the areas for concerted government attention right across the spectrum of social affairs: in law and order, where there have been moral panics about the 'new juvenile crime'; in education, where there is an endless debate about declining standards; in the family and in the field of public morality where both marital breakdown and the growth of teenage motherhood are taken as symptoms of social decay; and finally

180

in leisure where rave parties and particularly those organized by young squatters and travelling people are subjected to intensive policing and surveillance. Issues around the state, social institutions and governmentality, however, are much too important to ignore. It was the regulative and repressive practices of social control which gave an urgency to the early work in cultural studies on youth. Perhaps it is not so much that cultural studies has abandoned youth in the intervening years; more that a moment of convergence marked by the emergence of cultural studies represented the drawing together of such a diversity of concepts and ideas that this was quickly followed by a splintering, and then by a reconvergence and realignment of interests. If we look at the work of the Centre for Contemporary Cultural Studies (CCCS) in Birmingham we could suggest that the publication within a few years of each other of six volumes – *Resistance through Rituals* (Hall and Jefferson, 1977); *Learning to Labour* (Willis, 1977); *Policing the Crisis* (Hall *et al.*, 1978); and *Subculture: The Meaning of Style* (Hedbige, 1979); followed by *The Empire Strikes Back* (ed. Gilroy, 1982) and then by Gilroy's *There Ain't No Black in the Union Jack* (Gilroy, 1987) – led to an emphasis on four areas of key importance, not just to the study of youth but to the whole future development of cultural studies. These were race, state and nation; sexuality and representation; education and ethnography; and more recently postcoloniality and postmodernism.

What can also be witnessed during the 1980s is a rejection of the primacy of the youth and social class couplet which had underpinned the development of 'subcultural theory' (Hall and Jefferson, 1977) and its replacement by another set of concerns, the most significant of which are race and sexuality. One problem is that feminist work on youth in the 1980s, with a few exceptions, is more interested in representations of sexuality than in sexual behaviour, sexual activity, or the way in which sexuality is spoken about by young women themselves. The new 'Madonna scholarship' (Schwichtenberg, 1993) exists almost entirely within the framework of media or film studies. In her earlier work Madonna performed very much for a young female audience, but this dimension tends to get buried when her music, her videos and her film and TV appearances are understood as 'texts of sexuality' in a language which draws on feminist film theory. In Jackie Stacey's analysis (1988) of *Desperately Seeking Susan*,[2] for example, the film is not so much about patterns of female adolescent identity formation through friendship and fascination, as about what happens when one woman (Susan, played by Madonna) becomes the object of another woman's gaze (Roberta, played by Rosanna Arquette).

A similar process of textualization has taken place in the cultural analysis of music. With the exception of Keith Negus's recent account of the music industry (Negus, 1993), Finnegan's work on young musicians

181

(Finnegan, 1989), Sara Cohen's ethnography of musical production in Liverpool (Cohen, 1987) and Sarah Thornton's account of subcultures, youth and music (1993), we find a reduction of a whole field of social activities, including the participation of fans, audiences and young musicians in the production of musical culture, to that of musical texts. This has admittedly been encouraged by the visualization of pop music through the growth of commercial pop videos, but it does not excuse the narrowing of focus in the study of MTV, for example, to that of the status of texts of postmodernity, or not, as Andrew Goodwin argues in reply to E. Ann Kaplan (Kaplan, 1987; Goodwin, 1991).

The suggestion is therefore that during the 1980s the focus on youth which had been such a visible characteristic of cultural studies in the 1970s, was replaced by a number of other interests which overlap with or touch on youth without really acknowledging this fact. The over-shadowing of youth as a useful sociological or cultural category can even be seen in the work around 'new ethnicities'. It is after all black *youth* who have been making much of the music Paul Gilroy examines in *There Ain't No Black in the Union Jack* (1987) and also in his new volume *The Black Atlantic* (1993a). Despite this the processes of what Stuart Hall has described as 'becoming not being' (1992a) have not been explored in relation to the experience of black or Asian young people. We have to look almost exclusively to the sociology of education to find any recent material on this important subject. This is a pity because the whole question of identity which is posed by the new ethnicities work has a special resonance for youth. There is a particular intensity to the processes of separation and detachment from parents and the simultaneous attachment to symbols of freedom and adventure such as those provided in music and found in the spaces of the street and night-club. If this is not directly theorized in the work of the new ethnicity writers (with the exception of Cohen, 1992), it is possible to see a good deal of the work of the new black writers and film-makers as engaging directly with the experience of being young and black. *Young Soul Rebels* is a 'youth movie'. It records the sense of fear, adventure and freedom experienced by the film's central character as he explores the city, his own homosexuality and his blackness, against a backdrop of Britain in the late 1970s.

While these processes of identity formation (in the examples offered above, a largely male phenomenon) remain to be more fully explored in the new ethnicities work, writing on race, at a more general level, has moved cultural theory away from its focus on textuality. Neither Stuart Hall nor Paul Gilroy has ever been an exponent of the kind of purely structuralist or poststructuralist approach which otherwise has been so dominant in the field. In recent work by both Hall and Gilroy there is an even more noticeable shift away from emphasis on the text. Gilroy shows how consistently black expressive cultures refuse the framework of the 'Eurocentric' structuralisms as useful tools of analysis. Structuralism, poststructuralism and even psychoanalysis are urgently in need of critique if they are to be of any use in dealing with the hybridic, inter-textual and antiphonic forms of black popular culture. These forms, he argues, require at least an approach which integrates text and context through the social practices of performance, production and participation. The antiphonic (call and response) aesthetic of much of Afro-Caribbean musical culture means that its meanings are open-ended rather than closed. Answering back or talking back in an improvised or immediate way is what gives black expressive culture much of its character. This feature can be found in jazz, in rap, in sampling, in hip-hop music, and in the whole technology of musical production which is, of course, participated in and produced by young people.

This is also a way of creating new meanings by adding and replying to the cultural 'bank' of black history. Thus the Was Not Was remix (two white American producers, with black musicians) of the soul classic 'Papa Was A Rolling Stone'[3] has 'Papa's children' rapping back at him for failing in his parental obligations, for leaving 'Mama' to work to provide for her family and for letting his children down. This example of 'generational consciousness' is indicative of a desire to rewrite the classics from the viewpoint of youth who have grown up aware of questions of sexual inequality.

The idea of extending existing cultural forms in this way and in so doing producing new forms and new meanings is central to Gilroy's analysis of black expressive culture. His analysis tends to be restricted to music, but the same process can also be seen in dance, and since this is where the participation of young girls is perhaps more visible, the culture of ragga girls in Britain in the 1990s serves as a good example. If the cultural analysis remains at the level of ragga music as a text (an import from the dance-halls of Jamaica) then the question of the sexism of the lyrics and the overt homophobia found in the music of the singer and performer Shabba Ranks requires that this be engaged with directly. But the sexist meaning of the lyrics is challenged by ragga girls in their highly enthusiastic embracing of ragga as well as their distictive 'calls and responses' to it through dance. Shabba Ranks's sexism is talked back to. Ragga girls, as the *Sunday Times* recently reported (Willis, 1993), recognize ragga style as the strongest and fiercest reference point in contemporary youth subcultures. It conveys an uncompromising sense of blackness and for this it has already provoked a string of attacks in the press.

This moral panic has made ragga all the more attractive to young people, and it has been taken up by young Asians (raggastanis or bhangramuffins) and also by white girls, with their hair scraped back tightly into buns, wearing gold jewellery, trainers, leggings and fake-fur winter coats. The particular fusion of ethnicity and masculinity which dominates this subculture, however, virtually bars white boys from being raggas. (Though there is always the rare exception, slightly self-conscious in his baggy string vest, even baggier trousers and baseball cap.)

Black ragga girls participate in and energize the music through a form of dance which has been described as sexually explicit, even obscene. Its display of 'virtually simulated sex' has provoked outcries from black and white moral guardians alike. Spencer argues, in relation to the sexually explicit lyrics of rap, that this is a means of retaliating to the old white fears of black 'illicit sexualities' by verbalizing these fears and through appearing to celebrate precisely such a 'subjugated sexuality' in what he describes as an 'irruption of speech'. This argument can be extended to ragga music and also to the 'irruption of dance' (Spencer, 1993). The *Sunday Times* journalist who described the girls 'hitching their skirts and 'wining' onto men's faces' conceded that there is more, it seems, to this kind of dancing than sexism. As the anthropologist quoted in the article says, 'This is more about women enjoying their own sexuality than about seduction. I suspect they end up going home alone.' The journalist also included a quote from one of the girls: 'So long as you realize that a lot of it is tongue in cheek it isn't really offensive' (Willis, 1993). If then we connect to ragga music the participatory dynamics of its greatest fans, young teenage girls, we can see that this adds a further dimension of meaning not visible in the music or the lyrics alone. While these girls are so 'rude' that they would almost make Madonna blush, they also seem to have learned something from Madonna. The clothes are strikingly similar (bra tops and tight lycra shorts) and the rhetoric of a proud young female sexuality is combined with the sheer physical enjoyment of dance, working together to produce a euphoria of pleasure and of power.

This reflects a new, bold, visible and hybridic ethnicity, where young black British girls participate directly in the language of sexual relations and sexual conflict which has been prominent in Jamaican dance music, producing for themselves in the process a 'loud' and provocative image and identity. Likewise they could also be seen as participating in a 'changing mode of femininity' where their blackness and their sexuality are forged in a striking visual image which is both excessively and transgressively feminine and includes, for example, a school uniform of bright blonde wigs, gold cat suits, heavy jewellery and trainers.

INTERACTIVE CULTURAL SOCIOLOGY

What is needed, then, in relation to the study of youth, with particular reference to ethnicity and sexuality, is a research mode which prioritizes multiple levels of experience, including the ongoing relations which connect everyday life with cultural forms. This would be a way of breaking down the division which has emerged between the study of cultural texts and the study of social behaviour and experience. It has been argued in this chapter that questions of the state and social control, questions of institutional practice and policy, and also of lived experience, have been neglected in cultural studies over the last few years and that as a result there has been little opportunity to ground the concepts of difference, identity and subjectivity in these experiences.

At the same time cultural studies has wrongly been characterized, in sociology and in related fields such as social policy, as being a subdiscipline of literary studies, or else as a field which is much closer to the arts and the humanities than to the 'hard' social sciences. But what cultural studies needs to think about is how ideas like difference, subjectivity and other even more troublesome concepts – fascination, for example – which also figure frequently in discussions on race and sexuality, need to be fleshed out and explored within the landscape of everyday social relations. Sociology, meanwhile, needs to give more time to the concept of culture itself. If culture is dominant, then the social sciences need to find a way of engaging with this, other than either relegating it to the field of the arts and literary criticism or else packaging it up within the political economy of mass communications. The main crossover text in this context has been Paul Willis's *Learning to Labour* and, given the central place which it still seems to occupy in the sociology syllabus, it is surprising that no social scientists have embarked on a project of updating or revising this material which was published over fifteen years ago.

One potential solution to the dilemmas outlined above and to the cleavage which has developed in an area that might usefully provide common ground, is suggested through the kind of work which Gilroy proposes (Gilroy, 1993a). He argues that black expressive culture, particularly music, exists as a set of open-ended structures which invite and find creative cultural responses in the form of various styles of sampling, rapping, dance and performance, which in turn emerge as distinctively new aesthetics. This argument allows for the posing of more sociological questions of practice and production in what would otherwise be seen, more traditionally, as a set of closed cultural forms. In the section that follows I will make a number of suggestions about what might be important areas to study, and I will consider some of the work which has been carried out on patterns of inter-ethnic friendship, an area which is precisely one that deserves more attention. Do the shared cultures of music, fashion and style offer the possibility for a kind of popular anti-racism? If so, what are the gender dynamics which bring black and white youth together, and how sustainable are such relations within a wider social context of racial and sexual inequality?

INTER-ETHNIC FRIENDSHIP

Cultural studies has insisted on the importance of anti-essentialist approaches to the study of both race and sexuality through the concept of difference (i.e. there are many ways of being black, just as there are many ways of being a woman) but what is missing is a clear sense of what these different identities look like, how they are lived, and within what institutional frameworks they are pursued. What are the discourses within which 'different, youthful, subjectivities' are constructed? How are they expressed? One of the most noticeable changes in the commercial world of women's magazines and advertising is the way in which the male body has become commoditized and sexualized to such an extent that Richard Dyer's seminal argument (Dyer, 1989) about the extreme discomfort men feel through being made the 'object of the gaze' seems quite outmoded. No longer do male pin-ups look abstractly out and beyond the look of the viewer, as though to counteract the subordination of the camera through refusing to meet the female viewer's gaze. Now they engage directly with the camera, displaying a whole range of responses from the flirtatious and friendly to the overtly sexual, and then also to the purely narcissistic and seemingly self-absorbed.

How are these changing modes of masculinity reflected in language and social experience? It seems that for women ways of looking at and talking about men have changed. From the popularity of the Chippendales to overhearing a couple of female students exchange comments about whether or not the boy in the holiday snapshot had a good body, where all that could be seen across the picture was an expanse of chest, men appear to be enjoying the kind of attention which in the past has been part of how men view women and not the other way round. The beauty stakes have gone up for men, and women have taken up the position of active viewers. For feminists it seems ironic that sexual equality, with the support of the commerical world of magazines, commodities and advertising, should be 'won' along precisely the lines upon which it had always been most obviously lost. However, while this phenomenon of the 'new man' has attracted attention in cultural studies (Chapman and Rutherford, 1988), it needs to be backed up by more sustained empirical work than is at present available.

Earlier I pointed to the way in which an initial focus on youth in the CCCS work carried out in Birmingham in the late 1970s and early 1980s, quickly gave way to a series of other concerns. Of those mentioned on this list, the least developed was that of education and ethnography. These two areas of study straddled both sociology and cultural studies, but became increasingly the focus of attention in sociology. It is here that we have to look if we want to fill in the spaces left behind by cultural theory. In the sociology of education there has been a consistent interest in ethnicity in the school and in the shared environment of the multi-cultural classroom. Most of this work is also quite clearly anti-essentialist in its understanding of the relations between ethnicity and education. Donald and Rattansi (1992) provide an exhaustive account of how essentialist categories of various 'racial types' have been damagingly applied even in the conventional sociology of race as well as in the realm of popular common sense as a way of explaining 'under-achievement' in education. By drawing on ethnographic methods of research, the new sociology of race and education demonstrates how the direct experience of institutional exclusion and powerlessness means that ethnicity exists as a complex and fluid mechanism and resource for negotiating structures of both success and failure.

In Gillborn's work (1990), for instance, ethnicity on the part of young black males is expressed as a distinctive style which is on display in the school and taken by the teachers as an index of perceived or predicted failure. Other writers including Fuller (1982) and Mac an Ghaill (1989) point to the tightrope along which young black girls walk in their bid to succeed in school without surrending their ethnicity. In each case ethnicity is also the point at which racial hostility is aimed and responded to. It is thus a moment of tension and a focus for identity. It is in and through this particular 'difference' that inequality and disadvantage are resisted and perpetuated and nothing could be more obvious to the young black people themselves. Heidi Safia Mirza (1992) connects these processes with the wider structural forces which depress the aspirations of black and Asian girls by channelling their expectations and limiting their opportunities. These include inadequate careers advice, compounded by teachers' complicity in supporting a culture of under-achievement through adherence to essentialist categories.

However, work like this would need to be extended to the whole variety of educational institutions including art schools, drama schools, medical schools, etc. There would have to be a shift away from the bare interface of success and failure towards a more extended ethnographic mode which sought to capture the interactive web of relations which bring young black and white people together and which also keep them apart. Thus while the sociology of education and ethnicity is immensely important, it is weakened by two factors. The young people who are the focus of attention tend to be presented as virtually ethnically exclusive in their day-to-day experiences, and their interaction with white students is not explored. Attention to institutional practices is important in explaining the way in which inequality is reproduced but this mode of research is also constrained by the exclusive emphasis on the frameworks of the school, the teachers and the dynamics of achievement. There is another connected world of cultural and social relations, at home, on the street and in leisure, which also impacts on how ethnicity is experienced and used.

My suggestion is then that to understand the three issues which are being addressed here – new ethnicities in relation to youth, the changing modes of youthful femininity and masculinity which have emerged in cultural forms, and with these the constellations of 'different, youthful, subjectivities' – it would be necessary to pay greater attention to the space of inter-racial, interactive experience and to explore the processes of hostility, fascination and desire which penetrate and shape the nature of these encounters. Sociologists might immediately object that concepts like fascination and desire have no place in the discipline as organizing categories. It is true that in terms of existing debates around ethnicity such terms have been drawn from psychoanalysis and from the theoretical language of film and media studies and used in understanding, for example, the repetition and recurrence in culture of the racial stereotype (Bhabha, 1983). But feminist sociologists have also used 'desire', 'fascination' and similar terms to understand the appeal of romance, and the social construction and organization of sexuality, and these have been explored in empirical work; for instance, Radway's work on female readers of romance (Radway, 1985). What is at stake in the interest in fascination and desire is the deep absorption of subordinate self-images so that even when these are recognized and understood as oppressive they continue to exert a strong and powerful influence which impedes change. Sociological studies of domestic violence, for instance, have shown how such deeply internalized 'structures of feeling' (fascination with and desire for the abuser) produce patterns of complicity and collusion. In relation to race, cultural theorists like Stuart Hall and Homi Bhabha (Hall, 1992a, 1992b; Bhabha, 1990) would argue that any understanding of the experience of ethnicity which does not take into account the psychic complexity of blackness as explored in the work of Fanon remains partial (Fanon, 1992).

In relation to youth this would mean taking much further the rich and suggestive comments made by Dick Hebdige in *Subculture: The Meaning of Style* (1979) where he explains British youth subcultures as a response to the presence and experience of young black people in the UK in the postwar years. The implication, which remains somewhat cryptic in the book, is that white subcultures show an overt fascination with black culture and music, a fascination which may, as in the case of the skinheads, tip over into hostility, rivalry and hatred. Only two British studies since Hebdige's go any way in engaging with ethnic relations and interaction among young people. One is sociological in focus (Hewitt, 1986), while the other exists more firmly within the field of cultural studies (Jones, 1988).

Hewitt's study of interracial friendship patterns among boys in South

London shows such friendships to be strained to the point of breaking as the short-lived shared space of the school gives way to the more segregated spaces of adult life and employment. Racial aggression on the part of white boys is only constrained in those areas where they perceive themselves to be in a minority. Where they outnumber their black counterparts their language shows itself to be more openly racist. They see black boys 'encroaching' on their territory, which includes 'their' girls. And they see white girls who go out with black boys as 'niggermeat'. So much for inter-ethnic friendship. White women emerge as less overtly racist, but here too tensions appear; a mother who has put up with one of her daughters going out with a black boy is relieved when her other daughter finishes a mixed-race relationship and finds a new white partner (Hewitt, 1986).

Simon Jones's study (1988) was much smaller in focus and carried out in the Balsall Heath area of South Birmingham. He pays more attention to the dynamics of mixed race relationships and he gives a much fuller account of the hostility and aggression which white girls who fall in love with black boys have to endure, often from their own families. Jones shows how in this rundown area of Birmingham where young black and white people have been living alongside each other and going to school together for many years, black expressive culture, in particular, music, is a resource, as well as a source of envy and admiration on the part of young whites. This is because of its strength of feeling, its cultural richness, its ability to offer and confirm to young black people a sense of their own identity. *Black Culture, White Youth* is also important because it is more hopeful. The enduring friendships and relationships which Jones describes take place in a cultural space which is far removed from the institutional language of anti-racism or from the politics of race relations. He sees fascination translate into friendship, and desire into love, commitment and children. If there is a connection here with broader social processes beyond the neighbourhood, it is with the emergence of the two-tone youth culture and style and in particular the music of the Specials, UB40 and the Selector in the early 1980s, when Jones was carrying out his research. The problem with the book is that the sample is so small that the enthusiasm of a few of the respondents for black culture and rastafarianism verges on the idiosyncratic and obsessive. These white rastas, immediately identifiable by their careful re-creation of rasta style, do not strike the reader as reflective of the less exaggerated adoption of elements of black culture by ordinary white people in Balsall Heath. This makes it difficult to feel that the study reveals an absolutely accurate picture of inter-ethnic friendship and relationships.

WHO GOES OUT WITH WHOM?

There seems to be no work to date that takes as its object of study the experience of black and white girls as they sit next to each other in the classroom, as they read the same fashion magazines, as they listen to the same music, as they go to the same clubs, as they inhabit shared 'cultures of femininity' (McRobbie, 1991), as they negotiate the fear of sexual violence and as they also negotiate the battles of separation from their parents and the move into independence. The concluding pages of this chapter will make some attempt to suggest how such work might be framed within the fields of both sociology and cultural studies.

We can see some evidence of both 'new ethnicities' and 'changing modes of femininity' in the field of popular culture. *The Oprah Winfrey Show*, for instance, offers rich opportunities for thinking about a community of women, of all ages, and across ethnic and social backgrounds, brought together within the orbit of popular entertainment, and for whom the opportunity afforded by this occasion emerges from their shared experiences as women. Painful personal stories are exchanged in front of the cameras, on the expectation of a strong response both from the audience and from Oprah Winfrey herself. But the programme is not just about telling or confessing, it is also about personal transformation and empowerment. The underlying logic of the programme is to encourage change. Framed inevitably within the language of American pop psychology this show none the less engages with social and political issues including those of race and ethnicity. Winfrey's success as presenter cannot be separated from her distinctive political voice. While the programme is not wholly given over to women's issues, these do provide the framework, and as they are explored they also provide, within the context of global television, a new environment for bringing black and white women together.

At a more local level it is possible to point to the representation of mixed-race relationships in the British mass media and the way these construct spaces for subjectivity and identity on the part of viewers and passers-by. The recent billboard advertisements, for instance, for Joe Bloggs jeans ('You can snog in Joe Bloggs'), which became collectors' items and quickly disappeared from their bus-stop sites, showed a young, mixed-race couple locked in passionate embrace. The long overdue but now increasing visibility of black and Asian models in fashion magazines also allows for these processes of projection and identification. But this should not be seen as an exclusive one-to-one relationship between text and reader. It is not simply a question of looking at the images. Instead these circulating images have to be considered as potentially extending the notion of shared cultures of femininity. They also portray images of friendship and intimacy between girls from different ethnic backgrounds.

It might therefore be suggested that in the contemporary youth cultural media there are clear signs that British society is mixed-race and that this in turn produces a new vocabulary of interracial desire.

But this still leaves the question of how ethnicity is lived out by girls and young women. How is 'difference' understood by girls of different ethnic origin as they come together in some situations, and remain apart in others? How do black girls experience subordination and inequality in and through a culture of femininity they share by virtue of gender with their white female counterparts; a culture, for example, that still offers them only a token presence in the magazines, in the glossy images and in the written text? Once again there is little ethnographic material which deals with these kinds of exchanges and experiences. As a starting-point some research questions can at least be formulated. What, for example, is the dominant language of white female racism? Alternatively what is the language of white female 'disidentification with racism' (Mercer, 1992)? How do young white women let it be known that they are not racist and that they do not want to be associated with such practices? How do young black and white women share the mixed-race space of the school and the college? Do the same kind of patterns of relatively ethnic exclusive friendships appear within girls' groups as they do in Hewitt's study of young males? Or, less competitive than their male counterparts, do girls find it easier to break the ethnic divides?

Friendship, fascination and shared cultures of femininity are not, how-ever, unstructured processes. Post-school experience raises the same ques-tion of different ethnic pathways for girls as it does in Hewitt's study of boys. In many respects the labour market, especially at the upper end, remains ethnically as well as sexually segregated. The institutions of higher education also show clear signs of ethnic boundary-marking with the old universities remaining overwhelmingly white and the new urban universities attracting much higher numbers of black students. Equally important is the question of sexual identity and the familial and social processes which often seek to confirm intra-ethnic sexual relationships. The sexual dynamics of interaction between young people in a mixed-race culture are heavily codified within a sometimes latent and sometimes overt language of difference. Who 'goes out with whom' is not an innocent question.

What also remain problematic are the concepts which though now comfortably ensconced in cultural studies are still relatively untranslated into the world of contemporary sociology. Fascination and desire, differ-ence and subjectivity, continue to present a challenge to a field of study which is more concerned with the material structuring of social processes than with, for example, the psychic processes which underlie the social practice and articulation of racist behaviour. How then can we usefully employ these terms which have emerged from Lacanian psychoanalysis,

191

feminist film theory and theories of postcoloniality in the more sociological field of ethnicity, sexuality and youth? And how can we do this while avoiding the temptation to move back to the texts of culture as the sites where subjectivity is constructed? Such a move leads too easily into reading the texts and ignoring the interactive relationship of social groups with the texts of culture.

In recent work on identity and subjectivity it is argued forcibly that since full identity is never achieved, the question of the self is never resolved and fixed and is therefore always open to change, to transformation and to realignment. The deconstruction of the 'real me' has been a major theoretical task for feminist psychoanalysis, and for writers like Stuart Hall who recently showed how the search for subjectivity was always predicated on the ideological premise that it could be found. Once that is exposed as mistaken, identity becomes much more fluid, much more open to change.

This work challenges notions of full subjectivity and replaces it with fragile, 'shaggy', hybridic identities. It is surely significant that it is young people who seem to be at the forefront of exploring and inventing these categories often within the language of popular music, and that, as Paul Gilroy has recently pointed out, such new identities show signs of endless diversity and intensive cultural crossover (Gilroy, 1993b).

Different, youthful, subjectivities, for all the reasons of generational and institutional powerlessness which are the product of age and dependency, require and find in youth cultural forms strong symbolic structures through which 'who you are', 'who you want to be' and 'who you want to go out with' can be explored, not in any finalized way, but rather as an ongoing and reflective social process. This is to suggest that there is no clear sociological divide between 'lived experience' and 'texts and representational forms'. The one is always merging with the other, sometimes socially, in the club, listening and dancing to the music, at other points alone, in front of the television, or else with book or magazine in hand. The sounds and images addressed almost exclusively to young people represent identity-formation material, the success of which lies in its ability to reach into the adolescent unconscious and literally form a generation through the shared experience of particular books, records, films, videos, TV programmes and social activities such as dance. But old 'material' must endlessly be replaced by new sounds, new images, new faces, new 'kids on the block'. The commercial requirement of novelty as a condition for profitability reflects precisely the uncertainty of subjectivity, the need for more images to look at and the need for further confirmation about who you are and what you look like, a set of needs more than responded to by teenage magazines.

The sociological line separating lived experience from representational forms is broken in the space of fantasy, in the state of distraction, in the daydream, as the eye flickers across the advertising billboards. In this important context fascination and desire acquire a particular force, a peculiar intensity. We cannot ignore the strength of these privatized (but also social) experiences. To be 'lost in music', for example, is to be absorbed in a complex process of working out who to be. In this way whole subjectivities can come to be projected (usually for boys) into the possession of a 'record collection' as Gilroy describes (Gilroy, 1987).

The power which black cultural forms have for young black people is reflective of the historical processes of exclusion and marginalization experienced in high culture. These processes occur within the education system as well as in the traditions of British popular culture which have been reconsidered precisely on the grounds of their frequent confirmation of a simplistically monolithic notion of national culture and national identity. But what is also important about black cultural forms, in opposition to the more closed forms of British popular cultures, is that these also 'reach out and touch' many, often socially subordinate, white young people, male and female, as Alan Parker's film *The Commitments* showed. Such young white people can also 'disidentify with racism' through strongly identifying with aspects of black culture. Music, fashion and style thus make available a symbolic language for popular anti-racism.

If this appears optimistic to the point of losing track of the whole range of forces which maintain and underpin the perpetuation of racial inequality and injustice, then it has to be said that, within the narrow confines of this discussion, such a strategy is deliberate. The emphasis indeed has been on the upside rather than the downside of inter-ethnic exchanges between young people, simply to make the case that such a possibility is rarely considered as of interest to the sociologist or cultural theorist. It is largely cultural theory that provides a language for beginning to understand fascination and desire. The anti-racist subjectivities of young white people which can and do emerge from participating in these open-ended forms come into being therefore in and through the 'seats' available for them in this non-stop performance of black expressive culture (Gilroy, 1987).

The questions raised in this chapter relate to young people, and to the social conditions and experiences which play a role in constituting their subjectivities and identities. Although cultural studies has been, since its inception, a subject which engages with ideas and material arising from very contemporary social phenomena, and is sometimes criticized for having a journalistic tone, the issues raised here, while they are of a contemporary nature, require a much more detailed ethnographic approach. Indeed it would be both refreshing and helpful to have available also some good participant observation studies on youth in Britain today, particularly if such material was able to explore the emergent and 'hybridic' cultural and ethnic crossovers described above. The overall focus in this chapter has therefore been on the work that should be done and also on the sort of theoretical questions which would have to be asked. For instance, participant observation might gain something from the cultural studies' critique of the transparency of meaning in relation to spoken language. This would mean that producing the kind of work which Paul Willis carried out with young working-class boys in the late 1970s in the West Midlands might now entail a different kind of interpretive mode. Structuralist criticism would require that what the boys say be considered as potentially having been already said for them. They would be seen as activating certain given structures which accord with their position as gendered, 'classified' and ethnicized subjects in language. But this would not mean that they be seen as captives of language or as victims of their social position. What they said would be 'read' by the author and this would be presented not as the truth but as an account. Likewise other critics would be free to produce other readings of the same material. In some ways this is exactly what happens in 'Settling the accounts with subcultures: a feminist critique' (McRobbie, 1991: 16–35) where Willis's material is reconsidered from a feminist perspective. It would have been equally possible to produce a reading of Willis's ethnography from the viewpoint of race.

In short, ethnographic work would have at least to consider structuralist critiques of language as a way of producing a more complex understanding of meaning. And so, although the emphasis in this chapter has been to encourage cultural studies away from an exclusive concern with texts and meanings, this is not to say that such an approach has no value whatsoever. Here I have been arguing for a return, not to the real world, as it is sometimes seen, but rather to the terrain of how young people live and how they experience the changed world around them. If we, as sociologists or as cultural theorists, cannot do this then we must, in some way, be failing not just the disciplines we represent but also the politics which has underpinned so much of the most valuable work in these fields. A new sociology of youth would then need to demonstrate 'material steadfastness' while also being attentive to the 'wild style' of cultural studies.

This chapter was first presented as a paper at La Questionne Postcoloniale conference at Naples University, Italy, in May 1993.

NOTES

1 For a good example of this kind of boundary-marking and scepticism towards cultural studies, see Stan Cohen's recent introduction to the new edition of his classic study *Folk Devils and Moral Panics: The Creation of the Mods and Rockers*, Oxford, Blackwell, 1990.

2 For films cited in this chapter, see p. 197.
3 For music cited in this chapter, see p. 197.

REFERENCES

Bailey, David A. and Hall, Stuart (1992) 'The vertigo of displacement', *Ten 8 Critical Decade* 2, 3, Spring: 9–24.

Baker, Houston A., Jr (1993) *Black Studies: Rap and the Academy*, Chicago: University of Chicago Press.

Barrett, Michèle (1992) 'Words and things: materialism and method in contemporary feminist analysis', in Michèle Barrett and Anne Phillips (eds) *Destabilising Theory: Contemporary Feminist Debates*, London: Polity Press, p. 2.

Barthes, Roland (1977) *Image, Music, Text*, London: Fontana.

Bhabha, Homi (1983) 'The other question: the stereotype and colonial discourse', *Screen* 24, 6: 19–35.

Bhabha, Homi (ed.) (1990) *Nation and Narration*, London: Routledge.

Chapman, Rowena and Rutherford, Jonathan (eds) (1988) *Male Order: Unwrapping Masculinity*, London: Lawrence & Wishart.

Cohen, Phil (1992) ' "It's racism what dunnit": hidden narratives in theories of racism', in James Donald and Ali Rattansi (eds) *'Race', Culture and Difference*, London: Sage, pp. 62–103.

Cohen, Sara (1987) 'Society and culture in the making of rock music in Liverpool', unpublished PhD thesis, Oxford University.

Donald, James and Rattansi, Ali (eds) (1992) *'Race', Culture and Difference*, London: Sage.

Dyer, Richard (1989) 'Don't look now', in Angela McRobbie (ed.) *Zoot Suits and Second-Hand Dresses: An Anthology of Fashion and Music*, London: Macmillan, pp. 198–208.

Fanon, Frantz (1992) 'The fact of blackness', in James Donald and Ali Rattansi (eds) *'Race', Culture and Difference*, London: Sage, pp. 220–43.

Finnegan, Ruth (1989) *Hidden Musicians*, Cambridge: Cambridge University Press.

Frith, Simon (1992) 'The cultural study of popular music', in Lawrence Grossberg, Cary Nelson and Paula Treichler (eds) *Cultural Studies*, London: Routledge, pp. 174–87.

Fuller, Mary (1982) 'Young, female and black', in Ernest Cashmore and Barry Troyna (eds) *Black Youth in Crisis*, London: Allen & Unwin, pp. 142–58.

Gillborn, David (1990) *Race, Ethnicity and Education: Teaching and Learning in Multi-Ethnic Schools*, London: Routledge.

Gilroy, Paul (ed.) (1982) *The Empire Strikes Back*, London: Hutchinson.

Gilroy, Paul (1987) *There Ain't No Black in the Union Jack*, London: Hutchinson.

Gilroy, Paul (1993a) *The Black Atlantic*, London: Verso.

Gilroy, Paul (1993b) 'Between Afro-centrism and Euro-centrism: youth culture and the problem of hybridity', *Young: Nordic Journal of Youth Research* 1, 2 (May): 2–13.

Goodwin, Andrew, (1991) 'Popular music and postmodern theory', *Cultural Studies* 5, 2: 70–89.

Hall, Stuart (1992a) 'New ethnicities', in James Donald and Ali Rattansi (eds) *'Race', Culture and Difference*, London: Sage, pp. 252–60.

Hall, Stuart (1992b) 'The question of cultural identity', in Stuart Hall, David Held and David McGrew (eds) *Modernity and Its Futures*, London: Polity Press, pp. 273–327.

Hall, Stuart and Jefferson, Tony (eds) (1977) *Resistance through Rituals*, London: Hutchinson.

Hall, Stuart *et al.* (eds) (1978) *Policing the Crisis: Mugging, the State and Law and Order*, London: Macmillan.

Hebdige, Dick (1979) *Subculture: The Meaning of Style*, London: Routledge.

Hebdige, Dick (1988) *Hiding in the Light*, London: Routledge/Comedia.

Hewitt, Roger (1986) *White Talk – Black Talk: Inter-racial Friendship and Communication amongst Adolescents*, Cambridge: Cambridge university Press.

Jameson, Fredric (1984) 'Postmodernism, or the cultural logic of late capitalism', *New Left Review* 146: 53–92.

Jones, Simon (1988) *Black Culture, White Youth*, London: Macmillan.

Kaplan, E. Ann (1987) *Rocking around the Clock: Music, Television, Postmodernism and Consumer Culture*, New York: Methuen.

Mac an Ghaill, Mairtin (1989) *Young, Gifted and Black*, Milton Keynes: Open University Press.

McRobbie, Angela (1991) *Feminism and Youth Culture: From Jackie to Just Seventeen*, London: Macmillan.

McRobbie, Angela (1993) 'Shut up and dance: youth culture and changing modes of femininity', *Cultural Studies* 7, 3: 406–26 (reprinted in this book as chapter 9).

Mercer, Kobena (1992) '1968': periodising postmodern politics and identity', in Lawrence Grossberg, Cary Nelson and Paula Treichler (eds) *Cultural Studies*, London: Routledge, pp. 424–50.

Mirza, Heidi Safia (1992) *Young, Female and Black*, London: Routledge.

Murdock, Graham and McCron, Robin (1977) 'Consciousness of class, consciousness of generation', in Stuart Hall and Tony Jefferson (eds) *Resistance through Rituals*, London: Hutchinson, pp. 175–92.

Negus, Keith (1993) *Producing Pop*, London: Edward Arnold.

Pajaczkowska, Claire and Young, Lola (1992) 'Racism, representation, psychoanalysis', in James Donald and Ali Rattansi (eds) *'Race', Culture and Difference*, London: Sage, pp. 198–220.

Radway, Janice (1985) *Reading the Romance: Women, Patriarchy and Popular Literature*, London: Verso.

Schwichtenberg, C. (1993) *The Madonna Connection: Representational Politics, Subcultural Identities and Cultural Theory*, Boulder, CO: Westview Press.

Spencer, Jon Michael (1993) 'Introduction' in *The Emergency of Black and The Emergence of Rap*, Durham, NC: Duke University Press, pp. 1–15.

Stacey, Jackie (1988) 'Desperately seeking difference', in L. Gamman and M. Marshment (eds) *The Female Gaze: Women as Viewers of Popular Culture*, London: Verso, pp. 4–23.

Thornton, Sarah (1993) 'From record hops to raves: cultural studies of youth, music and media', unpublished PhD thesis, John Logie Baird Centre, University of Strathclyde, Glasgow.

Walkerdine, Valerie (1991) *Schoolgirl Fictions*, London: Verso.

Willis, Paul (1977) *Learning to Labour*, London: Saxon House.

Willis, Tim, (1993) 'Young, gifted and slack', *Sunday Times*, 2 May.

Films cited in this chapter

The Commitments, directed by Alan Parker, 1991, Orion.
Desperately Seeking Susan, directed by Susan Seidelman, 1985, Twentieth Century Fox.
Young Soul Rebels, directed by Isaac Julien, 1990, BFI/Sankofa Films.

Music cited in this chapter

'Lost In Music', sung by Sister Sledge, Atlantic, East-West.
'Papa Was A Rolling Stone', remix by Was Not Was, Fontana, Phonogram.

11

THE MORAL PANIC IN THE AGE OF THE POSTMODERN MASS MEDIA

The starting-point for this chapter is the central place occupied by the theory of the moral panic in sociology. Indeed if 'radical sociology' has made one major contribution to the kind of popular social analysis found in much of the quality press and on television, it is with the concepts of 'moral panic', 'deviance amplification' and social control. The moral panic is now a term regularly used by journalists. It has become a standard interview question to put to conservative politicians: are they not whipping up a moral panic as a means of laying the foundations for punitive legislation, or else as a foil to deflect attention away from other more pressing economic issues?

Although it is my argument that moral panics still exist, their high rate of turnover in the context of the massively expanded mass media makes it impossible to rely on the same old model with its stages and cycles, its ebb and flow. It is deeply in need of revisiting and revamping. Moral panics remain one of the most effective strategies of the right for securing popular support for its values and its policies. And this point needs to be made, that the moral panic has been inextricably connected with conservatism and that it also marks a moment of connection between 'the media' and 'social control'. In one crucial sense the moral panic is the supreme practice of consensual governmentality, a point that was strongly argued in *Policing the Crisis* (Hall *et al.*, 1978).

However, it has become, over the years, a standard response, a familiar, sometimes weary, even ridiculous rhetoric rather than an exceptional, emergency intervention. Likewise it has become standard journalistic practice to construct moral panics in the media and then, either quickly to grow tired of them or else, in some cases, to participate in a form of self-blame. 'Is it not the media itself which has helped to create this phenomenon?' asks Sue Cameron on BBC2's *Newsnight* on the question of 'new juvenile crime'. One suggestion here is that the 'moral panic' is the way in which home affairs or social and current affairs are constructed on a daily basis. However, these daily moral panics are less monolithic than the old model implied. They are also continually contested. The

198

whole terrain of the moral panic has become one on which the fiercest political battles are fought. The moral panic is the right's campaigning arm, but the right has increasingly had to contend with the pressure groups which have become the campaigning arms of the opposition. No sooner does a moral panic emerge than it is angrily disputed, and its folk devils are fiercely defended by any one of a range of pressure groups which have emerged as a key force in opposing the policies of the new right during and after the Thatcher years.

These new political relationships will be the subject of this chapter. But it should not be forgotten that at root the moral panic is about instilling fear in people and, in so doing, encouraging them to try to turn away from the complexity and the visible social problems of everyday life and either to retreat into a 'fortress mentality' – a feeling of hopelessness, political powerlessness and paralysis – or to adopt a gung-ho 'something must be done about it' attitude. The moral panic is also frequently a means of attempting to discipline the young through terrifying their parents. This remains a powerful emotional strategy. But the pressure groups which deal specifically with youth-related issues make the isolation of both the young person and the worried parent less intense. And the self-help movement has also shifted this delicate balance of power. Finally the moral panic still desperately tries to encourage an image of family life which is increasingly unviable and unsustainable as the whole fabric of relations between men and women undergoes deep and seemingly irreversible transformations. The less able the conservatives and the right are to control these changes, the more frantic their repertoire of moral panics becomes, to the extent that the panics are no longer about social control but rather about the fear of being out of control.

NEW JUVENILE CRIME

The death in February 1993 of 2-year-old James Bulger, allegedly killed by two 10-year-old boys, prompted the start of what sociologists have traditionally called a moral panic in the mass media. The James Bulger case received enormous publicity. The fact that he was dragged away from the shopping centre where his mother momentarily lost sight of him, in broad daylight, and that security video cameras later showed him being taken by the boys, contributed an additional dimension to the horror of the crime. In the following months the media gave a good deal more coverage to offences carried out by young people than would normally have been the case. This coincided with ongoing debates about the inability of the law to deal effectively with young criminals. The *Daily Mail* reported the frustrations of judges who were 'powerless to punish' violent young offenders because of the lack of provision in the law to deal with the level of violence which the legal system was now

199

experiencing. Stories, illustrated with photographs showing eyes blocked out to protect the identity of the young offenders, but also heightening the dramatic effect, appeared in most of the tabloids. (The *Daily Mail* ran one headline: JUDGE BRANDS BOY OUTLAW.) These stories were frequently about 14-year-olds living rough with a catalogue of offences to their names including robbery, burglary, criminal damage, theft and rape. But if the system was soft on young offenders, with police officers having to make use only of 'cautions' and magistrates restricted to giving out 'care orders', it was not long before the finger was pointed more firmly at the family.

From this point on it was the family and in particular the single parent family which became the scapegoat. For a couple of weeks in July 1993 teenage mothers were caught in the full glare of publicity. Not only were their parenting skills cast in doubt, but their moral recklessness, in the form of their willingness to have children without the support of a father and breadwinner, was spotlighted. Most seriously it was their dependency on the state and on welfare ('Married to the State' as the newspapers put it) which confirmed their parasitical and deviant status.

Indeed throughout the early 1990s, the figures which recur as giving particular cause for concern are the young offenders, young mothers and single parent families living on housing estates. While the political response to crime and welfare dependency has in the main been divided along party lines, with several of the panics being initiated by emotive speeches strategically delivered by Tory politicians as part of a bid to turn public opinion against those social groups and populations who are most reliant on welfare, there has also been a much wider range of responses, some of them less predictable.

It will be the increasing complexity of what, once again, sociologists used to characterize rather monolithically as the 'social reaction', which will form a key part of the work of reconceptualizing the 'moral panic'. This can be signalled in the above example by the convergences and divergences across left and right on the 'new juvenile crime'. Opposition spokesperson Tony Blair, while acknowledging environmental influences like poverty and unemployment, none the less came out in favour of 'effective punishment' and the need for moral regeneration in society. At the same time the then Home Secretary Kenneth Clarke, on Radio Four's *World At One*, referred, surprisingly, to the need for 'affection' as part of any programme of treatment for youngsters while simultaneously promising that fifteen new secure units would be built. On BBC2's *Late Show* a round-table discussion comprised four academics and journalists drawn equally from the left and right, all of whom ended up deploring the moral vacuum which characterized British society in the 1990s.

Now, while it might well be possible to explain these overlapping positions as a sign of the new political middle ground that has been opened up as the Tories try to hold on to power after Thatcher, and as the Labour Party tries desperately to redefine socialism to make it more palatable to an electorate used to Tory government, they are by no means the only sources of response to these issues. There are two additional forces which have to be taken into account in the proliferation of voices which now accompany the emergence of a moral panic, and the diversity of positions from which these voices speak.

First there is the growth of interest groups or pressure groups, one of whose aims it is to be able to respond instantly to media demonization of the group they represent, and to provide information and analysis designed to counter this representation. As we shall see later, the effectiveness of these groups and in particular their skills at working with the media and providing highly professional 'soundbites' more or less on cue make them an invaluable resource to media machinery working to tight schedules and with increasingly small budgets. These allow the media to be seen to be doing their duty by providing 'balance' in their reporting. At the same time they show how 'folk devils' can and do 'fight back'. And if, as in the case with child offenders, they are not in a position to do this themselves, then the campaigning organizations (Childline, Child Poverty Action Group, National Children's Bureau, the Howard League) will do it on their behalf. The proliferation of these groups and the skill with which they engage with the media is an extremely important development in political culture. On occasion it is amost as though such groups, in the absence of an immediate and articulate response from Labour on a whole number of social issues, function as a virtual form of opposition to the government. A 'new' political sociology, taking into account the prominence of the media, might fruitfully explore the precise sphere of influence and the effectiveness of these organizations.

The second major development is the expansion, diversification and amplification of the media themselves so that they can no longer be seen as something separate from society; rather they become something within which the social is continuously being defined. Or, as postmodern theorists might polemically put it, the media are society. The media can, to all intents and purposes, call the shots and do so by creating their own agenda of social and political issues and then pursuing these to the limit. If during the Thatcher years newspapers like the *Daily Mail* practised and perfected the characteristics of hegemony, in a way which was consistently in uncanny harmony with Thatcherism, the same process of reaching out to win consent through endlessly defining and redefining new social questions continues unabated. In the 1990s the *Daily Mail* is openly critical of John Major, and it remains adamantly within the strongly hegemonic mode of address associated with Mrs Thatcher, while at the same time continuing to take the lead by presenting itself as being on the cusp of social change. The precise way in which the *Daily Mail* (the only national daily newspaper with more female than male readers) presents itself as the moral voice of the new middle class deserves further sociological consideration. And as the world of the media becomes more competitive one strategy for maintaining healthy circulation figures is for a newspaper to cast itself in the role of moral guardian, ever alert to new possibilities for concern and indignation. At the same time, in the interest of maintaining 'balance' and thereby attracting a bigger cross-section of the reading public, which in any case is more fragmented than it once was, the paper will also reflect a greater diversity of opinion on these issues than might have been the case in the past. Professional journalistic style, carefully tuned to the popularity of 'human interest' stories, draws on a moralistic voice. Moral panics thus become the norm of journalistic practice, the way in which daily events are brought to the attention of the public.

In the United Kingdom the *Daily Mail* might be seen to take the lead in forging new patterns of public opinion, but it is not alone in the sophisticated journalistic techniques it deploys in this bid to attract more and more readers. The global deregulated media are also anxious to scandalize, sensationalize and marshal public opinion, to the extent that in the last few years the quality press in the UK has not only made increasing use of more visual material but also adopted an increasingly tabloid style of reporting. One of the characteristics of the new format of the quality press is the proliferation of tabloid-style supplements together with the use of exaggerated, sensational and moralistic headlines. Thus the cover feature of the 'G2' section of the *Guardian* on 9 August 1993, which was on the increasing use of firearms by young drug dealers on mountain bikes in Manchester's Moss Side, carried the headline 'BLOOD ON THE STREETS: They're Packing Pistols In Manchester'.

The suggestion here is that the *Guardian* knows full well that such a 'shock horror' headline is sensational. It almost seems to be poking fun at itself for borrowing such a tabloid-like mode. This is borne out by the more measured copy which follows. But by such overt use of irony and by seeming to put its own headlines in quotation marks, the *Guardian* is embracing a postmodern style of journalistic practice. Verging on parody, a headline like this produces an ambivalent response. Is this a real moral panic about violent crime, so serious that even the *Guardian* uses the most emotive of language, or is it merely a 'grabby', witty, 'hard-nosed' style of caption-writing, a poor copy of the popular press?

It is the extent to which the moral panic remains a key concept in the sociological vocabulary for understanding processes of social control and regulation which has prompted the critique presented in the pages that follow. So dramatic have the changes been both in the political culture and in the mass media of the 1980s and 1990s that such an exercise seems appropriate. At the same time, given circumstances like those surrounding the death of James Bulger, where a horrific event gives rise to a spiral of anxieties and leads to punitive measures being taken, and to new groups of stigmatized individuals emerging in the landscape of the public imagination, it is not surprising that the moral panic is still drawn on by sociologists as a means of explaining and understanding such chains of events.

THE WORK OF STAN COHEN AND JOCK YOUNG

Although the concept of the moral panic and the argument that it can play an active role in creating deviant behaviour owe their existence initially to the work of the criminologist L. Wilkins (1964), it was the pioneering studies of Jock Young (1971) on the social meaning of drug-taking, followed by Stan Cohen (1972, 1980) on the dramatic and much publicized confrontations between the mods and the rockers on various beaches in Britain between 1964 and 1966, which provided a radical counter to the empirically based sociology of deviancy. This type of sociology, dominant in most of the universities, tended either to be excessively descriptive or else to explain the 'predicament' of the young offender almost entirely in terms of poverty and deprivation.

First the new sociologists showed how agents of social control, the police in particular, played a role in 'amplifying' the deviance, and second, by picking up the sensational coverage in the press of what appeared to be new forms of juvenile delinquence, they not only pointed out the power of the media but also began to develop a vocabulary for understanding it. This meant going beyond those sociological accounts which looked to patterns of ownership and control as signs of complicity between the media and government. Attention was now being paid to the ideological role of the media and the active construction of certain kinds of meaning.

In addition this work showed how deviant behaviour was interactive rather than absolutist. It was more often the outcome of complex chains of social interaction, than it was the product of young people with a predisposition, individually or environmentally, towards crime or rule-breaking behaviour. Finally this approach challenged the moral guardians by suggesting that their overreaction was counterproductive. It merely contributed to further social polarisation, though this might have been the desired political effect, as Stuart Hall et al. in Policing the Crisis (1978) later went on to demonstrate.

Stan Cohen's book, Folk Devils and Moral Panics, is rightfully a classic, demonstrating a much greater degree of complexity than the many summaries of the work indicate. For example, he acknowledges that social control is uneven and much less homogeneous and mechanistic than the model of deviancy amplification suggests. Indeed one group of respondents (drawn from the ordinary public) criticizes the media for over-reporting the clashes between the mods and the rockers, while others describe how they came down to the beach to have a look at 'the fun'. Not only does Cohen have a sophisticated grasp of how these events fed into popular folklore ('Where are the mods and rockers today?' was the question he was repeatedly asked while carrying out his fieldwork) but he is also able to show clearly the intensity of some of the responses, verging on the hysterical, while simultaneously recognizing the entertainment effect and the commercial potential of these richly symbolic groups with their ritualistic encounters. Cohen also recognizes that the establishing of an identifiable set of roles in society for the mods and the rockers created a kind of handbook for new recruits. Finally when the panic has run its course and de-amplification has set in, the characters in this drama settle into history as recognizable social types belonging to a particular period, sometimes referred to, even by the agents of social control, with a hint of nostalgia.

Jock Young's study of drug-takers and in particular of young people who smoked cannabis, though published a year before the first edition of Cohen's book, focuses on a period which followed that considered by Cohen. The late 1960s saw attention being shifted from young working-class males to their more middle-class counterparts. Here too we see a form of behaviour being condemned, stigmatized, with those involved becoming marginalized from the rest of the community, a process which, according to Young, increased the likelihood for further deviance. By building on public indignation, particularly where there is a scarcity of accurate information, Young argued that the media can contribute to social problems. Segregating young people away from the community creates a greater risk of long-term social disorder since 'a society can control effectively only those who perceive themselves to be members of it' (Young, 1971: 39).

As is the case with Cohen's study, there is a great deal that could be engaged with in *The Drugtakers* from the viewpoint of the changes in British society in the twenty years or so since it was first published. For the purposes of this critique it is more appropriate to raise a few questions. Is moral indignation around drug-taking still so visible? If not why not? Has the social isolation of deviants continued, or was this always more apparent than real? On what grounds did these sociologists assume segregation? Was it not more likely, as I argued in a critique of subcultural theory in the early 1980s, that the male sociologists, like the journalists, restricted their gaze to the streets and other sites of public display and never thought to follow the deviants home at night, to their families and to the more mundane activities which they also took part in, like shopping, eating and going to college or to work, and even getting married (McRobbie, 1991)? Has the social or symbolic isolation of even hard drug-takers actually happened? Perhaps Young's suggestions that steps could be taken to avoid deviancy amplification and social segregation had a quite profound effect on social policy, with social workers and others making every effort to avoid stigmatization and isolation by keeping drug-users in the community, a radical tactic which is now, ironically, embedded in the conservative philosophy of 'care in the community'.

In relation to *Folk Devils and Moral Panics* it might be significant that these events did indeed become legends in the history of British postwar popular culture. The figure of the mod especially became the focus of an endless series of revivals, to such an extent that mod style has become a permanent feature of British fashion and youth culture. The sheer scale of the social reaction to the mods has also been an object lesson in overreaction, since the references to vermin and disease, to ratpacks and 'Sawdust Caesars', to which Cohen refers throughout the study, were so obviously prejudicial and pernicious that a generation of student radicals responded not just with humour but also with anger, and, like the new criminologists, saw the moral crusaders as powerful ideologues for the right. The politics which emerged from these studies, even though they were located within sociological interactionism rather than Marxism, none the less alerted readers to the political significance of cultural and social phenomena and to the politics of youth. Cohen and Young both showed how fairly unspectacular events or practices could on occasion provide opportunities for dominant groups in society to exert themselves by intro-ducing a series of sanctions, from more intensive policing to legislation and sentencing.

HOOLIGANS, HISTORY AND HEGEMONY

Engaging directly with the law and order rhetoric of Thatcherism in the late 1970s and into the 1980s, Geoff Pearson (1983) focuses on the way in which the social ills of the day and the moral panics these give rise to inevitably entail looking back to a 'golden age' where social stability and strong moral discipline act as a deterrent for delinquence and disorder. The shocking events of the day which have triggered the moral panic are compared unfavourably with what it was like twenty years ago. However, when Pearson investigates the media of twenty years ago, the exact same process can be seen in operation: 'the kids of today' were seen as rowdy and undisciplined and as having too much money, unlike their counter-parts of the previous decades. The same anxieties appear with startling regularity. These involve the immorality of young people, the absence of parental control, the way in which having too much free time leads to crime, and the threat which deviant behaviour poses to national identity and to labour discipline. Pearson shows how there were scares about 'cosh boys' and Blitz kids, during the 1940s, and how during the interwar period there was a string of moral panics about the misuse of leisure time and the decline of the British way of life through the popularity of Hollywood cinema. Pursuing this chain of investigation back through the nineteenth century, Pearson argues that the nature of the complaints and the social response to them provides a normative and consensual language for understanding the turbulence of social change and discontinuity.

The value of this historical study is to cast a critical shadow over any claims about the dramatic rise in violent crimes carried out by young people. It shows how moral panics in society act as a form of ideological cohesion which draws on a complex language of nostalgia. Instead of seeking to understand the dynamics of social change, and thus encourage people to be in a better, more informed position, the mass media employ a variety of strategies, many of which owe more to the conventions of popular entertainment than to those of analysis or critique. Pearson shows how the recurrent representation in the popular press over the last hundred years, of rowdy youth as animalistic and subhuman, paves the way for a more coercive state apparatus and harsher sentencing policies.

In the three studies described above, the moral panic can be seen as acting on behalf of the dominant social order. It is also a means of 'orchestrating consent' by actively intervening in the space of public opinion and social consciousness through the use of highly emotive and rhetorical language which has the inevitable effect of requiring that 'something be done about it'. The argument about deviancy amplification is precisely that where such strategies are indeed followed by social and legislative action, they also reassure the public that there is strong government and strong leadership.

It is only with the theory of ideology that the idea of the media's moral panics as defining and distorting social issues gives way to a more integrated and connective understanding of the construction of meaning across the whole range of media forms and institutions. *Policing the Crisis* by Stuart Hall and his colleagues from the Centre for Contemporary Cultural Studies (CCCS) in Birmingham, marks a turning-point, in this respect. As Muncie and Fitzgerald (1981) point out, the loose notion of social control found in earlier studies of moral panics is replaced with more specific references to state control. A more Marxist and a more theoretical vocabulary is introduced into a terrain which, though admittedly less empirical than conventional British sociology, none the less remained hostile to French or Italian neo-Marxism. And *Policing the Crisis*, unlike much of the structuralist and semiological analysis of the mass media which followed, also remained more palatable to the British sociologists, first because of its focus on the moral panic, and second because it was concerned with history and political culture. As a result this volume can be seen as bridging the gap between sociology and cultural studies, one which, however, was soon to be broken when further work from the CCCS in Birmingham, connected to the 'mugging' project and more explicitly on race, turned its full attention to the shortcomings of British sociology (Gilroy, 1987). Likewise the work which drew on structuralism and on textual analysis as ways of understanding the mass media and as methods for interpreting deviant behaviour and youth subcultures in particular (Hebdige, 1979) provoked a strongly critical reaction on the part of the sociologists like Stan Cohen for being unconcerned with 'real' political issues or for being too literary, too instinctive a mode of analysis for any 'real' social scientist.

Policing the Crisis introduces the Gramscian concept of hegemony to analyse the way in which the moral panic around mugging and the alleged criminality of young Afro-Caribbean males created the social conditions of consent which were necessary for the construction of a society more focused towards law and order and less inclined to the liberalism and 'permissiveness' of the 1960s. This particular analysis of the moral panic shows it to be not an isolated phenomenon but a connective strategy, part of the practice of hegemony which enlarges the sphere of influence of the state into the private sphere of the family, leisure and everyday life, what Gramsci labelled 'civil society'. The moral panic then becomes the envoy for dominant ideology. In the language of common sense, it operates as an advance warning system, and as such it progresses from the local issue to the matter of national importance, from the site of tension and social anxieties to the full-blown social and political crisis. This is a much more substantial force for maintaining and managing social cohesion than the earlier model of the moral panic and social control developed by Cohen and others. It is also a more pessimistic model because the moral panic here is deeply integrated into the practices of government. There is no question of social change being effected through the replacement of such distorted media messages by more truthful ones. The value of *Policing the Crisis* might not, in the end, lie in its argument about the stages of crisis. While the authors are alert to the complexity of historical and social relations there is a tendency in the book to suggest a kind of teleology of crisis and social breakdown which can then be managed only through the escalation of control and coercion. This is debatable but what is of greater importance is the recognition that ideology is a suffusive social process, and that it is not a simple question of the distortion of truth, but rather that ideology is a force which works continuously through the mobilization of popular common sense.

SEXUAL MORAL PANICS

Mica Nava's (1988) analysis of media coverage of what came to be known as the Cleveland affair reflects not just the way in which the sexual abuse of children generated a sudden explosion of attention in the 1980s, but also how the popular press no longer seemed to be in broad agreement on an issue so damaging to its victims that a unanimous cry of outrage, with virulent calls for tougher action being taken to stop it, might have been expected. No so. An altogether more complicated picture emerges, where at one point the female doctor (Marietta Higgs) who acted on behalf of the abused children is cast as the folk devil rather than the 'moral guardian'. It is uncertainty and ambivalence which characterize this moral panic, rather than simple condemnation of the guilty. This is not just because of the complexity of the case itself, where the evidence pointed to the fact that not all the children taken into hospital had actually been abused, though, as it later emerged, all were on the social services 'at risk' register, many had a history of abuse, and a substantial number were taken into the care of the local authority following their being sent home from hospital. Nor can the divided opinion of the huge number of experts, alongside the moral crusaders called in by the media to comment on the affair, be attributed entirely to the controversial technique for diagnosis pioneered by Dr Higgs.

Indeed the response to Cleveland in the media tells us more about changes in the media itself by the mid-1980s, than it does about the chain of events which culminated in this particular panic. For example, the *Daily Mail*, now with a clear commitment to women's issues including all forms of sexual assault and violence against women, claims that, in addition, it 'revealed the scandal (of child abuse) to the nation'; it also gives generous space to the supporters of Dr Higgs while at the same time championing the case of the parents. Even the *Sun* prints a story about one family who claimed they were saved by Dr Higg's intervention. While the social workers involved in the case are attacked for their 'fashionable zeal', it is clear that despite the vilification of Dr Higgs, there is, in the end, no one social group, least of all those who perpetrated the abuse, who can be blamed.

The conventional moral guardians, who refuse even to consider the possible guilt of some of the parents, on the grounds of their commitment to family values and to the overriding importance of keeping families together, are discredited by the fact that they are wholly male, and usually with strong religious beliefs. This is unpalatable to the feminist journalists, many of whom are now on the staff of the mass circulation dailies and women's magazines which also get involved. Media celebrities like Esther Rantzen, hardly known for her feminist views but none the less a major campaigner against child abuse and founder of Childline, acknowledge the prevalence of child sexual abuse, and if it is as widespread as is suggested then it is as likely to occur in Cleveland as it is anywhere else. It is not just the difficult and 'unresolvable' (all subjects of moral panics are by definition unresolvable) nature of this particular issue that makes the 'orchestration of consent' unmanageable, it is also the strong and vocal presence in the media and in the wider professional culture of 'experts', many of whom are women who dispute and contest the opinions of the editors and politicians as well as the conventional moral guardians.

If feminism shifts the balance which had established itself between the key protagonists in the scenario of moral panic, AIDS activists and writers like Simon Watney (1987) have developed the most sustained critique of moral panics and in so doing have also provided the foundation for a better understanding of how controversial social and political issues become inscribed with certain kinds of meaning across a wide variety of media forms. Watney rightly points out that the gradual and staged creation of a folk devil as described by moral panic theorists does not apply either to gay men and lesbian women or to people who are HIV positive. Instead there is a whole world of 'monstrous' representations. And since sexuality is by definition subjected to regulation and control, through a multiplicity of institutions each with its own distinctive discursive practices, its own textual strategies, the idea of the moral panic as an excuse for intensified social control is neither historically accurate if applied to the experience of homosexuality which has been controlled by definition, nor is it, as some have suggested, the key to understanding the fears and anxieties around AIDS. As Watney puts it:

> In other words, the theory of moral panics is unable to conceptualise the mass media as an industry which is intrinsically involved with excess, with a voracious appetite and capacity for substitutions, displacements, repetitions and signifying absences. Moral panic theory is always obliged in the final instance to refer and contrast 'representation' to the arbitration of 'the real', and is hence unable to develop a full theory concerning the operations of ideology within all representational systems. Moral panics seem to appear and disappear, as if representation were not the site of *permanent* ideological struggle over the meaning of signs.
>
> (Watney, 1987: 41)

Given that we live in a world of incessant image-making, meaning-making and mass communications, moral panic theorists, with their focused interest on 'media coverage', ignore the daily endorsement (not to say enjoyment) of heterosexuality as an ideological norm in the world of the mass-produced text and image and the consequences this has for those who are excluded.

Policies and practices which are concerned with 'policing desire' do not according to Watney emanate from one or two centralized agencies of social control. They are endemic in society, and in this context the moral panic is a local intensification ('the site of the current front line'; Watney, 1987: 42) rather than a sudden, unpleasant and unanticipated development. The moral panic is therefore a concept which is not able to deal with the kind of questions which more recent media theory, informed both by structuralism and by psychoanalysis, has attempted to engage with. Watney argues that it cannot explain the ambivalence and the excessive interest displayed by the moral guardians and their representatives in the media in the objects of their distaste. There is no space here for analysing in depth the fascination with the 'other', and his or her repeated appearance in the horror show of fictional representation as well as in apparently factual reportage.

In the conclusion I will argue that this is indeed a much more fruitful line of inquiry to pursue, one which has already been explored by Homi Bhabha (1983) in his seminal analysis of the racial stereotype. Bhabha uses Foucault's idea of the search for knowledge, in this case knowledge of the racial other, as part of a strategy of power and control. To be able to know him or her, and to speak as an expert on his or her characteristics, is to be in a position of power. The expert can record such knowledge in print and in the mass media and can transmit it in other wider discourses, including, for example, the powerful field of education. This requires surveillance of, and repeated looking at, the other. Hence the frequency of his or her appearance in the relevant discourses of inquiry. And in seeing difference there is also the frisson of fascination.

As Heather Nunn has recently put it, 'Put simply, that which is deemed as socially marginal often becomes symbolically central' (1993: 7). There is no reason whatsoever why the monstrous image of the other, the black person, the person with AIDS, the serial killer, should not display the same characteristics in non-fictional discourses as he or she does in the world of popular entertainment, since in the world of representation there is no rigid dividing line between the two. The same representational strategies (a sinister soundtrack, for example, a close-up to the facial expression as a clue for deviant intentions) frame the presence of the folk devil in both fact and in fiction, and in both cases the narrative is structured around the search for knowledge and the desire to retrieve what Foucault (1988) labelled 'subjugated knowledge'. Through considering the meanings which have developed around AIDS and homosexuality, Watney replaces the vocabulary of the moral panic with that of representation, discourse and 'the other'. In so doing he is able to bring to his work concepts drawn from the fields of psychoanalysis, cultural studies and film theory to produce a deeper account of processes of exclusion and regulation than that available in the old sociology of social control.

MORAL PANICS AND THE POSTMODERN MEDIA

In describing the central place occupied by the moral panic in a variety of areas of sociological study including crime and deviance, sexuality and gender, youth and ethnicity, the media and communications, an attempt has been made here to show how important it is that this concept does not in a sense bask in its glory and find no reason to redefine its place in the curriculum of sociology and cultural studies. What follows represents some possibilities for beginning this work. Broadly speaking it could be argued that the rectangular relationship of positions and processes which held the old moral panic model together (the sociologists on behalf of the deviant; the agencies of social control; the media; the moral guardians and experts) has been replaced by a more diverse and more fluid set of institutions, agencies and practices which sometimes interlock.

What now exists, in the 1990s, is an immensely complex scenario, the ground rules of which are increasingly set by the working practices of the mass media. To get some sense of this complexity it is worth drawing attention to the 'media flow' for the week beginning 16 August 1993. While by no means exhaustive, some of the examples that follow indicate the way in which the media provides a kind of non-stop floorshow upon which political issues of the day are presented, paraded and transformed, no longer into straightforward moral panics, but rather into a seamless web of narrativized news and media events. Central to the examples which follow is the launching of a pressure group campaign designed to attract the maximum attention of all the mass media at a traditionally quiet time, i.e. during the summer. The campaign organized by the Howard League for Penal Reform was aimed at drawing attention to the high number of suicides among young people held in adult prisons, and was designed also to present a counter to the moral panic of the previous months which had resulted in calls for more punishment for young offenders. The press indeed reported the campaign extensively. Articles referring to the research findings and the report published by the Howard League appeared in the newspapers on Monday 16 August alongside whole-page advertisements for a 'drama-documentary' titled *15: The Life and Death of Philip Knight*, a programme based on the events leading up to the death in 1991 of 15-year-old Philip Knight while he was being held in Swansea Prison. Tuesday's *World at One* on Radio Four had an interview with one of Philip's 'real-life' social workers, while the drama-documentary itself was broadcast with additional advance TV publicity on Wednesday evening on ITV. A discussion programme was scheduled for the following evening. Wednesday's *Daily Mail*, as though to stem any tide of sympathy for a more liberal attitude to young offenders, printed a full-page interview with a woman prison governor (Lynne Bowles of Whitemoor Prison, Cambridgeshire) who was arguing for tougher treatment for all offenders. The headline ran 'VICIOUS THUGS CONTROL THE JAILS THANKS TO THE DO-GOODERS'. Below this piece, which took up almost the whole page, was a shorter piece on a children's home which sent a girl offender 'to swim with dolphins as part of her care programme'. On the following page was another major piece, this time by the father of a 14-year-old girl; one of the girls who had beaten up

211

his daughter had already been sent to swim with the dolphins, for previous offences. The Rev. Glyn Thomas described the horrible attack on his daughter by two 'hefty 16-year-olds' and then went on to point the finger at the leniency of the social workers and, in contrast, to praise the common sense of the magistrates. 'Fortunately wiser counsels prevailed on the magistrates' bench. The girl was sentenced to custody in a young offenders institution. Now she is locked up. I have to say I am glad – it will do her more good than swimming with dolphins' (*Daily Mail*, 18 August 1993: 8).

In the exact same week the Conservatives released plans to hand over the responsibility for running secure units for disturbed, criminal and 'dangerous' youngsters to private bodies. This too provoked a ferocious debate across the entire range of media institutions including the BBC's 'flagship' late-night news programme *Newsnight*. Wednesday's *Newsnight* (18 August 1993) ran an additional social services and welfare feature on young single mothers. The general momentum of a range of such concerns continued throughout the week across the media with coverage of teenage joyriding incidents which had resulted in the death of a toddler, and again on Radio Four (*You and Yours*, 20 August 1993) on the question of juvenile crime.

In the context of such a crowded week, a strong case can be made *not* for the construction of a moral panic, *nor* even for the emergence of a series of concurrent interlocking moral panics. Instead, what is happening here is that politics is being created and pursued within the wide and welcoming embrace of the media. This week is little different from any other in this respect. Indeed it is more than likely that detailed analysis of any other average week would reveal a similar level of media management of political and social affairs.

What this series of events shows is the organization of news, information and drama on TV as well as in the press and on the radio, along the lines of what Raymond Williams (1975) described as flow. How precisely decisions are taken which lead to such an intensity of social issues being broadcast in any one week would require study of the occupational culture and the editorial and professional practices of media personnel. What is significant here is first the connections between an ever-expanding field of media and communications, with their 'shared agendas' and differential responses; second, the established scenario of anxiety and concern around 'new juvenile crime' (dating back to events earlier in the year) and its connection with other debates around the cost of welfare and social services, including those required to deal with situations like that of Philip Knight; and third, the political agenda already in place for further de-regulating the field of welfare and the social services as a means of cutting costs, running down provision and completing the project of privatization set in motion by Thatcher.

The coverage given to these questions can no longer be seen starkly in terms of folk devils and moral panics. The whole political culture is so changed that in the absence of strong and vocal opposition from Labour (fearful of being seen as soft on crime) the media must rely on other agencies and experts to provide opposing perspectives. The question for political sociologists might then be that of the effectiveness or ineffectiveness of the pressure groups. The same question could be asked of lobbies like that of the National Council for One Parent Families whose spokeswoman Sue Slipman has played a leading role, on an almost weekly basis over a period of three to six months, in diminishing the demonization by the Tories of young single mothers and the attempt further to penalize young mothers for having children without being married.

In short a 'new sociology' of social regulation would need to shift attention away from the conventional points in the circuit of amplification and control and look instead, for example, at the space of the expert as increasingly the space of opposition. In addition the growth of pressure groups would need to be examined in more depth, not just their numbers, the issues they represent, the people who work for them and their background and training (social science graduates with good knowledge of theories of social control and the role of the media?) but also their own professional practice as media workers. Is working for a pressure group in effect working in or near to the media? Does 'planning a campaign' in effect mean the preparation of a whole sequence of media-friendly facts, soundbites, information and analysis, backed up by human interest case studies, with high-profile experts on call, if required?

It would not be at all inappropriate to apply Baudrillard's (1985) idea of the 'ecstasy of communication' to the sheer speed, intensity and extensiveness of the media as they effortlessly create a web of interconnecting meanings each of which has its own momentum, its own pacing, its own narrative structures, its own accompanying images, its own experts and witnesses and victims and, when appropriate, its own parliamentary spokespersons, according to the story or issue of the day. These issues 'converse' with each other across the outlets and they also interact with and are connected to additional emergent or new 'news' issues. So sophisticated and efficient is this machinery that from the outside even the sociologist can only admit to being dazzled and impressed by so successful an industry which draws on the latest of computer technology and image-making processes to define its own centrality as reference point for the construction and maintenance of national life and political culture.

One of the suggestions in this debate has been that 'folk devils' have, over the last ten years, found themselves defended vociferously not so much by the mainstream opposition political parties (Labour, the Liberal Democrats) but rather by the pressure groups and self-help groups which have sprung up across the country and which now play a major role in contesting what they perceive as dangerous stereotypes and popular misconceptions. Some 'folk devils' themselves become organizers and campaigners in such groups.

This phenomenon of becoming an expert having been a deviant, has of course a history in the field of serious crime, drug abuse and juvenile delinquency. What is perhaps less evident is the extent to which so-called folk devils now produce their own media as a counter to what they perceive as the biased media of the mainstream. Thus *The Big Issue* is now a national media landmark as newspaper voice of the young homeless. Other groups and agencies produce a never-ending flow of newsletters and press releases many of which are written in a house-style customized to the needs of the journalists on the national and local media. More than this, as Sarah Thornton (1993) has pointed out, specific youth subcultures have historically nurtured a particular kind of relationship to the media which, as she demonstrates with the case of rave, seeks and plans for a sensational reaction on the part of the press and TV, as part of their own identity formation by staging a commitment to remaining 'underground'. In chapter 9 of this book I have argued that youth cultures make an explosive entrance into the world of the image and the text through a frenzy of communication, in style, in sound, in posters, fanzines, video, and in flyers and other publicity information. Without all of this and alongside the pretensions of preferring to remain pure and uncontaminated by the media, youth cultures require this kind of self-publicity to provoke the reaction they do.

So established and have successful have these forms of youthful communication become that the youth media are no longer restricted to the music and style press, the teenage magazines, *Top of the Pops* and the occasional pop programme. Television producer Janet Street-Porter, drawing on the cut-up graphic style of punk, and indicating a new commitment on the part of broadcasters to take youth seriously, pioneered 'Youth TV' in the mid-1980s through her *Def II* series on BBC2. In keeping with this commitment several of these programmes were explicitly aimed at countering youth folk devils and moral panics, particularly around drugs. Thus an informative and unsensational BBC2 *Reportage* programme on the use of Ecstasy in rave culture can be set against the much more traditionally sensational and fearful *Cook Report* (ITV) on the same subject (1992).

The other side of the implosive effect of the postmodern mass media described by Baudrillard (1985) and also relevant to this reconceptualization of the moral panic, is the media 'black-out'. This too marks a series of developments which have occurred perhaps in response to the impact of moral panic theory itself, i.e. the sociologist as expert. At least some of the agents of social control must have been listening when figures like Jock Young or Geoff Pearson were invited to add their voices to

214

these debates, because in recent incidents where there have been fears that rowdiness, disorder, or outbreaks of rioting might spread to other areas or to other cities, the playing down of the scale of such incidences has been a recurrent feature and a point of recommendation by the police in relation to the media.

The space of the black-out is an interesting one for sociologists. At one level it marks the power of the agents of social control, in the last instance or in the supreme moment of crisis, over the autonomy and the professional practices of the media. But since it has been argued here that this kind of binary model is no longer appropriate, then a different account becomes necessary. First, black-outs have a short lifespan. They can last for only a couple of days. There is a limit to the time that the various media institutions, including the foreign media, will hold to such a ruling. Second, they can only be applied to particularly visual and dramatic events, like the 'hotting' incidents on the Blackbird Leys estate in Oxford in 1991. Media black-outs are hardly relevant to the so-called new juvenile crime which takes place more routinely and outside the glare of the cameras (though perhaps 'caught' by the surveillance cameras). Third, just as events like those which took place on the Oxford housing estate had been going on before the cameras moved in, so also did they continue when the cameras were told to hold back. And finally there is also the 'signifying space' of the black-out itself. What are the meanings constructed in this space of apparent silence? Does the black hole of non-communication merely fan the flames for an 'ecstasy of communication' when reporting restrictions are lifted? What meanings circulate during this period of quiet, what other informal or illegal communicative systems move in to fill the gap? Sarah Thornton in her study of youth culture 'undergrounds' argues that these imagine themselves as 'black holes' in opposition to 'the media' and that the record companies and the public relations departments play to this when fuelling a moral panic (Thornton, 1993).

In what other ways have the old positions occupied by the figures behind the scenes of the moral panic been replaced by a new and much more fluid and intertextual set of relations, positions and cultural practices? To answer this question, it would be necessary to reconceptualize the audience who, in the old moral panic theory, played a minor role and remained relatively untheorized. They too were, with a few exceptions, the space of consensus, the space of media manipulation, the space of a fairly easily convinced public, or at most the space of social groups divided along the broad lines of class whose opinions or political inclinations are reflective of this particular mode of differentiation. Recent work on audiences, notably that of David Morley (1993), has challenged this model and has shown the whole process of being part of an audience to be a much more active role and a much less predictable practice. Social processes of fragmentation and the growth of identity politics over the last twenty years, and with this the decline of class politics, would also have to be taken into account.

In every way the reader or viewer or the various social groups categorized under the heading of public opinion would need not only to be given more of a place in the new model for understanding the representation of social issues, but also to be credited with possessing a greater degree of 'media literacy' than they did in the past. The ownership of home video-cameras, the possession of degrees in media studies, the existence of 'right to reply' programmes and 'video boxes' as well as the new space for broadcasting home video material on national television (in a series of programmes titled *Video Diaries*) have gone some way in breaking down what was once seen as the unbridgeable divide between media professionals and the 'punters'. Also important here was the introduction of a distinctively amateurish (rather than professional) style of presentation, developed in Channel Four's *The Tube* of the early 1980s and best reflected in the 'fluffed' mannerisms of its two presenters, Jools Holland and Paula Yates. And finally the increasing reliance on the audience as resource for successful television, as participants in Saturday evening prime-time programmes, seems to give a positive place to the audience in the process of programme production.

These kinds of phenomena not only point to a new and apparently more active and fluid position for the viewer, they also fit closely with Baudrillard's perceptions of the postmodern mass media. Baudrillard's pessimistic thesis is that the media appear to extend themselves generously to their audience in a gesture designed to demonstrate democratic embrace while in fact merely extending the sphere of their influence and control. A less pessimistic postmodernist account might instead emphasize not just the flow of images and texts as they circulate through the new economy of the sign but also the flow of active agents, whose role in the production and distribution of the image is not as robotic as Baudrillard would suggest. Such an account would also require much more analysis of the occupational culture and experience of media workers employed in this postmodern de-regulated sector, as well as of their audiences. If we are to take the role of the expert or the spokesperson for the pressure group more seriously as an active voice in this public sphere of contestation and debate then it would be only logical to extend this to the producers and editors who seek out their opinions and who request their appearance and participation.

The final point is perhaps obvious. The kind of social issues and political debates which were once included on the agendas of moral panic theorists as sites of social anxiety, and even of crisis, could now be redefined as part of an endless debate about who 'we' are and about what 'our' national culture is. These are profoundly 'home affairs'. The daily intensity and drama of their appearance, and the many voices now heard not in the background but in the foreground, punctuating and producing reality, point more to the reality of dealing with social difference than to the unity of 'current affairs' (Hall, Connell and Curti, 1981).

What has been argued therefore is that the model of the moral panic is urgently in need of updating and revising precisely because of its success. While the theory began its life in radical sociology, the strength of the argument quickly found its way into those very areas with which it was originally concerned. As a result the police, as agents of social control, now show some awareness in areas of potential deviancy amplification, of the dangers of overreaction, while sectors of the media regularly remind viewers or readers of the dangers of creating a moral panic, and thus of alienating wide sections of the community by falsely attributing to them some of the characteristics of the so-called folk devils. Last but not least the theory has, over the years, drawn attention to the importance of empowering the folk devils so that they or their representatives can challenge the cycle of sanctions and social control.

The problems with the old model of the moral panic are as follows. First it assumed a clear distinction between the world of the media and the world of social reality. But in one simple sense the media are as much a part of social reality as any other component can be. We do not exist in social unreality while we watch television or read the newspaper, nor are we transported back to reality when we turn the TV off to wash the dishes or discard the paper and go to bed. Indeed perhaps there is no pure social reality outside the world of representation. Reality is relayed to us through the world of language, communication and imagery. Social meanings are inevitably representations and selections. Thus when the sociologists call for an account which tells how life really is, and which deals with the real issues rather than the spectacular and exaggerated ones which then contribute to the moral panic, the point is that their account of reality would also be a representation, a set of meanings about what they perceive as the real issues.

The second point is that the delicate balance of relations which the moral panic sociologists saw existing between the media, the agents of social control, the folk devils and the moral guardians, has given way to what seems like a much more complicated and more fragmented set of connections. Each of the categories described by moral panic theorists has undergone a process of fissure in the intervening years. New liaisons have been developed and new initiatives pursued. In the above chapter attention has been paid to the growth and increasing importance of pressure groups who have, among other things, strongly contested the vocality of the traditional moral guardians.[1]

It has also been argued that the old days of the clearly defined and highly visible moral panic have been replaced by a much more

217

sophisticated way of representing social and political issues to the public. Stories with a moral panic 'angle', initiated, let us say, by a conservative politician, now are forced to confront much tougher opposition as the (diverse and fragmented) media, which are the stage upon which the drama is usually set, exploit their power and relative autonomy by refusing to concede ground entirely to the loud voices of the moral guardians. To analyse exactly how this is done would require lengthy examination of particular instances (interviewing technique, editorial decision-making on how to broadcast a story and whom to invite on). And this in turn would require a clear understanding of the different ways in which meaning is constructed across different types of media forms. At a general level what can be seen is the presence of experts whose views are in sharp contrast to those who are usually orchestrating the panic, and who are now as skilled as if not more skilled than the moral guardians at presenting their arguments in the language of 'good television.'

NOTE

1 On Sunday 10 September 1993 I was invited to appear as a sociological expert on Granada TV's *The Judy Finnegan Show*. The topic was single mothers and in addition to the presence on the panel of a Labour MP, a Tory MP, a Tory supporter of 'family values' and the well-known single mother Sara Keays, representatives from a number of pressure groups were dotted across the audience, which, as it happened, was overwhelmingly supportive of single mums and condemnatory of the Tories – Cecil Parkinson in particular! The groups represented were Campaign Against the Child Support Act, Dads Against Divorce, Families Need Fathers, Gingerbread and Wages For Housework. Also present was single parent Heidi Colwell who had left her 2-year-old daughter 'home alone' while she went out to work, because she couldn't afford a childminder. The audience was openly sympathetic to her and angrily refused to see her condemned by the Tories present on the platform.

REFERENCES

Baudrillard, Jean (1985) 'The ecstasy of communication', in H. Foster (ed.) *Postmodern Culture*, London: Pluto Press, pp. 126–35.

Bhabha, Homi (1983) 'The other question: the stereotype and colonial discourse', *Screen* 24, 6: 19–35.

Cohen, Stan (1980) *Folk Devils and Moral Panics: The Creation of the Mods and Rockers*, Oxford: Blackwell.

Foucault, Michel (1988) *Politics, Philosophy, Culture – Interviews and Other Writings, 1977–1984*, London: Routledge.

Gilroy, Paul (1987) *There Ain't No Black in the Union Jack*, London: Hutchinson.

Hall, Stuart, Critcher, Charles and Jefferson, Tony (1978) *Policing the Crisis: Mugging, the State, and Law and Order*, London: Macmillan.

Hall, Stuart, Connell, Ian and Curti, Lidia (1981) 'The "unity" of current affairs television', in T. Bennett *et al.* (eds) *Popular Television and Film*, London: BFI, pp. 88–118.

Hebdige, Dick (1979) *Subculture: The Meaning of Style*, London: Routledge.

McRobbie, Angela (1991) 'Settling the accounts with subcultures: a feminist critique', in Angela McRobbie, *Feminism and Youth Culture: From Jackie to Just Seventeen*, London: Macmillan, pp. 16–35.

McRobbie, Angela (1993) 'Shut up and dance: youth culture and changing modes of femininity', *Cultural Studies* 7, 3: 406–26 (reprinted in this book as chapter 9).

Morley, David (1993) *Television, Audiences and Cultural Studies*, London: Routledge.

Muncie, John and Fitzgerald, Mike (1981) 'Humanising the deviant: affinity and affiliation theories' in Mike Fitzgerald *et al.* (eds) *Crime and Society: Readings in History and Theory*, London: Routledge, pp. 403–29.

Nava, Mica (1988) 'Cleveland and the press: outrage and anxiety in the reporting of child sexual abuse', *Feminist Review* 28 (Spring): 103–22.

Nunn, Heather (1993) 'The happy limbo of non-identity: re-reading Herculin Barbin', unpublished dissertation essay for an MA in cultural studies, Thames Valley University.

Pearson, Geoff (1983) *Hooligan: A History of Respectable Fears*, London: Macmillan.

Thornton, Sarah (1993) 'From record hops to raves: cultural studies of youth, music and media', unpublished PhD thesis, John Logie Baird Centre, University of Strathclyde, Glasgow.

Watney, Simon (1987) *Policing Desire: Pornography, AIDS and the Media*, London: Methuen.

Wilkins, L. (1964) *Social Deviance*, London: Tavistock.

Williams, Raymond (1975) *Television: Technology and Cultural Form*, Harmondsworth, Mx: Penguin.

Young, Jock (1971) *The Drugtakers: The Social Meaning of Drug Use*, London: Paladin.

INDEX

212, 217; *Oprah Winfrey Show* 190;
   youth 159, 214
textuality 39, 48
Thatcher/ism 31, 35, 45, 62, 157, 160,
   180, 199, 205; reactions to 162–3
Theory, Culture and Society 98
Third World 16, 122, 127, 128, 129
Thompson, E.P. 45
Thornton, Sarah 179, 182, 214, 215
Tiedermann, Rolf 106
Time Out 144
transformation 52
trivial, analysis of 4
truth 70

unity 27–8, 127
urbanism 22, 105, 109, 115–16

vintage dress *see* second-hand clothes

wage/labour relation 49
Waters, Lizzie 118–19
Watney, Simon 209

welfare dependency 200
Weston, Edward 91
Williams, Raymond 45, 82, 112, 212
Williamson, Judith 55, 94
Willis, Paul 39, 181, 185, 194
Willis, Tim 183, 184
wish-image (*Dialectics of Seeing*) 108,
   109–10
Wolf, Christa 85
Wolfe, Tom 138, 151
Wolff, Janet 7, 47, 80
work/ers 35–7, 157; core/periphery 36;
   flexible specialization 37

Yale French Studies (YFS) 121, 123,
   124
Young, Jock 203–5, 214
youth culture 137, 156, 163, 205; black
   182–4; focus on 182; and sociology
   180; traditional argument 179 *see
   also* culture

Žižek, S. 40